Springs of Hope

SPRINGS OF HOPE

by

DIANA WITTS

The Memoir Club

© Diana Witts 2005

First published in 2005 by
The Memoir Club
Stanhope Old Hall
Stanhope
Weardale
County Durham

British Library Cataloguing in
Publication Data.
A catalogue record for this book
is available from the
British Library

ISBN: 1 84104 133 5

Typeset by TW Typesetting, Plymouth, Devon
Printed by Antony Rowe Ltd, Eastbourne

Dedication

Near the small village of Trefnant in North Wales, inside the ruins of an old church in the corner of a field, is a spring called Fynon Fair (Mary's Well). The spring never dries up, even in the hottest summer, and the water is clear and sweet. From the dark mud at the base of the well bubbles rise up that spin and dance their way to the surface, sparkling in the sunlight. I have often spent time sitting on the stone rim of the well, marvelling at the beauty of the fragile, life-giving bubbles that spring from such unpromising mud. Over the years I have similarly marvelled when meeting people from dark places of suffering and loss whose lives are filled with vibrancy and hope: men and women caught up in the chaos of civil war in Sudan, survivors of years of imprisonment during the cultural revolution in China, child victims of anti-personnel mines in Afghanistan, and many others. Such people have deeply challenged and enriched my life and this book is dedicated to them all.

Contents

List of Illustrations ix

Foreword xi

Acknowledgements xv

Chapter 1 Growing Up 1

Chapter 2 Off to Canada 13

Chapter 3 Arrival in Africa 20

Chapter 4 Move to Kikuyu 30

Chapter 5 From the Himalayas to Gordonstoun 40

Chapter 6 Amongst the Maasai 51

Chapter 7 Exploring Zaire 76

Chapter 8 Visits to Uganda 98

Chapter 9 Theological Education by Extension 103

Chapter 10 Life in London 107

Chapter 11 West Africa 111

Chapter 12 Growth and instability in Zaire 125

Chapter 13 Southern Africa 132

Chapter 14 Sudan: the gathering storm 138

Chapter 15 The New Sudan 153

Chapter 16 Sudan: politics and refugees 169

Chapter 17 New responsibilities 179

Chapter 18 Widening horizons (India, Romania, Afghanistan,
           Middle East) 182

Chapter 19 East Asia (China and Hong Kong, Japan, Nepal) 197

Chapter 20 Bicentenary celebrations (Britain, New Zealand,
           Australia) 208

Afterword 218

Index 220

List of Illustrations

My father (third from left) at the Royal Hospital 7

Ailsie, Francis, Diana and Elizabeth at Mortehoe 8

Setting off for a day's skiing 14

On the summit of Margherita 36

My mother at The Dingle in her later years 44

Nambulong 55

Tipape ole Seitah 56

Tailoring class 67

Enjoying the Meto Hills 69

A main road in Zaire 79

Robeni Mukulungani with community health workers 85

Bishop Patrice Njojo by the Semliki River 105

Nyakato Kabarole and Tim Rous 126

Refugee from Chad at Angi-Koti 143

Bishop Nathaniel Garang at Malek 157

Bishop Seme Solomona building a Bible School at Kaya 160

Camp for displaced families from the Nuba Mountains, Kadugli . . . 171

With Metropolitan Daniel and Mark Oxbrow at Tirgu Neamt 186

Mine victim in Kabul offering us a rose 188

Colonel Aziz on the north side of the Salang Pass 191

With Elizabeth Ludbrook (left), healing the hurt of 150 years 213

Gathering of CMS General Secretaries at my farewell service 216

Maps

Meto 53

Zaire 77

Republic of Sudan 139

Southern Sudan 154

Foreword

Amongst the multitude of recallings of vivid scenes and moving moments given us by Diana Witts throughout this whole, fascinating record of her adventurous life, one tiny incident stands out for me. It occurred on her visit, as General Secretary of the Church Mission Society (CMS), to Sudan for the joint celebrations of the centenary of the Episcopal Church of Sudan (ECS) and of the bicentenary of CMS, which had helped to bring that church into being. The setting was Yambio, in the area of Southern Sudan controlled by the, then 'rebel', Sudan People's Liberation Army (SPLA). Diana describes how she robed in the cathedral with ten of the southern bishops and then processed across the grass to the place where a service was to be held outside, and how, as guest preacher and General Secretary, she walked with the others through two lines of welcoming pastors and church workers. Then she noticed how the faces of the Mothers' Union workers in those lines lit up as they suddenly saw a woman walking amongst the leading men.

'It was rather like watching a sunrise,' she says, 'seeing the faces of the women break into expressions of delight and joy, and those closest stretched out their hands to touch me. It was so moving I was almost in tears before I reached the end of the line. The women in the ECS have borne much of the pain of their people in recent years as their sons and husbands have been killed in the fighting and they have borne the brunt of responsibility for caring for their battered communities. They form the backbone of the church, and their worn faces show a strength and calmness that springs from their faith and years of patient endurance.' Women do indeed hold up more than half the sky throughout Africa, Asia, South America and indeed the whole world, especially amongst the poor.

What struck me on reading this, and indeed so many other of Diana's graphic accounts of her meetings with such people through a lifetime of working for the liberation and fulfilment of people in so many parts of the world, a lifetime of 'mission' in the fullest sense of the word, is that no previous General Secretary of CMS could quite have done what she did, or meant what she did, in those visits to Churches and in that particular sharing in the struggles of developing peoples rent by war and

deprivation which she accomplished so effectively. Her appointment as
the first woman General Secretary was thus enormously significant for
many people everywhere. And this is true not only because she was a
woman. It is also because she is a remarkable woman, essentially a 'doer'
of theology, never happier than when, as in the greater part of her earlier
working life, she was in the front line of the struggle for the spreading
of the gospel and for a just society in Africa and throughout the world.

From the moment when, before joining CMS, she pioneered the
introduction of girls into a British boys' public school, itself in this
respect highly conservative, to the (strangely similar!) task of expanding
educational opportunities for girls in the deeply conservative society of
a nomadic people in Kenya, the Maasai, Diana was a courageous and
enterprising innovator, inspired by the social implications of the gospel
of Christ. She was loved by her Maasai pupils and became known as
Ngoto Ntoyie (mother of the girls), as well as being hailed by the local
Maasai as *Di-ya-na*. She went on into years of highly demanding and
creative work in community development and theological education in
Zaire (now the Congo), and was then plunged, as a regional Secretary
based at CMS headquarters, not only into West Africa and Zaire again,
and later Southern Africa, but also into the tragic conflict of Sudan.
There was a time when some of us couldn't help seeing her as almost
the Kate Adie of CMS!

Of all the CMS General Secretaries Diana was, perhaps the most
evidently, a *practitioner* of mission, not so much primarily as a theorist, or
even a prophet or visionary, as a person of *action*, willing to be a steadying
presence in the midst of any agonising situation, supremely capable of an
intuitive embodying of CMS in the midst of the devastating chaos of the
Sudanese civil war, or of expressing in New Zealand amongst Maoris and
in the company of a descendant of Henry Williams, an early missionary
wronged by CMS in the nineteenth century, a healing repentance which
was at once effective.

Indeed, through her strong but gentle presence, Diana embodied, as
she does in this whole story, one of the most essential tasks of CMS
today. She brought us close to, and linked us firmly with, so many
growth points in Christian mission across the world, supremely amongst
the poorest and most wounded in a variety of places. She was befriended
and beloved by outstanding women as well as men across the world
scene, people who became for her, as she makes them become for us,
'springs of hope' indeed. And in the quiet humour, courage and faith
with which she was ready to face so many seemingly perilous forces, not

least, more recently, in her own personal encounter with cancer, she herself has been made again and again a spring of hope, a witness to the creative and redemptive power of God's mission in Christ, to which her whole life and this book offer such a vivid and telling testimony.

Bishop Simon Barrington-Ward, KCMG

Acknowledgements

I am grateful to family and friends for encouraging me to put my memoirs on paper, and in particular to Susan Robinson who gave me much helpful advice and to my sister Elizabeth for her interest and creative comments. I am very grateful to Bishop Simon Barrington-Ward for so kindly writing the foreword, and to Eileen Finlayson of the Memoir Club who was constantly helpful through the editorial process. I also owe a huge debt of gratitude to members and supporting parishes of CMS, without whose prayer and giving over the years this book could never have been written.

CHAPTER 1

Growing Up

RUNNING BAREFOOT ACROSS THE LAWN, climbing trees in the woods, building dams in the stream, playing hide-and-seek in the bracken on the common. My most vivid childhood memories are of an active, open-air life, endless creative fun, and the security of being part of a loving extended family. The context for this rural idyll was Gaines, a large Queen Anne house in Herefordshire that belonged to my grandparents. I was born in the house and lived there for most of my first nine years, together with my older sisters Ailsie and Elizabeth.

My father, who was in the British Army, was posted to India when I was barely a year old. My mother went with him and left us in England, as she had been advised that the climate in Karachi was unhealthy for children. Loyalty and a deep sense of duty led her to do this and in later years she shared with us what an agonising decision it had been. She was away for over a year and then returned as events started to move towards the outbreak of war. When she came back she seemed almost a stranger.

This was not as traumatic an experience for us as it might otherwise have been. We were left with our grandparents and exceedingly kind aunts at Gaines where a new nanny, Agnes Ritchie, had recently arrived. She was there when I was born, in May 1936, so we had a special bond. She had an instinctive understanding of children and was a warmly selfless and loving person, always full of fun and ready to dissolve all our tantrums by joking us out of our paddies. I can remember once trying to involve her in a game of monopoly, but the whole game fell apart as she kept trying to help the other players. Nanny stayed with us through the first of the war years and then collapsed through overwork (like our aunts she was called on to be a nursing auxiliary as well as helping at Gaines) and had to have an extended period of recuperation.

We lived together as a family for a short period in Yorkshire when my father was recalled from India and posted to Catterick camp. Then, as war loomed and he was sent to France, the rest of us returned to Gaines where we stayed for the duration of the war. We lived there as part of an extended family and the house was always full of children. In

1940 the Loewen family joined us. Charles Loewen, a Canadian officer in the British Army, was a friend of my father and when Charles was posted abroad his wife Kay and two sons Barney and Johnny came to Gaines and stayed with us till the end of the war. Barney and Johnny were the same ages as Ailsie and Elizabeth respectively, so the two families got on well together and the boys were like brothers to us. Francis, the youngest child in the Witts family, was born in 1941 so there were six permanently resident children. Cousins Johanna and Nicholas, children of our mother's brother Arthur, came to stay regularly, and when the bombing became bad in Birmingham or Coventry evacuees were sent to Gaines until things became quieter at home. These children were city-born and bred and were often quite uncomfortable in such a rural setting. We were astonished that they did not know how to climb trees and were frightened of cows.

My mother had five sisters who all came to Gaines from time to time, but the ones we knew best were Aunt Mary and Aunt Edie who stayed at home to help to run the house. They both enjoyed children and made everything as much fun for us as possible. Despite the constant anxieties and practical difficulties generated by the war, the house was always full of laughter.

Grandfather was a Lancashire cotton-spinner who lived in a succession of large houses in Gloucestershire before finally settling at Gaines. He had been a skilled horseman in his time but in his later years he suffered acutely from arthritis and was confined to a wheelchair, spending most of the time in his study. When I was twelve years old I had an extended stay at Gaines to recuperate from paratyphoid and went to his study every evening before going to bed. I sat on a stool in front of the log fire and was transported to new worlds of the imagination as Grandfather read to me. He had a wonderful reading voice. Granny was the matriarch of the household and had spent many years organising her own family and those of the retainers whose services they had enjoyed in the pre-war days. I was allowed to enter her 'bogey-hole' from time to time, an Aladdin's cave where she kept anything that might ever be needed by anyone, always restocking by the dozen.

Beyond the lawns and garden immediately surrounding the house there were fields and woods, and a stream running through one of the woods fed three small lakes in the valley. We were given total freedom to roam the grounds on our own as long as we went back to the house promptly on hearing the kitchen bell. Its ring could be heard for miles around and, as it was usually rung to summon us for meals, we responded with alacrity. There were also fierce rules about not going anywhere near the lakes without adults, but apart from this we were free to wander in the woods, build tree-houses, play in the stream and explore the outhouses including such magical places as the hay loft. It was all a wonderfully outdoor life.

Immediately outside the front door there was a magnificent cedar tree and a thick rope with a knotted end hung from a high branch. This was known as 'the magnet' as every child arriving at the house would immediately run to the rope and swing in heady circles in the awesome space under the branches. The room that I was born in was just opposite the cedar and a large picture window offered an impressive view of the great tree. When I visited the room half a century later I was fascinated to find cedar branches, heavy with cones, almost touching the window. It had never occurred to me that the immense cedar, like myself, would have grown during that time.

We had just as much fun in the winter as in the summer, even though the house was very cold and there was often ice on the inside panes of the windows in our bedrooms. During the hard winter of 1941 we skated on the ponds for several weeks and had wonderful toboggan rides down a sloping field that led to the stream. During the long freeze of 1943 I went down one day to the lower pond with Francis (then just large enough to be able to run) and our mother. Francis went running out onto the ice and made at speed for the far bank, where the ice was dangerously thin under over-hanging trees. Our mother shouted to him to stop but he kept on running, and in desperation she set out on the ice after him. Mercifully the ice broke almost immediately under her weight so she was able to scramble up the bank, and Francis came running back at the sound of the cracking ice. He was blissfully unaware of the double tragedy that had been so narrowly averted.

During the winter evenings we had wonderful games of hide-and-seek, making full use of the three staircases to escape our searchers. We played games of monopoly that went on for days on end, and we had circular jigsaw puzzles that were perfect for several children to work on together. Every now and again we put on some entertainment for the long-suffering adults and as we had two whole trunks of an amazing assortment of dressing-up clothes to raid these were colourful events. Children's books were read to us at night and once we could read for ourselves we all became avid readers. I can remember numerous nights when I would read by the light of a torch under the blankets after our lights had been turned out. I think on the whole our imaginations were stimulated by enjoying a television-free childhood.

The older children in the house started to go off to boarding school in due course. Barney and Johnny were sent to prep school at Abberley Hall, Ailsie went to Bredenbury and Elizabeth went to Mathon Court for a few years. The rest of us had a governess, Mildred Shepherd, who coped with the difficult task of teaching whatever mixture of ages happened to be in the house at the time. All of us fitted without difficulty into our subsequent education so she must have done a good job.

Those years at Gaines were all lived against the backdrop of war. It must have been a desperately difficult time for the adults, but I was probably too young to realise how serious it all was and had no real fears for the future even though we all had contingency plans for what we would do 'when the Germans come'. We were issued with gas-masks with pictures of Donald Duck and Mickey Mouse on the covers, and had to practise putting these on and gathering under the little bridge across the ha-ha. I still remember the claustrophobic feeling of being shut into one of these masks, but luckily we did not have to wear them for very long even though we were supposed to take them everywhere with us. When the feared invasion was most imminent we were told that if we were out on the lawn and saw aeroplanes we should run for cover immediately – stories abounded of low-flying German planes strafing civilians with machine-gun fire. If the Germans arrived when I was in the house I decided that I would hide behind the hotplate in the passage from the dining room to the kitchen. There was a spare foot of space there that I often climbed into when we were playing hide-and-seek. Visiting children never had any idea that there was any space there so it was a perfect hiding-place and I was convinced that I would be safe there when the Germans came.

When we went on walks up to Bringsty Common we hunted for the silvery tracer foil that was dropped over open land as a decoy to confuse the bomber pilots heading for Birmingham. One time a German plane was shot down near Bromyard and we were allowed to see the crash site. Every night we had to be careful about blackout around the house and, on the rare occasions that we travelled, we got used to the absence of names on station platforms and of signposts on the roads. Fuel was extremely scarce, so a journey by car was a major event. One of our regular walks was down the drive to the main Worcester/Bromyard road to 'see the cars go by'. Often we were disappointed as no car appeared, sometimes we saw one car, and very occasionally (on real red-letter days) two cars would pass by.

Everything was rationed, from clothes to food. Being the third girl I wore the clothes that had been handed down from Ailsie to Elizabeth, and then from Elizabeth to me. I think I must have been about fifteen before I ever had any new clothes. Getting enough food for the large household at Gaines was a constant headache for the adults, and we were always very conscious of the importance of not wasting food. Fresh eggs and milk were a luxury, and any sweets were strictly rationed. We all grew very fond of a pig that was bought when meat was particularly difficult to get. We spent hours scratching its back with a stick and enjoying the ecstatic expression this induced on its face. When it was finally slaughtered none of us had much appetite for the pork that then started to appear. Some of the lawns were ploughed up so that potatoes could be planted to help the war effort, and land-girls arrived to help with the digging.

All the younger men in the community had gone off to fight, so the only regular men in our lives were those who were too old to enlist. Perigo lived with his wife in the lodge at the drive gate. He looked after the windmill that pumped water to the house and was the only person who understood how it worked and was able to keep it going. Pitt was the chauffeur. He still suffered from being gassed in the First World War and would have much preferred to have horses to look after instead of cars. He and his wife lived in the village and we often visited Mrs Pitt when we went on walks there. She spoke with a wonderfully soft, lilting Scottish accent, and gave us old-fashioned humbugs from a large glass jar on a shelf above her chair.

When Nanny returned to Gaines after her long illness we organised a Civic Reception at Knightwick Station to greet her. We sewed black letters saying 'Welcome' onto a white towel that Johanna and I held aloft on broom-handles, both wearing our smartest possible clothes and hats, and Nicholas carried a huge key on a plush red cushion to represent the Freedom of Gaines. Francis ran up and down the train carrying a length of red carpet to put on the platform for her to step onto when she got out, and Mitzi (an elkhound) rushed up and down wearing a huge bow that confused her greatly. A very small boy, Alan Lane, clutched an enormous bouquet that was about twice as big as he was and had to be propelled towards Nanny from behind when she arrived, as he could not see her through the flowers. The other people on the train all looked out of the windows to see what was happening and dear Nanny was quite overcome.

News came through in October 1944 of the death in action in Italy of my grandparents' only son, Arthur. He had been the one boy amongst six girls in the family, and left a German widow who was already facing the particular difficulties and hurts of being German in England at that time. It was a terrible blow to all the family, one that our grandparents carried with the greatest courage and dignity. When VE (Victory in Europe) Day finally arrived there were great celebrations and bonfires were lit on the common. Aunt Mary, in a letter to her sisters, described the children 'squealing round the garden waving flags and almost losing their heads with excitement.' We turned on all the lights in the house, opened all the curtains and then went out onto the lawn to enjoy the amazing sight of the lit-up house after all those years of blackout.

After the war we left Gaines to move to London but regularly went back on visits during the holidays. We greatly looked forward to such visits. When grandfather died in 1952 Gaines was sold and this marked the end of an era for us all.

Royal Hospital, Chelsea

In 1944 my father took up a four-year appointment as Lieutenant-Governor of the Royal Hospital in Chelsea. London was still being bombed at the time so the rest of the family joined him the following year, after the war had ended. We lived in a large house with a private garden and had free run of all the public spaces around the hospital, including the south grounds that ran down to the river. By London standards it was a very spacious environment, but in comparison with Gaines it felt cramped and we always looked forward to visiting Gaines during the holidays.

It was not an easy time for either of our parents. My mother had to cope with housekeeping at a time when there were still severe food shortages and we no longer had the advantage of being in the country and able to grow our own fruit and vegetables. We had to stand in long queues with our precious BUs (Bread Units) and fresh milk was very short. Feeding the family must have been a constant anxiety. My father was still trying to come to terms with his own career. We loved to watch him taking the parade on Sunday mornings, inspecting the line of pensioners in full dress uniform with a huge sword at his side and wearing an ostrich-plumed helmet; at such times I was proud of being a General's daughter. Yet his posting to the Royal Hospital was a retirement appointment, even though in 1944 he was only 55. When he returned to Britain in 1943 he was not given another post in active service; thus he moved from being the General Officer Commanding-in-Chief, Southern Army, India to finding himself unemployed. For a

My father (third from left) at the Royal Hospital

soldier at a time of war that must have been an extraordinarily demoralising experience.

We arrived in London in time to see the victory parade from a hotel in Oxford Street, and watched as seemingly endless numbers of men and women from all the services and from many far-flung parts of the world marched past. The music of the bands was wonderful. In the evening we went up onto the roof of the hospital to watch a spectacular fireworks display and on our way up the stairs climbed over the insensible bodies of pensioners who had been celebrating in the local pubs.

The hospital buildings had suffered a good deal of bomb damage and much work was needed during the next few years to rebuild the gaping holes in the Great Hall and the men's accommodation in the east wing. So there was plenty of practical work to be done, and our father also threw himself into the work of the St John's Ambulance Brigade. One of our jobs was to present bouquets to the visiting royalty who appeared every year on Founder's Day. Elizabeth once contracted chickenpox soon after presenting Princess Elizabeth with a bouquet, so we all watched the papers anxiously for a few weeks to see if she had passed on her chickenpox to the Princess.

On Sunday mornings a short service was held in the chapel. The shortness of the service was for the sake of the pensioners, but it was also ideal for children. We sat in a reserved box pew at the back of the chapel, which was also ideal as it meant we could play bears inside the box without anyone else in the chapel noticing.

I had my first experience of formal education at the Francis Holland School, Graham Terrace, which I attended as a day-girl. The school had closed during the war and I was amongst the first group of girls to enter the reopened school. I enjoyed my time there, though our year had a reputation for being rather wild as most of us had had minimal supervision before. The school had a well-equipped gym which I loved being able to use. It was the next best thing after climbing trees at Gaines. During my last year Francis joined the kindergarten. Ailsie and Elizabeth were both away at boarding school throughout our Chelsea years.

It was still not very easy to travel about and we all spent many hours waiting for the 137 buses to come across Chelsea Bridge. They were few and far between. Smog was still a factor of London life, especially in the winter, and I have vivid memories of one occasion when the smog was so thick that I totally lost my bearings in the middle of a road.

Ailsie, Francis, Diana and Elizabeth at Mortehoe

I had no idea where either pavement was and for a moment of terror felt utterly abandoned in a silent, sightless world.

We made up for the restrictions of the war years by going to a party or theatre nearly every night of the final winter that we were in London. We were always in a fever of anticipation by the time the show started as my father always insisted on arriving half an hour before the curtain rose. During the summer holidays we twice went to the coast of Devon, staying at the Haven Hotel in Mortehoe. It was a perfect place for a family holiday, with rocky coves and sandy beaches all within walking distance of the hotel. During our last stay there, in 1948, I picked up paratyphoid from eating ice-creams and was not well enough to start at boarding school in the autumn as planned. Instead I was sent to Gaines in an ambulance to recuperate while the rest of the family moved to Cirencester.

In Cirencester my parents bought a house called Magpies where they lived until my father died in 1969. My father threw himself into all sorts of good works and was greatly sought after to chair committees. My mother continued her role of supporting him and caring for all the family as we came and went. For my next ten years of school and university Magpies was the home to which I returned every holiday.

My father and I had a rather stormy relationship and every now and then we reached an impasse that ended (for me) in tears. But one night after such an episode, when I had gone to bed feeling miserable, he came up to my room, knelt beside my bed, and asked me to forgive him. I knew that my own behaviour had been totally out of order, so I was profoundly humbled by his coming to me in this way. I think that moment laid the foundation for a new relationship and in later years, when my Christian faith had come to life in a fresh way, we came together in real understanding and affection.

For four years I went to Brondesbury-at-Stocks, the boarding school where both Ailsie and Elizabeth had gone ahead of me. I felt a misfit from the start and was very unhappy at times. The school was more geared to turning out debutantes than to equipping girls to earn their living, and I left the school knowing how to do a court curtsy but never having heard of Physics and Chemistry. Having discovered these interesting subjects I signed up for crash courses in them at the technical college in Cambridge. Two years later I had acquired enough A levels (Physics, Chemistry, Maths and English) to read Physics at Bristol University.

It was all a bit of a scramble, but I greatly enjoyed my time in Cambridge. I stayed in a house in Storey's Way run by Dr and Mrs

Bevan, commonly known as 'The Bevanry'. There were usually about half a dozen English girls in the house, and the same number of Swedish girls. It was a fairly chaotic household, but great fun, and we were all swept into the social life of the university in different ways. During the winter of 1953 there was a prolonged freeze and the Cam froze for several weeks from the Backs alongside the colleges right up to Grantchester. We got hold of skates and had a marvellous time skating along the Backs and up the river as far as time allowed. People had parties on the ice and racing was organised on the lakes at one of the local sewage farms.

At Bristol I was introduced to rock climbing. Members of the climbing club used to go out on Saturday afternoons to climb the limestone cliffs above the Avon Gorge which rose for three hundred feet above traffic on the Portway. It was my first experience of rock-climbing and I loved it.

During my second summer vacation from Bristol I went up to Cumbria and spent three weeks working in the Bridge Hotel in Buttermere. I cleaned the rooms with Lizzy from Cockermouth who loved trying on the guests' clothes. I was always in an agony of suspense lest the guests should walk in when Lizzy was admiring herself in the mirror dressed in their best finery. She had two expressions, 'Ee, it's 'ot' and 'Ee, I'm sweating' and a little ditty that ran: 'Down in jungle living in a tent, better than a pre-fab, no rent.' I rarely heard her say anything else.

On free afternoons we swam in Crummock Water, and on my day off I walked along the hills opposite, Red Pike and High Stile, looking down on the brilliant blue waters of Buttermere and Loweswater and the distant sea. I fell further in love with the hills. At the end of the three weeks I joined Ann Metcalfe-Gibson, a friend from the Bevanry, who lived in the beautiful village of Ravenstonedale. From there we drove up to Scotland and toured the west coast, camping whenever it was dry. Although we had some very wet weather, especially on Skye, it was my first taste of Scotland and an introduction to hills to which I later returned many times. We had one fine day when we enjoyed the Celtic peace of Iona.

In Cirencester one year the British Legion organised an open-air pageant in the grounds of Cirencester Park. Almost the entire population of the town was enlisted to take part and it was done on a lavish scale. My father played General Gordon and was assassinated by dozens of secondary schoolboys dressed up as dervishes. They threw spears towards him with alarming enthusiasm, and he wore a red fez and a sword that had been passed down to one of Gordon's descendants. I was enlisted to play Nell Gwyn, because of my red hair, and had two King Charles spaniels in attendance plus two real live Chelsea Pensioners. King Charles was played by the handsome master of the local hunt and Ailsie and Elizabeth were ladies-in-waiting. The floodlit setting in the trees was very beautiful and we had four fine evenings.

We made regular visits to Gaines, and after the house was sold we used to visit Granny and the Aunts at Middle Chinnock in Somerset. Aunt Mary and Aunt Edie continued to make visits there almost as much fun as we had had at Gaines, though the house and garden were much smaller. Granny used to get up early every morning and write all her letters before breakfast – she was a copious correspondent – and she knitted quantities of socks and jumpers for us all.

We also made regular visits to the small Cotswold village of Upper Slaughter that had been home to the Witts family for over two hundred years. Our forebears had been Lords of the Manor since 1852, and for four generations they were also rectors of St Peter's Church. Our grandfather, great-grandfather and great-great-grandfather were success-ive rectors of St Peter's for over a century between them. Our great-great-grandfather, Francis Witts, kept a diary, parts of which have been published in a book entitled *The Diary of a Cotswold Parson*. The family lived in a large home that served as both rectory and manor.

My father grew up in Slaughter, the youngest in a family of five boys and three girls, and he went to the village school with some eighty other local children. He met my mother when he was at home on leave one year. The Wrigley family were then living at Wyck Hill House, just a mile or so away, so they met regularly out hunting and at dinner parties, and my father finally proposed on a skiing holiday in Switzerland. Being the fifth son, my father never had any expectation of inheriting the Slaughter estate. In the event, two of his brothers, Edward and George, never married. His brother Frank married but died before having any children. His brother Jack married and had one son, Stephen, who sadly suffered from schizophrenia. So the estate finally came to my father when Uncle George died in 1958. By that time he was too old to cope with a move from Magpies, so the Manor was let to a series of tenants, the last of whom ran it as a guest house. It was a great sadness for him that the house came to him too late for our family to live there.

As children we were taken over to Slaughter regularly from Magpies. We enjoyed playing in the garden that had a great sweep of lawn, a skating pond, a bridge across the stream where we could play Pooh sticks, and lots of exciting barns, but we were always slightly overawed by Uncle Edward and his sister Aunt Agnes, who were quite unused to children. We always felt that we had to be on our best behaviour at the Manor, in contrast to our experience of Gaines. When Uncle Edward died in 1956 the next brother George moved there together with his sister Aunt Edith, and when Uncle George died Aunt Agnes and Aunt Edith moved to a cottage in Wyck Rissington and the contents of the house were sold.

Our family moved into the house for just three weeks before the sale to try to sort things out and it was a huge job. It seemed as though no one had thrown anything away for the previous two hundred years. There were books, papers, furniture and pictures, not to mention cupboards full of linen and lofts full of a mixture of useless, rusting machinery and rare museum items. Much of the paper was of no value, but hidden amongst the rubbish were items that were seized on as treasures by the county archivist, so we could not simply throw it all away. The auctioneer, Arthur Negus, was extraordinarily patient as Aunt Agnes and Aunt Edith regularly changed their minds about what they wanted to take with them to the cottage, and items went in and out of the catalogue every day.

During the later days at Magpies my father started to lose his memory and became more and more agitated when unexpected things happened around him. Those years took a real toll on my mother, but she cared for him faithfully until he had to go into hospital for his last few weeks. He died in 1969, shortly after his eightieth birthday and their ruby wedding. The following year Magpies was sold and my mother moved to The Dingle, a dower house built in Upper Slaughter by my grandfather.

CHAPTER 2

Off to Canada

AFTER LEAVING BRISTOL IN 1958 I got a job as a hospital physicist at the Charing Cross Hospital in central London. I worked in the radiotherapy department, using a radioactive isotope of iodine to monitor iodine uptake in patients suffering from malfunction of the thyroid gland. It was fairly routine, undemanding work, and I used most of my energy enjoying the evenings in London and going on interesting expeditions at weekends. Ailsie and I shared a room in the flat in Candover Street that Ailsie had found when she was nursing at the Middlesex Hospital.

In February Ailsie, Elizabeth and myself went to Obergurgl in Austria on a skiing party organised by our cousins Peter and Gill Wimperis. It was my first experience of skiing and I loved every minute of it. We had great fun for those two weeks and the skiing conditions were excellent. This and other trips abroad whetted my appetite further for being in the mountains and for travelling, so Ann Metcalfe-Gibson and I started talking about finding jobs in Canada. Ann worked in the chemistry laboratory at the Hammersmith Hospital and her head of department had contacts in Montreal. He eventually found jobs for us both, at the Montreal General Hospital for Ann and at the Royal Victoria Hospital for myself. In November 1959 we set sail for Montreal on the *Empress of England*. Nanny came to wave us off from Liverpool, and a bagpiper piped a lament as we sailed off down the Clyde from Greenock.

On arrival in Montreal we were welcomed by Dr Bates (Ann's future boss) and taken to Harrison House where we stayed for our first year. Miss Harrison, an exceedingly kind but rather eccentric American lady, had a large house on Pine Avenue where she gave board and lodging to a mixture of English and Canadian girls. Ann and I were put in a circular turret at the top of the house that had no heating, so we nearly froze to death to start with. Yet it was a wonderful place to start our time in Montreal, and we made some lifelong friends while we were there.

My job at the Royal Victoria Hospital was almost non-existent for the first few months. I was employed as a research assistant to help an

Setting off for a day's skiing

American doctor who was researching into lung function. We had an elaborate method of monitoring lung function by getting patients to breathe in a radioactive isotope of Xenon gas and following its movements using a battery of Geiger counters. Readings from the counters were recorded on a multiple channel tape recorder that arrived six months after I did. So for those first months I did a few other odd jobs to help out in the department and otherwise saved my energy for the weekends.

Almost every weekend we went up north and skied in the Laurentian Mountains. The first winter we struggled to take our skis by bus but by the second winter we had our own car, an enormous Dodge, which made life much easier. By then we had moved out of Harrison House to a flat on Pine Avenue West that Ann and I shared with Sue Daniell. Sue and I had part shares in a ski shack at Christieville and we had wonderful weekends up there. When we arrived we often had to dig our way through several feet of snow to get to the door of the cabin, then we collected logs to get a fire going; it was sometimes bitterly cold with temperatures going down to as low as forty degrees below zero. But with a good fire, hot food and plenty of beer we soon warmed up, and sang rousing songs with the help of a guitar. In the morning all we had to do was to put our skis on outside the back door and set off to enjoy the day.

There was plenty of downhill skiing available in the area and we also enjoyed cross-country skiing through the forest where well-marked trails led into a silent, spell-bindingly beautiful world of frozen lakes and trees – a different world from the noisy clamour of the pistes. For yet more variety we went southwards across the border to visit the ski centres of New Hampshire and Vermont. It was wonderful to be able to ski so regularly through the winter, though when the temperature fell to forty degrees below zero we nearly froze to death on the chairlifts despite the provision of bearskin rugs, and we had to watch each other's faces for signs of frostbite.

In the spring the ice on the St Lawrence River started to break up, which was always a dramatic sight. Huge blocks of ice crashed against each other as they were swept downstream in the fast-flowing current. As the temperature rose the sap started to run in the maple trees, and we went to sugaring-off parties where sap was collected in cans that were emptied into a huge vat over a log fire. The boiling syrup was then thrown onto the snow where it crystallised into delicious sticky toffee. With the coming of spring, green fields reappeared in the country round about, a dramatic emergence from their five-month blanket of snow.

During the summer we went to many of the same places to walk in the hills and canoe on the lakes. In the Adirondack Mountains and around the shores of Saranac Lakes in New York State lean-to shelters were provided for hikers and canoeists, three-sided log cabins with stone fireplaces outside. After cooking a meal on a log fire we would throw our sleeping-bags onto the pine needles that covered the floor and watch the stars through the open side of the lean-to. Those were wonderful nights and occasionally we saw shimmering green displays of the Northern Lights. In the fall we paddled our way in Canadian canoes through still waters that reflected the brilliant colours of the trees: the red leaves of the maples set against the deep evergreen trees behind them and the golden leaves of the silver birches and their white trunks. Those were magical days and we relished the freedom of being able to explore so many beautiful places so easily.

During our second winter an ice storm hit Montreal, when several inches of freezing rain fell in a few hours, followed by high winds. We were up north when it happened, and returned on the Sunday night to find a city that had been plunged into darkness as power lines had collapsed under the weight of ten-foot icicles and a three-inch wrapping of ice around the cables. Icicles hung in enormous curtains from any lines that were still standing and from the road signs and billboards. Trees had tumbled as the weight of ice broke off huge branches, but the trees that were still standing were an amazing sight. Ice covered every tiny twig, and the avenues of trees lining the roads into the city stood like giant chandeliers over the deserted streets. The headlights from our car lit them up and the only other source of light came from the flicker of candles from behind curtained windows. The storm was a disaster as many people were left without heating or the wherewithal to cook food at the height of winter. But it was an extraordinarily beautiful sight.

Francis came out at one stage and I managed to get a job for him as a porter at the Royal Victoria Hospital for a few weeks. Then Ailsie arrived at Easter 1961, just as Ann and I finished our jobs, and joined us for a tour of North America in the Dodge. Another friend, Liz Palmer, also joined us, so we bought a tent that would sleep four and set off on what turned out be a 13,000 mile journey.

Basically we circled the continent, starting down the east coast and travelling south as far as Mexico City where we went to the Ballet Folklorica, an amazing evening of traditional Aztec and contemporary Mexican dancing that was all executed with huge verve and energy. Outside the city we visited the ancient stepped pyramids of the Sun and Moon at Teotihuacán and spent a night in Tasco, an old silver-mining village in the mountains to the south. Back in the States we explored the spectacular canyons of the west before reaching the west coast at San Francisco. We followed the coast as far as Vancouver and then drove back to Montreal via the Rockies on the trans-Canada highway. We camped everywhere except in the cities and experienced many different climates, from snow in the Blue Ridge Mountains of Virginia to the heat of the Mexican plains. It was a great trip and we finally arrived back in Montreal, eleven weeks after leaving, to a warm welcome from Sue and Egbert, our resident terrapin.

A few days after arriving in Montreal Ann and I set sail for Southampton. Our time in Canada was a wonderful experience, and after all the weeks of travelling we had got well into the rhythm of being on the move. Settling back into Britain after all that was not easy for either of us.

Teaching in London

My jobs as a hospital physicist in London and in Montreal had both provided good work experience, though neither job was particularly demanding. I enjoyed collating and analysing the data we collected, but at the end of the day I always had to hand over the information to the medical experts for interpretation of the results. I realised that without some medical training I would never really be able to engage fully with the implications of what I was doing. So I cast around for some other kind of work when we got back to England, and decided to have a go at teaching. In those days it was possible to get a teaching job on the strength of a university degree without having to have any teacher training.

Early in September I went along to the education offices of the London County Council and offered my services. Girls' schools were always short of Maths and Physics teachers, so I was offered a post immediately at Parliament Hill School, a girls' comprehensive school in North London. Two days later I arrived at the school, knowing nothing about the skills needed for teaching. The headmistress smiled, saying it was a risk for her to take me on, but she was obviously desperate to get someone into the classroom. So in I plunged, diving in at the deep end, and for the next few weeks struggled frantically to keep my head above water.

Parliament Hill was a relatively well-disciplined school by comprehensive school standards but I was given some of the least able and most difficult classes when I started and had no idea how to handle them. Gradually I learnt how to achieve some semblance of order, through hard and painful experience, and in my second year I was given a much more reasonable spread of ability. At that stage I shared a flat with two friends in Campden Hill Square; it was a lovely flat, but the journey to work was awkward and entailed a bus and two-stage tube journey. 1963 was another very cold winter so all our pipes froze and I seemed to spend an eternity at the start of each day freezing to death waiting for buses.

One great advantage of teaching was having the school holidays and I made full use of the opportunities that gave to do more travelling. Over the first Easter that I was back I went high-level ski-touring in the Oetztal in Austria which was a marvellous experience. We started off at Obergurgl and then skied from hut to hut over the mountains for ten days. We started each day early, before the sun had risen, and set off up the nearest glacier using skins. As the sun rose its rays lit up the snow around us and as we gained height the views expanded. Then after several hours of hard climbing we emerged on to a col and a whole new world opened up before us – snow-covered peaks as far as the eye could see with glaciers sweeping down to the valleys below. We took off our skis to scramble up the nearest rocky summit and get a heady sense of being on top of the world, then back down to the col where we put our skis on again, this time without skins, and had an exhilarating run down the glacier over deep, soft, untracked snow to the next hut.

We had an excellent local guide who was able to take us out each day, even when the clouds were down and visibility was almost non-existent. On one such day we crossed a glacier that was broken up by unseen crevasses and our guide roped us up to each other for safety. None of us were very professional skiers, and as soon as the guide told us that it was important not to fall we started tumbling like ninepins out of sheer nervousness. When one person fell the taut rope brought down the skier ahead, and then the skier behind crashed into them both. Eventually we were released from our rope, which was becoming more of a hazard than a help, but were still exhorted to be careful. We climbed all the major peaks in the area and after ten magnificent days of high-level skiing we descended to Solden. By then the snow had started to melt, so for the last few hundred yards we took our skis off and walked down through green meadows, trampling a multi-coloured carpet of spring flowers under our ski boots. It was an amazing time, the most memorable of all my skiing experiences.

The summer holidays offered more possibilities for travel, and during the summer of 1962 I joined three friends to go on a camping trip across Europe that took in Istanbul, Athens, Corinth and Venice, travelling whenever possible by water. The following summer I joined Ailsie, Sue and Ann on a visit to Dubrovnik and Korcula, sailing down the Dalmatian coast from Venice. That was another memorable trip. Over the Easter of 1963 Sue and I went up to the Lake District and climbed Great Gable in a sleet storm. We battled against icy rain that almost blew us off the mountain and then emerged on the summit to find that it was like Piccadilly Circus. We were astonished to find there were so many other people up there in such bad conditions and it was one of the events that confirmed my growing sense that I wanted to be off again to somewhere in the world where there was more space. None of us had found it easy to settle in Britain again after our Canadian odyssey, and I still felt very restless.

When I went back to Parliament Hill for the summer term I found a cutting on the notice board advertising posts for teachers in secondary schools in a number of different parts of the world, including East and West Africa. In those days the British Government gave aid to several countries in the form of teachers, particularly teachers of Maths, English and Science. So I got in touch with the Crown Agents and put in an application to go to teach Maths and Physics in East Africa. After a long delay I was called for an interview and advised to go to West Africa; I was told that schools in East Africa would not be able to offer teaching at sixth-form level (which was not in fact true). By then I had had a good look at a relief map of Africa and seen how many high mountains there were in East Africa, and how few mountains of any kind there were in West Africa. So I stuck to my guns and said that I wanted to go to Kenya.

By the time we went on our holiday to Dubrovnik and Korcula I had heard no more news from the Crown Agents, although by then I had given in my notice at Parliament Hill and said my farewells. When we got back to London again at the end of August I found a letter asking me to go to the Highlands School in Kenya, where the term started the following week. It was all a bit of a scramble, but off I went to Nairobi in early September, having signed a contract with the Crown Agents to teach in Kenya for the next two years.

CHAPTER 3

Arrival in Africa

I ARRIVED IN NAIROBI JUST IN TIME to join the school train to Eldoret. Although Eldoret is only two hudred miles from Nairobi, the journey takes twelve hours and it was a wonderful way to spend my first day in Africa. As the train reached the edge of the Rift Valley the crater of the ancient volcano Longonot came into view and the plains beyond stretched far into the distance. It was a huge view that reminded me of the Grand Canyon. We passed lakes that were pink with flamingo and we crossed the Equator at 9,000 feet at Timboroa, where it was very cold and mist swirled round the pine trees. For the last few hours the train took us through the blackness of an African night; no lights of any kind relieved the darkness outside the windows of the train. On that day I had a strange sense of having come home.

Eldoret lies at a height of 8,000 feet on the fertile Uashin Gishu Plateau. The area was first settled by outsiders when Afrikaner farmers from South Africa, in search of a new home after the Boer War, made a massive trek northwards by ox wagon and found the land of their dreams on the plateau. British settlers arrived in the area after the First World War when demobbed soldiers were encouraged by the British government to buy land in Kenya. The whole area soon became known as the White Highlands.

As the day for Kenyan Independence drew near many of the Afrikaners decided to go back to South Africa, and most of the British farmers, aware that the time had come for Kenyans to own more of the good farming land, were selling up as and when opportunity arose. Memories of the Mau Mau Emergency were still fresh and many people were predicting chaos and disaster after the handover of sovereignty. I was assured more than once that Jomo Kenyatta, the President elect, was the devil incarnate. There was still much racial prejudice about and, had Kenyatta stirred up trouble, things could have become very difficult for the European and Asian communities. In the event President Kenyatta showed remarkable generosity of spirit towards those who had imprisoned him, and repeatedly urged his fellow Kenyans to work peacefully together to build a multiracial society. He was held in such respect by the vast majority of Kenyans that others followed his lead, and this ensured a peaceful transition of power.

The Highlands School, which had only been open for a few years, was designed to meet the needs of expatriate parents who wanted their children to end up with entry qualifications for British universities. In 1963 the boarders were all European girls whose families lived in Kenya or Uganda, and there were a few day-girls from local Asian families. No African girls had at that time been admitted. I was disconcerted to discover that I had been sent to a high-cost European school and applied for a transfer to an African school. However, the headmistress refused to pass my request on to the Ministry of Education in Nairobi. Once I had digested the reality of the situation I settled down to enjoy the Highlands, not a difficult thing to do.

My home was a small cottage in the school grounds, only a two-minute walk from the classroom block. On the first morning I walked across the grass to the school past jacaranda trees and brilliantly coloured flowering shrubs such as frangipani, bougainvillea and poinsettia. Sunbirds added to the colours, bright blue lizards scampered about the lawns, and the sun shone from a deep blue sky. The air was clear and the sky was high in the way that is unique to plateau country. All a far cry from the icy greyness of London and struggling with buses and trains. At midday I swam in the warm waters of the spacious school swimming pool. Then when I started teaching I found I had small classes of well-behaved girls, who were both intelligent and motivated to learn. It felt like a dream that was almost too good to be true.

Independence Day was in early December, and I went to Nairobi just a week before the official handover ceremony, primarily to met up with Robert Chambers who had been a neighbour in Cirencester. Robert introduced me to the Mountain Club of Kenya, and on the Sunday John Blacker, a club member, took me out to Lukenya, a rock face about twenty miles outside Nairobi that was owned by the club. There I met Charles Richards who, with his wife Elizabeth, later became a close family friend. From then on Charles, John and myself climbed together whenever I was able to make the two-hundred-mile journey from Eldoret, and in later years we climbed together in Scotland, Wales and Arctic Norway. Robert himself dashed off that day to make final preparations for the climb he was leading up Mount Kenya to celebrate Independence.

It was a wonderful time to be in Kenya as in those days one could travel safely all over the country apart from some areas in the Northern Frontier District where Somali bandits raided their neighbours from time to time. We could travel freely across the borders into Uganda and

Tanzania with minimal immigration formalities and using the same currency, the East Africa shilling. We were free most weekends so regularly explored the varied and beautiful terrain within striking distance of Eldoret. We simply set off with food and tents and went wherever we wished. If it was cold in Eldoret we often drove down onto the hot plains of the Rift Valley floor, some 3,000 feet below. During the dry season in Eldoret, when it could get quite hot, we visited nearby Mount Elgon and cooled off on its 14,000 foot summit. I bought a second-hand VW beetle that survived thousands of miles on rough roads over the next two years without ever breaking down, and I had a tiny tent from the Gaines days.

Anne Horsfall, who had lived in Kenya for many years, took me for my first night's camping in Africa to a clearing at the base of Kadam, a handsome mountain rising from the plains of NE Uganda. We arrived to find that a professional hunting safari was already encamped with two white hunters, two clients who were Argentinian ranchers, and an entourage of camp attendants. They were very welcoming and invited us to dinner. This turned out to be a five-course meal served by robed bearers, and as we sat in a tent lit by flickering hurricane lamps a massive thunderstorm broke overhead. What with flashes of lightning, continuously rolling thunder and the sound of torrential rain, the whole setting was quite dramatic. The Ernest Hemingway scenario was completed when the second hunter returned from the outer darkness and threw the carcase of a leopard at our feet. I was sorry about the leopard, but even in death it was a superbly graceful sight. We had a very wet night, and our little tents almost floated away in the flash flood that swept through the campsite, but it was a unique experience, tasting the drama and luxury of an old-time hunting safari.

During the Christmas holidays I drove with Pat Pearce, a teacher at the Highlands, to Marangu in Northern Tanzania to climb Mount Kilimanjaro. It was a strenuous five-day expedition, climbing from the tropical rainforest to the snow-covered summit at 19,000 feet. The climax of the climb came on the fourth day when we set off from the top hut to climb the final four thousand feet. In a letter to my parents I wrote:

'Our guide woke us at 1.30 a.m. and we spent a bad-tempered half-hour putting on boots in an over-crowded hut by the dim light of our flickering paraffin lamp. Someone miraculously got a frozen primus to function and produced hot coffee all round. At 2 a.m. we emerged and started up the mountain in single file and in silence. Once outside in the fresh air it was quite beautiful, the clouds had cleared and we climbed steadily up the black mountainside under a starlit sky, the snow on either side lit up by a full moon. Then we were kicking steps in steep snow that seemed to stretch on forever and were aware of nothing but the hard cold snow and the silhouettes of the hooded climbers ahead. Gradually the sky in the east became lighter and the sun rose from behind Mawenzi, lighting up the snow and the clouds circling the peak. We reached the top after five hours and found ourselves standing on the rim of a volcanic crater, a great bowl filled with snow and ice. The rim itself was formed by dramatic ice-falls covered with thick fresh snow, and beyond the rim the plains of Kenya and Tanganyika disappeared into the blue distance beyond.'

It was a breathtaking sight; the whole of Africa seemed to lie at our feet. Then we began the long climb down. As we arrived wearily at Marangu the following day the porters presented us with wreaths of everlasting flowers that I still have. It was a great trip and my first taste of the snow-capped mountains of East Africa.

During the Easter holidays of 1964 I flew to Addis Ababa with Eirene Charles, another teacher from the Highlands, and spent two weeks travelling around Ethiopia by bus. We went north to Asmara, a three-day journey on an Italian-built road that wound its way through massive mountain ranges. Hairpin bends, similar to those in the Alps, took us over four passes above 10,000 feet and dropped us down into canyons below. The bus tilted dangerously on bends as it was so overloaded on the roof, and it had no self-starter. All the strongest passengers had to get out and push every time we renewed our journey and there was great excitement each time to see how many of the pushers had been left behind.

We returned to Addis on a more westerly route that took us through Axum, the ancient capital of Ethiopia, through the spectacular Simien Mountains, and on to Gondar where we explored the ancient castles and looked round wonderful churches that had ceilings covered in pictures of round-eyed angels. Then on to the shores of Lake Tana, the source of the Blue Nile, and the Tissisat Falls where the Blue Nile drops a hundred feet after leaving the lake. Nearer Addis the road crosses the dramatic Blue Nile Gorge and plunges over four thousand feet as it winds its way across. The road was lined with wrecks of lorries and buses that had come to grief over the years.

Ethiopia is certainly one of the most spectacularly beautiful countries in Africa, and it was very good to visit the country while Emperor Haile

Selassie was still in power. People were still wearing traditional dress; all the men trotting past us on their donkeys wore jodhpurs and topis and carried black umbrellas as protection from the sun. The donkeys had embroidered saddle-cloths and jingling bridles so it was all a most colourful sight and our greetings were courteously returned in triplicate.

★ ★ ★

Surprised by God

About six months after I first arrived in Eldoret events overtook me that came as a complete surprise and changed the course of my life. I had never been a particularly faithful churchgoer, despite having been brought up in a loving Christian family. As a child I had been taught stories of the Bible and had been taken to church and encouraged to pray. I was baptised as a baby and at fifteen was confirmed along with the rest of my form at school. Since then I had continued going to church rather sporadically, and by the time I arrived in Kenya I simply saw the Christian faith as a rather dull business of trying to be good. Despite all the advantages of a Christian home and education, I had failed to understand the crux (literally) of the faith.

During the early months of 1964 I began to reflect on the meaning of my life and was startled to discover that I had no idea what the answer was. The question had never occurred to me before. One weekend I went camping with some friends by the Suam river on the plains to the north of Eldoret, and as we drove back up the escarpment we stopped to enjoy the superb view that opened up behind us. The evening sun was low in the sky, lighting up the mountain ranges that rose from the plains below, and I was suddenly filled with awareness that it was God who had created all this beauty, and that my own life was a gift from God. It was a completely unexpected moment of revelation.

In the days that followed, awareness of the creative love of God continued to be with me, but I had a sense that there was more that I still needed to understand. The next Sunday I went to Holy Communion in the early morning, and as I knelt by the rail and put out my hands to receive the bread I realised that I had no idea what I was doing. Yet I also knew that I *must* know. Afterwards I asked the vicar if I could see him and in the evening we talked together. He listened to my story and then spoke about the cross, but at the time it made no sense to me and I left feeling empty and confused. Back in my flat, still in a state of total confusion and not even trying to pray, I suddenly saw a figure hanging from a cross. The vision appeared only fleetingly, but it was the most illumined and meaningful moment of my life. Even now I can be moved to tears by the memory. I knew that what I had seen was the most important event in the history of the cosmos, and I knew that I had come home.

In the days that followed I was filled with an immense sense of peace and a deep joy. The next day when I went shopping I wanted to tell the people I met in the greengrocers to stop worrying about the price of cabbages and instead rejoice that Christ had died for them. I have to confess that my British reserve prevented me from actually doing this, but the experience of that Sunday night left me with a deep desire to share with others the truth that I had been shown about the saving love of God. It was both a moment of new life in Christ and a call to mission.

During the rest of my time in Eldoret I became involved in the life of the local church, joining in the regular worship and teaching in the Sunday school. At the school I became involved in leading Bible studies with the girls, and was able to have fellowship with some of the other staff. Later that year Jenny Bryson, whose parents lived in Eldoret, arrived at the school to teach English and we started a close and enduring friendship. When I next went to Nairobi and climbed at Lukenya I found that I was able to talk freely about what was happening for me with Charles Richards, who had a wide and wise understanding of the Christian faith. He later accepted a post with the World Council of Churches that took him around the world helping to set up centres for the publication of Christian literature. I looked after his boots and whenever he came through Nairobi we went climbing together.

When my time at the Highlands came to an end I knew that I would need to spend time somewhere in the UK where I would be able to reflect further on the Christian faith and find out what God wanted me to do next. The Anglican Bishop in Nakuru suggested that I should join the community at Lee Abbey, which is what I did, and I had six very happy months there in the first half of 1966.

★ ★ ★

Travelling on
In August 1964 Hilary Birley, a friend from London, came to Kenya and we made a tour of Central Africa. Hilary was working for Heinemann's educational publishers and was chasing up authors for contributions to

their Africa series, so we had contacts almost all the way and we both had friends in Salisbury (now Harare).

Having driven down the Great North Road through Tanganyika (now Tanzania) we visited Northern Rhodesia (now Zambia) and Southern Rhodesia (now Zimbabwe) and came back via Mozambique and Nyasaland (now Malawi). Central Africa was poised for the move to independence, hence all the name changes, and it was an interesting time to see what was happening. In Zambia we found there was intense interest in the political changes that were taking place and we were drawn into many late night discussions about it all. In Harare, by contrast, the impending political changes were very rarely part of the conversation. We made a day visit by air to the Victoria Falls and I can still remember the wild beauty of the place and the drama of the thunderous volume of boiling, rushing water crashing down into the gorges below.

Our return journey took us through the length of Malawi. After a night with friends in Zomba we drove on to Lake Malawi and camped on the beach in the dark. The next morning we woke to see a rising sun reflected in the still waters of the lake, with silver fishes rising and brilliantly-coloured birds flying over the water. We cooked breakfast, had a swim and then set off again. The next night we spent in a rest house high up on the Nyika Plateau, a wild and beautiful moorland area, then on to Mbeya and back home on the Great North Road. In Nairobi Francis arrived to join us, en route from Aden and Hadramaut. Sadly, by the time we got to Eldoret Francis was feeling very unwell and it turned out that he was suffering from hepatitis. That put paid to plans for doing any more travelling, and once he felt fit enough to face the journey I took him to Nairobi and he flew back to London.

The school holidays presented a wonderful opportunity to explore East Africa. Kenya alone offered mountains, lakes, game-covered plains, deserts and an unspoilt coast of white sands, palm trees and coral reefs. At that time there were only a few designated game parks so we could camp anywhere and enjoy the game areas without being constrained by official regulations and surrounded by tourists. Lake Baringo in the Rift Valley was a favourite place for a weekend from Eldoret and we always had great fun there. There were no facilities for tourists in those days so we simply camped on the lakeshore and usually found a good supply of balsa wood logs that were ideal material for making a raft.

Climbing was still my favourite activity, and I drove down to Nairobi for the weekend whenever possible to join the Mountain Club of

Kenya. The clubhouse was at Wilson Airport and on arrival on a Saturday afternoon I would find Charles Richards and Geoff Newham, a close friend of his, working on the buildings. The next morning we would go to the early service at the cathedral and then spend the day climbing at Lukenya where there were wonderful rock faces to explore. We ate lunch in the shade of an umbrella tree and at the end of the day drove back into Nairobi and had a cold beer together at the clubhouse. From time to time the club organised weekend outings and occasionally I managed to join these trips, though it was always a bit tight getting back to school on the Sunday as the drive back to Eldoret took four hours.

One memorable weekend I joined a club expedition to climb Ol Doinyo Lengai (The Mountain of God), a volcano in the Rift Valley in northern Tanzania. The volcano is still live and periodically erupts lava that has a high content of soda and thus looks white. From a distance it looks as though the top of the mountain is covered in snow. It is greatly revered by the local Maasai because of its height, its appearance and its alarming volcanic activity. As the mountain was approaching another active phase, we decided it would be interesting to investigate. The mountain is on the open plains near Lake Natron and there are no roads in the vicinity, so we set off across country in a convoy of seven Land-Rovers. It took us all day to reach the foot of the mountain as we had to cross numerous dry river-beds.

We drove up the mountain as far as possible and then camped out for the night, lying in the wind and watching the stars. We were high up on the grassy shoulder of the mountain and had a stupendous view of the plains below; volcanic cones of all shapes and sizes littered the plains, cloud patterns swept over them, and Lake Natron lay beyond. When the sun rose the next morning, pink light diffused across the plains and it was as though a primeval world was being created before our eyes.

It took us about four hours to climb the 4,000 feet to the crater rim. Then we climbed 1,000 feet down into the crater and found ourselves in a weird white world. Writing to my parents afterwards I described the scene: 'The walls of the crater were white cliffs and the base was pure white, flat except for a few miniature cones of most dramatic shapes, also white, steam shooting out at intervals. Every now and again there would be sound like that of waves on the shore, magnified as it reverberated round the crater, and we could see the boiling lava inside one of the cones wallowing up and down. It all looked like a snow scene except for the astonishing shapes. It was a most extraordinary experience to be there.' The crater erupted the next year.

Later in that same holiday I made my first trip up Mount Kenya with Tony South and two other friends from the Mountain Club. We approached the central peaks from the east side of the mountain via the Choggoria track, which at that time was a little used but very beautiful route. After a wet night at the Choggoria hut we reached Hall Tarns and camped at 14,000 feet on a grassy shelf overlooking the dramatic Nithi Gorge and encircled by saw-toothed crags above, then on to Top Hut at the top of the Lewis Glacier. From the hut we had a superb view of glorious curving snow surfaces and green crevasses. Armed with ice-axes we gathered snow in saucepans to melt for water, had toboggan races on aluminium sheets down the glacier, and climbed the 16,300-foot peak, Point Lenana.

Before leaving Eldoret I made an exploratory visit to the Alliance Girls' High School at Kikuyu. I had already given in my notice at the Highlands School, and knew that if I were to return to Kenya I wanted to teach African girls and to be in a school with a Christian tradition. AGHS was the longest established school in Kenya that catered for African girls up to sixth-form level, and had been founded by an alliance of the Anglican, Methodist and Presbyterian Churches. It was next door to the Alliance High School, the school that pioneered secondary education for African boys in Kenya. Although I made no commitment to returning at that time, I experienced a strange moment of recognition as I walked through the gates of the school; it was almost as though the place was already a familiar part of my life.

When flying home in December I made a stopover in Cairo and flew on to Amman to visit the Holy Land. The old city of Jerusalem was then in Jordan and from Amman we were driven at breakneck speed by Arab taxi-drivers across the Jordan Valley to Jerusalem. It was a wonderful way to arrive; the road plunged down hairpin bends into the valley until we saw the moonlight glittering over the waters of the Dead Sea, crossed the Jordan River, and passed a signpost to Jericho. The road then started to climb and we had more dramatic moonlit views of the mountainous landscape until the lights of Jerusalem finally appeared, shining from the heights above. In Jerusalem I stayed at St George's Cathedral to visit the traditional holy sites, and on returning to Amman I made a day visit to Petra. It was all a wonderful experience. I travelled by taxi to Damascus, failed to find a way to get to the crusader castle Krak des Chevaliers, and then went on to Beirut by bus. As it was snowing hard in the mountains, the traffic on the pass was in chaos and it was bitterly cold, but we eventually made it and I flew back to London the next day.

It was lovely being back with the family and I arrived just in time for Christmas. After two years on the Equator it all seemed very dark; that hit me much more than the cold. Then in January I drove off to Lee Abbey where I joined the community for six months. Lee Abbey is a Christian conference centre, on the north coast of Devon just outside Lynton, and is beautifully situated between the sea and the north edge of Exmoor. The house has a dramatic approach through the Valley of Rocks and the coast in the area is rocky and rugged, with high cliffs overlooking the sea. The sheer beauty of the surroundings made it an ideal place to be in touch with God and to explore the way ahead. I worked on the house team, cleaning the rooms, and shared a room with Grace Sato from Japan. We became great friends and had much fun together, though I lost touch with her later as written English was so difficult for her.

The six-month period was a very helpful and important time. It was a time of spiritual growth and an opportunity to explore the Christian faith at depth with others from a wide variety of backgrounds. I learnt much from the formal epilogues each night, the regular worship, and the working through of relationships within the community. In terms of the future I felt deeply affirmed in the call I had already experienced to go back to Kenya, and made arrangements to start teaching at Alliance Girls' High School in September.

CHAPTER 4

Move to Kikuyu

ALLIANCE GIRLS' HIGH SCHOOL, KIKUYU, was founded in 1948 as the first secondary school for African girls in Kenya. When I joined the staff in 1966 it was still the only low-cost school that offered sixth form courses, so we had the pick of the country. Girls from all over Kenya competed fiercely for places and were highly motivated and many of them were extremely able. Teaching at AGHS was both demanding and very rewarding. The staff were mostly committed Christians and it was expected that we would all become involved in many extra-curricular activities on top of full teaching timetables. I came in as head of the Maths department and later took on additional responsibility as house-mistress for one of the boarding houses. The senior girls did most of the work of running the house, but I had to be on hand to give them support when needed. I taught Physics as well as Maths and inaugurated an Advanced level course in Physics. Several years later I came across some of the girls who had been in that first class and was delighted to find that five of them had gone on to become doctors; they became part of the first generation of Kenyan women doctors. The Christian tradition was very strong; there was a flourishing Christian Union and some of the senior girls walked many miles each week to take Sunday School classes in the local primary schools. I used to help with preparation classes for these girls and was always deeply challenged by their commitment and fresh insights. There was a beautiful chapel where the worship was lively and meaningful.

The headmistress, Miss Bruce, had been at the school for many years and brought her own Scottish traditions of excellence to Africa. She was a delightful person, very gifted and much loved by the girls. When she left Mrs Waithaka came in as the first Kenyan head and helped to build up a majority Kenyan staff. In 1966 there were only two Africans on the staff, but the ratio gradually changed as the British Government withdrew support for the teachers' programme and more qualified Kenyans became available. One of Miss Bruce's particular eccentricities related to the subject of vests. At 8,000 feet the school became a fairly chilly place during the rainy season and the girls used to pile all kinds of coats and scarves over their uniform. Miss Bruce would have none of it: 'They should be wearing vests' was her only response to pleas for some leniency over uniform rules. As a child in Scotland she no doubt grew up in vests, but such items of clothing were unheard of in Kenya.

On open days it was fascinating to meet the parents of the girls. Some of the mothers arrived barefoot from the villages and were often illiterate, never having had any opportunity for formal education themselves. But they were clearly immensely proud of their daughters and made great sacrifices to raise the modest school fees that were needed. By contrast other parents were highly placed in Kenyan society; we had two members of the cabinet and several senior church leaders and heads of commercial organisations when I first arrived. This could be very helpful when the school was doing battle with impossible directives from the Ministry of Education, and Miss Bruce never minced her words when crossing swords with bureaucracy. From time to time she would come into the staffroom saying that she had started to pack her bags, as she expected imminent deportation. This never finally happened, though there were some real crises when she refused to accept the children of politically powerful parents who had not qualified for entry. She was never willing to compromise her principles and was gloriously articulate in explaining the reasons for her decisions.

With girls in the school from all parts of the country political events impacted the school community from time to time. There were many girls from western Kenya, and when Tom Mboya was assassinated in 1969 the Luo girls became almost uncontrollable. Tom Mboya was an outstandingly gifted politician and Kenya felt the loss of his gifts for many years to come. As the next election approached the practice of oath-taking emerged once more amongst the Kikuyu. The purpose was to ensure that Kikuyu voted only for Kikuyu parliamentary candidates and they were made to swear loyalty to their own leaders. Many Christian Kikuyu refused to do this on the grounds that they could only swear ultimate allegiance to Jesus Christ. When this happened they were often beaten up or killed, and sometimes their houses were burnt with their families still inside. The Presbyterian Hospital at Kikuyu treated many of the survivors of such attacks, so we were much aware of the violence. Church leaders made a courageous stand against the oathing and eventually the practice was stopped.

The girls were so highly motivated that there were few discipline problems, but if sanctions were needed the most effective punishment was to take a girl out of classes for a day and get her to do some work around the grounds, such as cutting grass. Pregnancies were a regular occurrence, and normally resulted in the girl having to leave school. Often the younger girls had been forced into an unwanted relationship, but the men involved were rarely identified and never sanctioned. Double standards operated in Kenya as in many other societies. When a girl realised she was pregnant she was often terrified to go home, as she fully expected to be beaten by her father, and I often wished there was something more we could have done for them.

I lived in a stone-built cottage with a small garden and had a cook, Kinyanjui, and a gardener, Anna. Later on Dido (a collie/labrador mix) joined the household. So I was well provided for and it was easy to offer hospitality to passing friends. I had a log fire that was very welcome during the rainy season. For transport I bought another VW beetle, this time a grey model, and it went as merrily over the rough roads of East Africa as its blue predecessor had done in Eldoret. Kikuyu was only fifteen miles outside Nairobi so we went into Nairobi regularly to buy food, to visit government ministries and to socialise. Although Kikuyu was so much nearer Nairobi than Eldoret I went to fewer mountain club functions than before, simply because of the number of commitments in school. I sometimes managed to get to the regular Wednesday evening walk along the Ngong Hills, and of course the school holidays offered continuing opportunities to explore East Africa.

That first Christmas holiday Ailsie joined me for a wonderful five weeks together. She had finished nursing in Kashmir and on her way home sailed from Bombay to Mombasa and came up to Nairobi by train. We had a great reunion on the station platform in Nairobi and Ailsie recovered from her overnight journey fast enough to come rock climbing at Lukenya that day. After some socialising in Nairobi we set off up-country, arriving in Eldoret in time to attend Jenny Bryson's wedding to Fred Burgess. Fred was a widower whose first wife had died only a year earlier, and Jenny and I had taught two of his four daughters at the Highlands School. It was a very happy occasion.

After the reception we drove on to Mount Elgon where we camped with members of the Mountain Club, and the next day we climbed to the nearest summit at 14,000 feet. Most new arrivals would have had difficulty in going straight to that altitude, but Ailsie, fresh from Kashmir, was well acclimatised. Remnants of the Elgon party then went down to Lake Baringo where Anne Horsfall (who by then was teaching at Nyakasura School in Fort Portal), Tony South, Ailsie and myself stayed for four glorious days of swimming, rafting and bird-watching.

We slept under mosquito nets hanging from thorn trees and Ailsie woke the first morning to find a naked Pokot warrior standing above her with his spear, so she had a good introduction to camping in Africa.

The rest of the holiday was similarly active, and we spent Christmas with Peter and Liza Cox at a mission hospital in NE Uganda where Ailsie was able to see how a hospital functioned in the African bush. For the final week we went down to the coast and joined Anne in Kilifi where she and her brother Robin had recently bought a plot of land overlooking Kilifi Creek. We swam and sailed in the warm green waters of the creek before putting Ailsie on her boat home at Mombasa.

At the end of the next term I spent a weekend with Shelometh Gathua at her family home near Nyeri. Shelometh was one of the first two Kenyan teachers to be appointed to Alliance Girls and I greatly appreciated this opportunity to stay in a Kikuyu home. Shelometh taught me about Kikuyu traditions and I was warmly and graciously received by her family. Later on I had various opportunities to visit girls in their own homes which enabled to me understand more about their backgrounds, and I much valued this introduction to African hospitality.

Now that Anne Horsfall was based at Fort Portal I had a splendid opportunity to make a first visit to the Ruwenzori Mountains, Ptolemy's Mountains of the Moon, whose rivers were for many years assumed to flow from the mysterious source of the Nile. The mountains were fully explored for the first time in 1906 when the Duke of Abruzzi made a remarkable visit to the area and climbed all the highest peaks. The Ruwenzori represent the only permanently snow-capped mountain range in Africa, as both Mount Kenya and Mount Kilimanjaro are single peaks.

The Ruwenzori have the highest rainfall in Africa as rain sweeps in from the east (Uganda) and from the west (the Congo) and drenches the mountains for most of the year. There are reputedly two seasons in the mountains, the wet season and the wetter season. But if one has the time and stamina, and patience to wait out bad weather, the Ruwenzori offer a unique variety of vegetation on the approach routes and stunning views of rock, snow and ice on the high glaciers. The high rainfall ensures that the vegetation is prolific and grows to huge heights; heather trees reach forty feet, giant groundsel and lobelia grow in thick forests, and solid masses of helichrysum can make progress almost impossible. The general dampness of the area creates conditions for bogs that are a real speciality of the approach routes, and the prevailing winds from east and west carve out astonishingly beautiful double-edged snow cornices on the summit ridges of the glaciers.

On my first trip in August 1967 there were nine of us in the party and we approached the central peaks via the Bujuku Valley. Having left the cars at the road head at Ibanda, we spent three days getting to the Bujuku hut at 12,000 feet, finding shelter on the way at Nyabitaba and Bigo huts. We started off through open elephant grass, then the path led through the giant trees of the equatorial rain forest where we saw a variety of monkeys, brightly coloured birds, and orchids. Having passed through the bamboo belt, we entered the strange and beautiful world of the heather forest where the giant trees were all covered in moss. Green light filtered through the branches above and the whole scene looked like something out of a Hans Andersen fairy tale. It was very quiet amongst the trees, all sounds deadened by the wrappings of moss. Then we had our real baptism into life in the Ruwenzori as we came to the Bigo bog. Huge tussocks were scattered across the bog and to start with we tried to avoid the mud by tussock-hopping. The tops of the tussocks were so slippery that we all ended up in the bog anyway, and a couple of times we had to pull out porters who had fallen into really deep mud and could not get out because of the suction.

From Bujuku we went up Mount Speke (16,042 feet) and had a splendid climb across the snow, zigzagging our way up onto the ridge. When we reached the summit of Victorio Emmanuele the clouds were down and we could not see the view, which was a bit tantalizing, but we were happy that we had made it to the top and had fun glissading down the snow on our way back. For the next two days the weather really closed in and we were reduced to organizing a hyrax hunt to keep everyone occupied. When the weather cleared a little the third day, we went up to the Elena hut at the foot of the Stanley glacier. From there we tried to explore the Stanley plateau, but again the clouds closed in and we lost visibility. After wandering in circles for a few hours and nearly falling over the edge of the glacier into the Congo we admitted defeat.

The next day we decided to have another try and went back up onto the plateau. In a letter to my parents afterwards I described that morning: 'We were on the Elena glacier as the sun rose and the sky was clear, the icefall above us glowing red, the snow was sparkling, the sky turning deep blue, the cloud billowing in the valleys far below, the peaks still above us standing clear in every detail. It was superb; I have never seen anything like it even in the Alps. The peaks of the Congo all lay to the west and the views from the plateau when we got up there were quite breathtaking. We could see the whole extent of the Speke glacier and the great west wall and summit of Baker behind us, and rising up from the plateau ahead the twin peaks of Alexandra and Margherita. Margherita especially was a wonderful sight, huge crevasses splitting the glacier at her foot and a wonderfully corniced ridge leading up to the summit which was itself one huge cornice. We laughed at our wandering tracks of the day before, quickly reached the Alexandra ridge and crossed over to the bottom of the Margherita glacier. Then in two minutes the wonderful world we had just been gazing at disappeared and once again we were in the middle of a complete white-out. It happened so quickly that we could hardly believe it.' We tried to find a way between the crevasses, but in that visibility it was hopeless so we had to turn back and go down to Bujuku again. It was disappointing, but a great experience nevertheless.

The next day we went across the Scott-Elliott pass to Kitandara. It was snowing hard as we crossed the steep and rocky pass, but the weather cleared a little when we got to Kitandara and we were able to enjoy the hut there which is beautifully situated between two mountain lakes. From there we tried to climb Baker, but again the weather was against us. We had already experienced rain, hail, sleet, and snow, and as we reached the lower ridge of the mountain Anne remarked that we had met every kind of weather on the trip except thunder. The next moment there was a flash of lightning and a clap of thunder reverberated round the valley, so we decided to turn back. We returned to Bujuku and went back down the Bujuku valley, roping up to cross a fast-flowing river that had risen while we had been away.

On the second trip in January 1969 there were just three of us, Anne, Maggie Kirk and myself, so we were able to travel more lightly. This time we walked in via the Mobuku Valley, which is a most beautiful way to approach the central peaks. After a night at Nyabitaba hut we found our way up past waterfalls and steep rock faces to Bujongolo, where a large area of overhanging rock provides natural shelter. As we were able to find enough dry wood to build a large fire, it was very cosy and we gazed in awe at the pinnacles of Mount Baker above us, silhouetted in the clear moonlight. The third day took us over the Freshfield pass to Kitandara hut, where we made our base for the rest of the trip.

The next day we had a superb climb to the summit of Mount Baker (15,889 feet). Snow conditions were perfect and we approached the summit via a wonderful, curving snow ridge along the top of the Edward glacier. The snow swept down to the Kitandara valley on our

On the summit of Margherita

left, and to our right rock precipices dropped nearly 5,000 feet to the
Mobuku valley far below. At one point the ridge narrowed to a corniced
knife edge of snow, curving round for about fifty feet, so we roped up
and crossed very carefully, moving one at a time. The summit was in
cloud, but every now and again we had glimpses of dramatic views in
all directions. It was a great day.

Before setting off for Mount Stanley we had a lazy day pottering at
Kitandara, watching the sunbirds feeding on the lobelia, sunbathing,
sorting out equipment, and practising climbing out of crevasses by
prusiklooping up a rock overhang. Then off we set for Mount Stanley.
This time we bypassed the Elena hut and went straight on up onto the
plateau where we planned to bivouac in Anne's little tent. We found a
perfect bivouac site on the glacier, tucked in between a wall of snow
and a small rocky peak called Moebius, so we were well protected from
the wind. From the tent we looked out across the glacier to Alexandra
and Margherita, and outside the snow wall we had a grandstand view of
the whole east side of the range. Clouds boiled and churned their way
up from the valleys below and beyond them the plains of Uganda
stretched out into the blue distance. The light and the cloud formations

changed constantly and the view was breathtakingly beautiful through-out the day and by moonlight. From the top of Moebius we could see the whole of the western view into the Congo, rivers winding away into the distant plains.

We spent two nights in our little eyrie in the snow. We did not have enough fuel to melt snow so we all became quite dehydrated and lost our appetites. We were also feeling the effects of the altitude (just over 16,000 feet) and were very cold and cramped at night with three of us together in the little two-man tent. But it was a unique experience and this time the weather was kind to us; we had a totally clear day to climb Margherita, the highest point in the Ruwenzori. We simply walked up the Margherita glacier and followed two climbers (RC priests) who had gone ahead and had cut steps through the cornices onto the summit ridge. The view from the top was amazing, and the whole way up the wind had blown the snow into astonishingly beautiful feathered cornices. We were on snow and ice all the way and the summit itself was one enormous snow cornice. It was a wonderful moment when we got up there at last.

The next morning we were not sure how we were going to be able to carry the tent and so on down the glacier again in our weakened state, so we made a toboggan out of the rope and lashed the kits bags onto it. Anne and I belayed ourselves to it and tried to control its speed as we tobogganed down the glacier to the Elena hut. After a while it took off and we found ourselves glissading wildly behind it. Luckily we fell into no crevasses and arrived at the bottom in a bit of a heap but in one piece.

Back at Kitandara we decided to try a new route down and spent the next three days finding our way through the mountains to the copper mines at Kilembe. One of the porters said he knew the way, but it soon became clear that he had never been in the area at all so we had quite a job route-finding. There were no recognizable tracks and we had to cut our way through a lot of helichrysum. We spent the first night in a rock shelter at 14,000 feet on the Tatra pass, then on the second day we became seriously lost and eventually realised we had gone too far south. A violent hailstorm held us up for a while; we all sheltered from it under a rock overhang and the porters lit an enormous fire. We eventually managed to find a steep and slippery way down into the Nyanwamba valley and then had to climb up again to find a rather inadequate rock shelter for the night. We were all very tired that night and were starting to run out of food, so it was with great relief that we picked up a hunter's track the next day that led us down through the bamboo forest.

In the early afternoon we emerged from the forest and saw a road winding away far below us, a welcome sign that we were in Kilembe area. Two hours later we staggered into Kilembe and the mine manager was so surprised to see us that he immediately offered the use of a mines truck to take us back to Ibanda. We were very lucky to make it safely through in three days, given that no one knew the route, but it was very satisfying exploring an area that no other climbers, as far as we knew, had been in for many years.

In August 1968 I went back to Britain on leave. It was great to see the family, and I was particularly glad to see my father who was starting to go downhill at that time.

In October Elizabeth came out to Kenya for two weeks, travelling with Sue Daniell who came to see her brother Patrick. It was lovely having them both to stay and on our first outing we went for a Sunday afternoon walk with Dido along the nearby Ngong Hills. We followed a path along the ridge that commands superb views of the Rift Valley, and when coming back to the car we suddenly saw a lioness looking at us from the path ahead. It was the only time I ever saw a lion in those hills, and we did not know quite what to do. Eventually she moved into the long grass at the side of the path, but in order to reach the car we had to walk past the place where she had disappeared. I was afraid that she might take an interest in Dido, but mercifully Dido did not seem to be aware of her. It was a tense moment for us all. Patrick later took all three of us off in his Land-Rover to Secret Valley where we had an exciting evening watching leopard and other animals drinking from the nearby waterhole.

In early January 1969 my father had a small stroke that affected his speech. On 30 January he celebrated his 80th birthday and the next day was taken into hospital. On 7 February a lunch party was held to celebrate my parents' Ruby Wedding, but by then he was too ill to move. He died on 10 March in the early morning. Miraculously my mother was able to contact all of us very swiftly, even though Francis and myself were out of the country (Francis was in Tehran), and we both arrived the next day.

The funeral was held at St Peter's Church, Upper Slaughter, and the night before Elizabeth and myself kept vigil by the coffin. As we sat in the still dark church I had a strong feeling that we were not alone but surrounded by many loving presences. The funeral was a very dignified service, and afterwards our cousin Ronald Boone invited us all back to

Rockcliffe where he plied us with champagne. I was only able to stay for two weeks, as it was a very busy time in school, and was sorry to miss the memorial service that was held in April at the Royal Hospital, Chelsea. But I returned again in the August holidays and was glad to have time with my mother then. She clearly needed much support, so I decided to return to Britain when my contract at Alliance ended the following August.

CHAPTER 5

From the Himalayas to Gordonstoun

IT HAD LONG BEEN A DREAM OF MINE to see the Himalayas and when I left Kikuyu the Crown Agents agreed to route my return flight via Delhi. Anne Horsfall was free at the time, so she set off from London and we met in Kathmandu. It was not an ideal time of year as the monsoon rains were still falling, but we did not want to miss the opportunity to go. Anne offered to do some plant collecting for Kew Gardens and hoped she might light on something new by visiting the area at such an unusual season. The other advantage was that no one else was mad enough to start trekking in August so we enjoyed a tourist-free time in the mountains.

After I had spent a week in Delhi waiting for lost luggage, Royal Nepali Airlines flew me over the mountains to Kathmandu where I met up with Anne. She had succumbed to various unpleasant Nepali bugs, but had already done the work of buying the supplies we would need and organising Sherpas to carry them for us. So that freed us to have a few days riding round Kathmandu on Chinese bicycles seeing the sights. In those days Kathmandu was an exotic place, full of ancient palaces and temples, and the streets were filled with rickshaws and cows.

We were driven by Land-Rover to Dolalghat, about thirty miles to the east of Kathmandu, and spent our first night camping on a hillside at about 2,000 feet. Then off we set on foot and walked for the next thirty-five days. Our main aim was to reach the Everest base camp, which meant crossing a number of major rivers that carved out deep valleys across the route. We finally reached 19,000 feet at the top of Kala Patar but we reckoned afterwards that we had actually climbed some 90,000 feet in all as we kept climbing up to a pass and then down again to the next river. So it was an energetic exercise but immensely worthwhile. On the lower part of the climb we had a lot of rain and were continually attacked by leeches; they fell off the trees onto our heads and down our necks and climbed up the stocks of our ice-axes onto our hands. We soon became expert at leech-repellent techniques and found flypel was the best deterrent. Although we had hoped to camp for most of the time, the wet weather made this difficult, especially for the Sherpas, and we ended up staying in the villages. Usually some household offered floor space for the night and a share in the cooking space above the fire, and sometimes Anne and I slept in a Buddhist temple.

Nepal is a Hindu kingdom, but once we had left the Kathmandu valley and entered the mountains, signs of Buddhism surrounded us at every turn. Temples with wonderful painted interiors emerged from the mist, and domed shrines and prayer wheels appeared along the paths. Prayer flags fluttered from the passes and were stacked up in large numbers at the end of every bridge; the more rickety the bridge, the greater the number of prayer flags. In areas where grain was grown, water wheels over the streams provided power for grinding mills, and sometimes prayer flags, rather then a mill, were attached to a water wheel – an ingenious source of prayer power.

The people we met in the villages and on the paths were all very friendly, greeting us with the word *namaste* and a small bow, hands held together in an attitude of prayer. On one occasion we became totally lost and separated from the Sherpas. Darkness fell as we stumbled our way back to the last village we had passed through and we knocked on the door of the first house we came to. We were dripping wet, but the couple who opened the door immediately invited us in. They gave us mats to sleep on beside the fire and some cobs of dried corn to eat, and then disappeared. The next morning we found that they had spent the bitterly cold night outside on the balcony. Such is the hospitality of mountain people.

Gradually we gained height and after two weeks started to turn north, following the Dudh Khose river, and on day fifteen arrived at Namche Bazaar, the trading centre for the Everest area. At this stage the weather started to clear a little, much to our relief. Beyond Namche we passed through Sherpa villages set in veritable rock gardens and made the welcome discovery that we had arrived at the height of the new potato season. On to the famous monastery at Thyangboche, and then to Periche where we camped in a most beautiful yak pasture, surrounded by snow-covered peaks. An old man, a Tibetan, walked with us for part of the next day, spinning black yak wool as he went. We then climbed up the base of the Khumbu glacier where we camped in a stone shed built to provide shelter for yak-herders.

The next day was totally clear and we climbed to the top of Kala Patar (19,000 feet) opposite the Khumbu ice-fall. We were surrounded by an amphitheatre of huge snow peaks and looked across to the great north face of Lhotse, nearly two vertical miles high, with the pyramid of the Everest summit clearly in view beyond. Fluted, frozen snow led down from the crystal ridge of Lhotse and the hanging glaciers glowed green as the sun rose overhead. Snow and ice fell constantly in great avalanches from the face. Looking back the way we had come, we could see more great mountains to the west; it was a truly magnificent view.

The return journey was uneventful, apart from the culture shock of being hurtled into the twentieth century at Lamasango, on a newly built Chinese road, whence a bus took us the last few miles over hair-raising landslides to Kathmandu. From Kathmandu we flew back to Delhi and, on finding that a flight was leaving that afternoon for Kabul, decided to visit Afghanistan. Three hours later we landed in Kabul, amazed to see dry desert hills surrounding the city, so different from the lush vegetation of the Kathmandu valley. We spent a fascinating week in the country, first exploring Kabul itself and then travelling further afield. We much wanted to see the giant Buddhas at Bamiyan and managed to get a lift on the main road north on a truck carrying bags of cement. We had a grandstand view of the Hindu Kush as we crossed the 10,000-foot Salang Pass, lying on cement bags that had been warmed up by the sun and enjoying spectacular views of the mountains. But we failed to find any vehicles travelling on to Bamiyan, so returned to Kabul and took a flight to Bamiyan on Ariana Afghan Airlines.

The Bamiyan valley was then dominated by two giant figures of Buddha carved out of the cliffs, both of which were later destroyed by the Taleban. We climbed up behind the largest one (over two hundred feet tall) and emerged from a honeycomb of caves and passages to stand on the head of the Buddha. It was a most precarious climb over loose sandstone, but a spectacular experience and we marvelled at the industry and vision of the monks who had carved out such massive figures. We also visited the beautiful green lakes at Band-I-Amir, and the remains of an ancient castle that hung precariously to the mountainside, mute witness to the ravages of Genghis Khan many centuries earlier. Back in Kabul we had a last shopping spree on the banks of the Kabul River to buy Afghan rugs, then flew back to London via Tehran.

Return to Britain
We arrived back in Britain at the end of September and I went straight to Magpies to be with my mother. There were plenty of things that needed to be done as the move to The Dingle in Upper Slaughter was planned for the last week in October. The Dingle had been let out for

some years and the most recent tenants very helpfully moved out when they realised my mother wanted to move in. We spent our first night in the house on 29 October.

I needed to find a job, so I scanned the *Times Educational Supplement* for openings for Maths teachers, and drove over to Oxford in depressingly thick fog to explore possibilities there. Eventually I was offered a post teaching Maths and some Physics at Headington Girls' School and started in January. It was a well-run school, with some very intelligent girls, but there were not many extra-curricular activities and I felt stultified by the fixed ways of doing things. At Alliance, where the situation was constantly changing, we had to improvise all the time and everyone was expected to use their own initiative. At Headington people were most upset when anyone departed from the 'correct' way of doing things. I felt a real misfit and was not sure how long I could handle it. Then right at the end of term I saw a notice in the staff room saying that Gordonstoun School was about to go co-educational and that a Senior Mistress was needed in September to implement the change to co-education. I walked straight into the headmistress's office and handed in my notice to leave at the end of the summer term. It was a mad thing to do, as I had no certainty that I would get the job, but I had no hesitation. During the Easter holiday I was called for an interview with the headmaster of Gordonstoun, Mr Kempe, at Brown's Hotel, and then invited to spend a couple of nights at the school, meeting a variety of people including the chairman of the Governors, Lord Leven. To my huge delight I was then offered the job, which I accepted with alacrity.

In the summer I joined Charles Richards and John Blacker to go climbing in Norway. Charles had meetings to go to in Oslo, so for the first couple of weeks John and I went to Tromsø to do some climbing in the Arctic. We flew from Oslo to Tromsø, arriving at midnight when the sun was lurking only just below the horizon. Although we missed the midnight sun it was light throughout the night in that part of Norway. We hired a car and drove to the Lyngen peninsula, hoping to climb Jaekkevarre which at 6,000 feet is the highest mountain north of the Arctic Circle. There were no roads into the centre of the peninsula, so we had to carry bivouac tents and food. We soon reached the first snow, as glaciers on the peninsula come right down to the sea. We had a good try to get up Jaekkevarre, but the weather was not very good and we lost visibility for much of the time. As we were on heavily crevassed glaciers, we eventually had to give up, but not before we had reached a respectable height and seen some spectacular Arctic snow and

My mother at The Dingle in her later years (photo Judy Holder)

ice formations. We then sailed through thick sea mist from Tromsø to Trondheim and met up with Charles at Otta Station.

The three of us then spent another ten days exploring the Jotunheim. We climbed one technically tricky peak called the Skagastolstind and at one point I was helped by an obliging Norwegian who let me step off the top of his head to get onto a ridge that was beyond my reach. We climbed the Galdhopiggen which claims to be the highest mountain in Norway, though a neighbouring peak beats it by a couple of feet when it is covered with snow and ice in the winter. It was an enjoyable climb, and although not technically difficult the route was very exposed and slippery at one stage.

On 20 February that year Ailsie married Dennis Corble, a retired merchant banker. The wedding was held at St Peter's Church in Upper Slaughter, and it was lovely that they were able to get married in the church where there were so many family connections. My mother was still very tired all the time, but gradually she adjusted to being on her own and to the new life at The Dingle. She became deeply involved in the village community and everyone loved her. When she did eventually emerge from her physical and mental exhaustion, she moved into one of the most fulfilling periods of her life, free to be herself after years of being dominated by a strong mother and then by an even stronger husband. She was a very gentle and gracious person.

Gordonstoun

In September 1971 I drove up to Scotland to start the job at Gordonstoun. The heather was out as I crossed the hills and the countryside was looking very beautiful. Gordonstoun lies on the south bank of the Moray Firth, and on arrival at the school I was given a flat at the top of Gordonstoun House that almost looked out to sea and had a baronial turret in one corner of the sitting room.

Gordonstoun was the first of the major British boys' public schools to go co-educational throughout the school. Marlborough had started to take girls into the sixth form in 1968, but Gordonstoun decided to take girls into the third and sixth forms from the start, which meant that by the third year there were girls throughout the school. I thought that Gordonstoun must be very forward looking to be taking this pioneering step and looked forward to a stimulating relationship with colleagues. It was only after arriving at the school that I discovered that the decision to go co-educational had been made by the Board of Governors without any consultation with the masters. Six of the masters had resigned the term before I arrived by way of protest, and many of those who were still at the school were deeply opposed to the proposed change. I thus found myself under assault from all sides by masters who disagreed profoundly with what I had been brought in to do.

My job was to get to know the school that year by teaching the boys and to make preparations for the move to co-education the following year. These preparations included selecting the first intake of thirty girls and doing a PR job to persuade parents that it would be safe to send their daughters to the school at this experimental stage. I also had to work out a mass of practicalities about what the girls should wear, how they should be absorbed into the many activities such as sailing and climbing, whether they should be punished in the same way as the boys, and so on. At every stage the suggestions I made at masters' meetings were shot down with derision. To start with I found this quite bewildering and outfacing. At girls' schools a modicum of politeness is maintained at staff meetings. Eventually I realised that this was a tactic to scupper the change altogether and started to fight back. I did have some allies amongst the masters, such as Jim Rawlings who was in charge of mountaineering. He had a fund of good will and common sense and helped me to recover after particularly dotty and acrimonious meetings.

Three women were appointed to the teaching staff that first term and Norma Smith and I shared a flat when I moved into Hopeman House the following year. Norma too was very supportive and helped me to recover my perspective after doing battle with the masters. We realised that most of them had been at boys' schools themselves, had been to Oxford or Cambridge in the days when most of the students were men, had done national service in another male community, and had then gone back into all male communities as they had started teaching in boys' public schools. So perhaps the remarkable thing was that a few of them did support the change.

I had never taught boys before and wondered how different it would be from teaching girls. In general I enjoyed teaching the boys but one of my classes during the first year was a real nightmare. All the Gordonstoun parents wanted their sons to do Maths so that they could go into the Navy or whatever. At other schools children who could not add up were taught Arithmetic, but I was given a group of innumerate fifteen-year-olds and told to teach them Maths. After struggling unsuccessfully for some weeks I finally abandoned the Maths syllabus and started to teach them basic numeracy skills. Things then became more manageable, but it was still hard work. Maths was my main subject, but I also taught General Studies to the sixth form, and Religious Education to third formers, including Prince Andrew when he first came.

When the girls started to arrive I became housemistress for the first girls' house and was then on duty in the house round the clock seven days a week, as well having a significant teaching timetable. Norma helped to share the house responsibilities, but it was still a very heavy workload and I was often in the office up to 11 p.m. I used to arrive in the school at the start of term and then go into a kind of Gordonstoun tunnel from which I emerged at the end of term.

When the first thirty girls arrived in September 1972 there was much media interest. The BBC tried to film a mixed crew sailing a cutter round Hopeman Harbour, but the cutter capsized and most of the camera crew ended up in the water as they leapt to the rescue. Life at that time did have its entertaining moments. The girls, who came from the Bahamas, Canada, England, Iran, Ireland, Italy, Jamaica, Nepal, Scotland and Venezuela, were a great group and Aylie Lonmon, who came on exchange from Salem, made an excellent first head of house. One of the third formers, Caroline Montgomery, came in almost two years younger than the boys and ended the year with top results in Maths and Science. This started to silence some of the masters who were still making remarks about girls having nothing between the ears.

In general once the girls were actually there much of the prejudice against them started to fall away, though Hopeman House was still referred to as the Hopeman Maternity Home and housemasters got into a panic every time they found a boy missing during the night. They used to ring me up and insist that I make a round of the girls' house to see which of the girls was missing. None of them ever were, and eventually I stopped responding to calls of this kind. If I did have problems with boys fooling about with the girls, I used to go to the senior boys for help and they always responded very effectively. Hubert Beaumont was the Guardian (head of school) that first year and he became a great ally. Years later his father was my vicar when I lived in Kew. I first met Prince Andrew when he had strayed into an out-of-bounds area of Hopeman, but he immediately apologised and left, much to my relief.

As well as setting new standards of work in the classroom (on the whole the girls took their academic work more seriously than most of the boys), the girls played a full part in the many extra-curricular activities. Soon there were girls in the Mountain Rescue team and the Fire Service and mixed crews of boys and girls sailed the school yacht, Sea Spirit, round the Western Isles. Some of the girls were musically gifted and the school started to put on some high-standard musical productions. Plays with mixed casts transformed the drama possibilities. The girls were not allowed to play rugger or cricket, but joined in just about everything else. When ballet lessons were later started everyone was astonished that two boys joined the class. One of the things I noticed was how some of the quieter and more sensitive boys became much freer in expressing themselves once the school had started to become a mixed community.

There were of course problems, and at every stage I had to fight the system to effect changes that needed to be made in order to meet the needs of the girls. Some of the masters still hoped that girls would simply fit in and behave like boys, and recognition that a genuinely co-educational school would be different from a boys' school with a few girls in it came only slowly. But, as the numbers of girls rose, attitudes did start to change and things that were viewed as being unheard of initially became the norm in due course. For instance it was some time before the first girl was elected as a Colour Bearer (prefect), mainly because girls were not members of the rugger fifteen and did not shout at small boys to pull their socks up. But in 1978 the first girl, Georgina Housman, was appointed Guardian, a possibility that would have been dismissed with derision in the early days. At the stage when girls were still a novelty the boys showed off like mad on the rugger field and there were forty-eight fractures that first term, partly due to the hardness of the ground but mainly due to the presence of girl spectators.

Many of the girls enjoyed the opportunities that Gordonstoun offered for climbing and sailing and those in the Mountain Rescue Service particularly were highly respected for their competence and skills. I was able to join a number of camping expeditions to the hills of the west coast and did a little skiing and ice climbing in the corries of the Cairngorms, but generally I did far less in the way of exploring the Scottish hills than I had hoped, mainly because it was so difficult to get away from the house.

In 1974 a second girls' house, Windmill, was opened with Judy Cowx as housemistress. Judy stayed on at Windmill for the next fifteen years and did a great job, and it made a huge difference to me to have another woman at the weekly housemasters' tea. By September 1975 there were two full girls' houses, with a total of 130 girls, so by then I reckoned my contribution was complete.

All the family came to visit me at one time or another while I was at Hopeman, and my mother came twice. The second time (September 1974) I drove her up and then put her on a flight back to London from Kinloss. It was the first time in her life that she had flown, at the age of 72. She handled the experience with aplomb, and that set her up to fly to Cairo the following year. Francis was posted by his bank to Cairo in November 1974 and the next year my mother, Anne Horsfall and myself visited him for two weeks during the Easter holiday. Francis gave us all a great time; we were swept round Cairo by Ahmed, his chauffeur, and for a few days Anne and myself left my mother to enjoy the social round in Cairo while we went up the Nile to visit Luxor, Aswan and Abu Simbel. It was my first visit to Egypt and I was stunned by the size, beauty and grandeur of the ancient temples and tombs.

Francis opened the old family home in Upper Slaughter as a hotel in October 1972, calling it The Lords of the Manor. When I came back from Gordonstoun that Christmas there was a staffing crisis at the hotel, so we were all roped in to help. Ailsie and Dennis manned the reception and Elizabeth and I helped Mrs Rowlands with the washing-up. Mrs Rowlands had lived all her life in the village and by then she was almost toothless, but she led the washing-up team with gusto, getting steadily merrier through the evening as she drained the glasses of wines and spirits that came back from the bar. By the end of the evening we were all in a fairly blotto state, but it was great fun and the hotel kept going (just).

There were no plans to open a third girls' house at Gordonstoun immediately so once the first two houses were established I felt my own task had been fulfilled. I started to think about the future and somehow it seemed clear that the next step should be to approach the Church Missionary Society (CMS) to see if they could use me. I had come to know many CMS personnel in Kenya and much admired what they were doing. So I approached CMS and was accepted for a term's training at Crowther Hall in Birmingham in September. I made an open offer and had no idea where I might be sent, but I was at peace as it all felt very much of God's leading.

During my time at Gordonstoun I met someone who very much wanted to marry me and for a year I struggled to know how to respond. He was a good friend to me and as I was in my late thirties I realised it might be my last chance to have a family. But I was concerned about the balance of our relationship and eventually recognised that I could not commit myself wholeheartedly to a lifelong partnership with him. When it came to joining CMS I barely made a conscious decision – it just seemed the natural thing to do – and it was only later that I realised that the real turning point had been the much more complicated decision about not getting married. I had no idea at the time of all that lay ahead, but that decision freed me to offer to CMS and opened the way for the extraordinarily rich experiences of the next twenty-five years.

At the end of the summer term we had a house barbecue on the beach. It was light until nearly midnight, so we watched the sun set and then lit a huge fire and played games on the beach. At such events it was traditional for the boys to throw their housemasters into the sea, so the girls decided they needed to keep their end up and give me the same treatment. They came and asked me very politely beforehand if I would mind, and when the time came they made sure I had remembered to take my watch off. In the end we all plunged into the waves together and it was remarkably warm. I can still remember the magic of swimming in that black water by the light of the moon and looking up at the cliffs overhead. It was a good final memory to have.

During August Charles Richards invited Elizabeth and myself to join him in a chalet in Samoens in the French Alps that he had been lent by a colleague in the WCC. It was a very happy time, and Charles tried to teach me to count in Swahili as we climbed the mountain paths — by then it was becoming clear that CMS would be sending me back to Kenya.

CHAPTER 6

Amongst the Maasai

Time to Prepare

IN SEPTEMBER 1975 I WENT TO Crowther Hall, the CMS training college at Selly Oak in Birmingham. It was a complete change from Gordonstoun and the term I spent there was a real oasis – I felt as if my spirit was being watered after four years in a dry desert. It was not until I arrived at Crowther Hall that I began to recognise how hard those years at Gordonstoun had been and how much I had missed regular Christian fellowship. It was heart-warming to be back in a worshipping community where people genuinely tried to listen to and support one another.

During the time at Crowther I met many people who were to became long-standing friends, including Peter Vaughan (the principal) and his wife Elizabeth, and fellow students such as Andrew Wheeler, who later went with his wife Sue to Sudan. I met Simon Barrington-Ward (CMS General Secretary) for the first time and he and Jean often invited me to their lovely holiday-home in Scotland in the years to come. Similarly Tina and Christopher Lamb (tutors) regularly welcomed me to their cottage in Wales once I was back in the UK. Lesslie Newbigin was at Selly Oak at that time and I was immensely privileged to sit at his feet as he taught the Theology of Mission course. Dan Beeby opened my eyes to the Old Testament in new ways in the introductory biblical course, and I lapped up the chance to broaden my understanding of a wide range of mission issues.

Conversations with Margaret Beaver and others went on about my location, and it was eventually agreed that I would be sent to Meto, in Maasai country in Kenya close to the Tanzania border, to open a secondary school for Maasai girls. It all sounded very exciting. I was commissioned as a CMS missionary in London in December by Dame Diana Reader-Harris, then CMS President, who became another long-term friend.

In January I flew to Nairobi to start six weeks studying Swahili at the church-run language school. It was good to be back in Nairobi and

Margaret Njonjo kindly lent me a car so I was mobile and able to catch up with friends in Kenya. Derek and Pat Wilks soon took me out to Meto for two nights so that I could see the area and meet some of the key people, like Gideon Maridadi who was in charge of the ranch aid store. Derek and Pat were a wonderful support throughout my time at Meto. Derek used to visit regularly to do useful jobs and together they put me up in their house at Bishopsbourne whenever I came in to Nairobi.

On 24 January I had my first meeting with Archbishop Festo Olang who had a great vision for providing secondary education for Maasai girls, and at first asked me to start a secondary school. Having seen Meto I knew that an academic secondary school would not be appropriate in that area and suggested that we might start up a village polytechnic to offer more practical, vocational courses. To my relief he agreed. He continued to be very interested in all that happened at Meto and was personally warmly supportive.

Chris Carey, the CMS Kenya representative, lived nearby and he and his wife Rosemary were also very supportive. In due course Chris bought a car for me, a little Roho, so when the language course ended I was all set to go to Meto. I slept my first night there on 15 March, taken in by Derek and Pat. They camped and I slept in the little tin rondavel that was to be my home for the rest of that year. Two days later Robin (manager of the Maasai Rural Training Centre at Isinya) and Joan Slade drove in with their Land-Rover piled high with bed, cooker, table and chair and I settled in. The next day there was a meeting of the Meto Committee to make plans for the school, and that evening all the visitors left, skidding their way down the road after a cloud burst. I wondered what it would feel like being left alone with the Maasai and sat outside the rondavel watching the sun set behind the Meto Hills. It was a still evening, and as I gazed at the view, listened to the crickets, and enjoyed the quiet of the bush, I was filled with a profound sense of peace.

Early days at Meto
Meto is a tiny village in the heart of Maasailand, in the far south of Kajiado District in Kenya, close to the border with Tanzania. The village lies in a horseshoe of rolling hills and looks across the plains to the western face of Ol Doinyo Orok. It is beautiful country, and I never tired of walking in the area, exploring the hills and the river courses. But it was quite isolated at times as the last thirty miles of the dirt road in from Bissel crossed numerous dry river-beds that could become raging

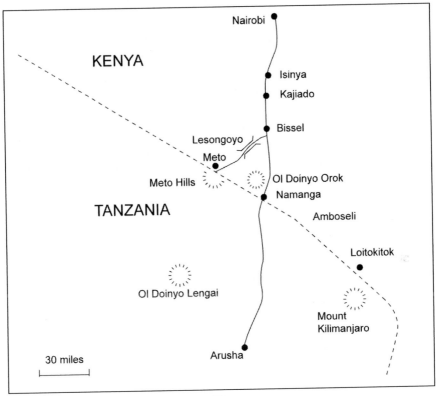

Meto

torrents during the rains, and there were no bridges. The road came to an end at Meto so there was no through traffic other than on foot. The nearest post office and telephone were fifty miles away at Kajiado, and we had no means of radio communication.

There was a ranch-aid store at Meto, a church, three small shops, a little primary school and a dispensary. But although Meto was so small, it was the centre for a large area, as many of the Maasai villages round about were dependent on the tap at Meto for water during the dry season. The water came from a spring in the hills five miles away in Tanzania, and there were constant problems involved in keeping the supply flowing. Wandering moran (warriors) would often break the pipe with their spears to get a convenient source of water, or to make buffalo traps, and Gideon would then have to walk the length of the pipe to find where it was broken and mend it. Water dominated life at Meto, whether when trying to keep the water from the pipeline flowing or when struggling with the floods that swept the road away during the rains.

Women from all the villages round about came to Meto to collect water. They left their donkeys outside the thorn fence and came with their water-tins to settle round the tap for a good gossip, so it was always easy to contact them. For the first few months at Meto my job was to get to know the Maasai way of life so that I could get an idea of what kind of courses would be most appropriate for Maasai girls who had completed primary schooling. Very few such girls found places in the secondary schools in the area, and there were at that time no other options open to them for continuing their education, whereas there were already well-established vocational schools for the boys. Tradition-ally there was no need for formal education for girls as they were expected to marry at puberty. Little girls as young as eleven years old commonly found themselves becoming the third or fourth wife of an aged elder and then spent the rest of their life carrying wood and water, looking after the children, cooking, and doing the heavy work of house-building whenever the family moved.

Throughout Africa it is common to find that women do most of the work, but amongst the Maasai the imbalance is even greater than elsewhere. The only work that the elders do is to sit around under thorn trees and make decisions about what should be done by the women, though they do make a contribution to house-building by putting in the four main posts that support the houses. Small boys do most of the herding. The moran have nothing to do at all. Traditionally their job has been to lead cattle raids and kill lions, but as both these activities are now illegal in Kenya the moran get very bored and often take themselves off to school and even university. In 1976 times were changing, and repeated episodes of drought and rinderpest, combined with the loss of traditional grazing grounds to other tribes, were already forcing many Maasai into a settled way of life for which they were ill equipped. So the church was not trying to enforce change but to help Maasai to be better equipped to respond to the changes that were already happening around them.

During those first few months there were three particular people who became great friends and who helped me to start understanding Maasai culture and customs. The first was Gideon Maridadi who ran the ranch-aid store. He was endlessly patient in interpreting local customs to me and in sorting out difficulties that we ran into from time to time with the local community. Then there was Nambulong, an old lady who lived on the hill opposite. Her sons still had cattle so they were on the move, but they left their children with Nambulong so that they could

Nambulong

go to the village school. She willingly shared her rather collapsing hut with six grandchildren so that they would have the opportunity of education. When the girls arrived she was very supportive of the whole enterprise, and gave much wise advice to the girls who regularly went to visit her. She was something of a matriarch in the local community and her support helped to gain acceptance for the opening of the school. Finally there was Tipape ole Seitah, a little boy at the primary school, whose family were destitute as they had lost their cattle. He used to drop in every day after school and devour any reading matter that I was able to find for him, and then we would go for walks together in the bush and he would share his astonishing knowledge of bush-craft with me.

When I had mastered enough of the language to understand the complex routine of greetings I had great fun watching Maasai trying to place me when me met on the bush paths. Greetings varied according to the sex of the person being greeted and their age group, i.e. whether they were likely to be of the same age group as oneself, one's parents or one's children. If I was walking through the bush wearing jeans I was often greeted with the greeting for a man, and they clearly had no idea of my age. At different times I was greeted with the words suitable for a small child right through to those used for a wrinkled old woman. The breakthrough came when they discovered my name, which seemed to

Tipape ole Seitah

trip very readily off a Maasai tongue: 'Di-ya-na!' they would call out in three equally accented syllables, and after that there was no problem.

I tried to communicate something of the Gospel stories by putting up pictures on the walls of my sitting-room. One of the pictures illustrated the parable of the Prodigal Son and was shown in an African setting, the father running out of his grass hut with arms outstretched, ready to greet his returning son. My Maasai was so limited that I was happy to let Nambulong explain what it was all about when visitors dropped in. Then one day I heard her merrily describing a great fight. Afterwards I tried to work out where the misunderstanding had come in, and eventually realised that in Maasai culture people don't embrace one another. The only reason that a man would have his arms outstretched as he ran towards someone else would be so that he could grab his spear and throw it at him. After that I was very careful about the stories I used and I studiously avoided the references that St Paul makes to the shamefulness of women who appear bareheaded – in Maasailand the women shave their heads and they all look most beautiful.

The Maasai language is not an easy one to learn, and I found it very difficult to hear what people were saying, even when I knew the individual words. It all comes out at great speed and there are some important tonal differences that my ear could not pick up. But I had seven weeks in Kajiado being taught by Lorna Eglin, one of the few non-Maasai who is fluent in the language. That gave me enough of a grounding to have a lot of fun with it, and coming out with a few halting words of Maasai immediately opened the way to warm relationships. Some of the structures of the language are very revealing about the way Maasai think. For instance there is no future tense in Maasai and the word for tomorrow is 'metabaiki' which means 'should it happen'. When I had been with the Maasai for ten months of drought and the cattle were starting to die, I began to understand why the future is treated with such uncertainty.

I arrived once at the Nairobi Show with a Maasai friend who looked around the milling throng and observed, 'There's no one here today.' A moment later he announced triumphantly, 'There's someone!' – he had spotted another Maasai. 'Maa' means 'person', so in the eyes of a proud Maasai they are the only real people.

As well as getting to know the Maasai I had some practical work to do in getting my own house built. For the first few months I lived in a little tin rondavel that just had room for a bed, a small cupboard, a gas cooker, a gas fridge and a plastic bowl on a stool (the bathroom). I kept everything else in a case under the bed and had a paraffin lamp for lighting. The fridge regularly refused to work and I would stand it on its head for forty-eight hours which sometimes (not always) got it going again. During the middle of the day the little hut was too hot to stay inside, so I would go in search of the shade of a thorn tree, or sit in the church and chat to people. I was much looking forward to having somewhere cooler and more spacious to live.

A workman arrived from Isinya to make blocks for the walls and tiles for the roof, but to make blocks and tiles he needed sand, cement and water. We got the sand from a nearby dry river-bed where a team of Maasai threw the sand up onto the trailer and were paid according to the hours that they worked. One day the sand-diggers went on strike as they said those who were of senior age groups should be paid more than those of more junior age groups. Age groups are so central to the structure of Maasai society that I was not sure how to handle this and left it with Gideon to sort out. It was wonderful having Gideon at such moments as he was a most diplomatic negotiator and soon got them all working again. Then the cement had to come in from Isinya on the trailer which regularly got stuck in the Lesongoyo, the nearest and largest of the drifts across the road. And getting enough water to mix the sand and cement was always problematic. But gradually the walls did start to go up.

The water supply was a constant problem and one week a group of volunteers went to dig out another spring in the hope of increasing the flow of water into the pipe-line. Gideon and I went up to see how they were getting on: Gideon rolled up his trousers and climbed into the mud to help with the digging, and they decided my job should be to cook the food. I was led into a little shelter and told that there were many hungry men, then abandoned. All I could see were several large hunks of dismembered goat hanging from a tree, three stones on the ground and two cooking pots. So I was somewhat at a loss. I was rescued by our spear-carrying escort who sized up the situation in a trice and, grinning broadly, gave me a superb demonstration of bush-craft. First he produced a flame with a few deft twirls of his fire-sticks, then when the fat was sizzling merrily on the fire he chopped up a leg of goat with his wickedly sharp knife. With the same knife he fashioned an excellent spoon from a branch of the nearest tree and we ended up with a really delicious stew. He chivalrously disclaimed any involvement in the whole operation and I was acclaimed as a successful Maasai cook.

During those early months I travelled round the district to visit as many of the primary schools as possible in order to spread the news about the proposed school for girls. By this time it had generally been agreed that we should open a Village Polytechnic (VP) and I needed to start alerting primary school leavers about the opportunity to come to Meto the following year. There were not very many Maasai girls in the final year of the primary schools, which was discouraging at the time, though in the end we were well over-subscribed. Those visits also gave me the chance to talk with the primary school heads. At the same time I was pursuing discussions with the Ministry of Social Services, as we were going to need government funding for instructors' salaries to ensure the ongoing support of the VP. CMS produced some funds that enabled us to start on a building programme, and Oxfam later produced a £20,000 grant for equipment. We also had a local *harambee* (fund-raising event) and Charles Njonjo kindly came as the celebrity to draw support.

We started putting up the first building (a dormitory) in the middle of the bush, and one day a road-grader arrived at Meto. Being thoroughly opportunist I chatted up the road-grader driver and an hour later we had a beautiful access road leading from the village to the VP site. I had not realized that joining CMS would involve hijacking bulldozers, but life at Meto was certainly not short of new experiences. I did wonder whether I should have got planning permission, but no one seemed to object.

A number of visitors came to Meto that first year, including Anne Horsfall who had just arrived back in Kenya to be headmistress of a school near Kapenguria. Charles Richards was also around for part of the time and he very kindly escorted my mother and sister Elizabeth when they came to visit for two weeks in September. He hired a car and drove us all to Meto for the day. It was so good that they were able to see Meto, even though there was nowhere for them to stay, and my mother made great friends with Nambulong. Afterwards we had a few days in Amboseli where we saw lots of game, including elephants that surrounded the lodge.

In my tiny tin hut there was not much room for friends so I used to go and visit them instead, and always loved being invited into Maasai homes. I had to bend right down to get in through the narrow, low entrance, and then it was so dark inside that it always took me a few minutes to be able to see anything. A little light filtered through a small hole in the wall but the only way I could tell how many people there were inside was by listening to their voices. I would sit on the edge of the hide-covered sleeping shelf, and if there was a fire going would soon be offered a large mug of sweet tea.

In the evenings I often went down to the nearest dry watercourse and walked along the river-bed. It was cooler at that time of day and the animals would come down for water. Impala were often there and they would bound away in high leaps when they heard me coming or caught my scent. Monkeys chattered in the trees and it was fun watching them jump from tree to tree. There were also usually a few baboons around and lots of birds. Occasionally giraffe would be drinking straddle-legged from pools in the river. Sometimes I was woken at night by odd noises and would look out to see the house surrounded by impala, a wonderful sight in the moonlight. I never felt lonely at Meto and the free evenings were an amazing luxury after the incessant demands at Gordonstoun. It was wonderful to have that space, and no one ever visited me after dark unless there was a full moon; there were no street lights at Meto and few Maasai had torches.

During 1976 there was a little rain in April (just enough to make the road difficult for the Roho), and then for seven months there was no rain at all. By the beginning of November the grass had disappeared and the grazing lands had turned to dust. Water holes had dried up and the Maasai were having to take their weakened cattle further and further to find water. Every day some of the animals collapsed and then died where they lay, and I almost stopped going for walks as the stench from rotting carcases pervaded the bush. Milk had long dried up and the people were getting seriously weak and malnourished. The National Christian Council of Kenya were concerned about this and sent a certain amount of relief food for us to distribute to the most needy families in the area. As soon as word got about that food was being given out at Meto more people moved into the area, so there was never enough food for everyone and the distribution operation became something of a nightmare. As always, Gideon was invaluable and helped to identify the most destitute families.

Then one day in November the sky grew black, the heavens opened, and rain poured down on the parched land. It created havoc with the roads but the rain transformed the landscape almost overnight. Three days later the countryside round Meto was green again and the water-holes everywhere were filling up. It was a truly amazing transformation and I started to understand why one of the words that the Maasai use for rain is the same as that for God. Rain, after all, is the source and sustainer of life. I grumbled like mad about the rivers that poured across the roads, but I noticed that the Maasai never, ever grumbled about the rain. Many of them got pneumonia as their huts leaked, and it was very cold, but they never mentioned this and simply gave thanks to God for the life-giving gift of rain. Spirits lifted and the first questions that followed greetings were: 'Where are you from? – has it been raining there?' If the response was positive the reply would be 'Thank God!' An elder asked me one day if it was true that in England it could rain on any day of the year. I rather gloomily agreed that it could and he immediately exclaimed: 'Then England must be like heaven!' That year in Maasailand completely changed my attitude towards rain, and I still find it extraordinary that people in Britain equate wet weather with bad weather.

The first time that I tried to leave Meto after the rain had started I nearly got benighted. The Roho sank into a wet stretch of black cotton soil and without a few pushers I was helpless. Usually someone would come wandering out of the bush after a while, but that afternoon the road seemed deserted. I had already pitched my little tent and started to settle down for a rather damp night when I heard the sound of an engine and saw headlights ahead on the road. A truck appeared and the two men inside helpfully towed me out of the mud and set me on my way again. I eventually arrived at Isinya just before midnight feeling very cold and hungry and covered in mud. Having visited some of the primary schools around Loitokitok I then tried to get back to Meto and this time met a raging, impassable torrent.

I was worried about not being able to get back as we were expecting the Archbishop the following day and I should have been at Meto getting things ready. He was coming in for a confirmation service and the hope was that my house (which was still waiting for doors and floors when I left Meto) would be able to accommodate the archiepiscopal party. Anyway I went back to Isinya and the next day the Archbishop arrived there and we (Robin and Joan Slade, the Archbishop, the Vicar of Kajiado and myself) set off in Robin's Landcruiser, with the Isinya truck carrying thirty confirmation candidates. The road still had a lot of water pouring across it at various points and the truck quickly got bogged down and we had to send it back to Isinya. The Landcruiser got through (just) and when we arrived I was astonished to discover that my house was ready and furnished. The cement on the floors had only just dried and Pat and Derek, who were already at Meto, had been up at crack of dawn to move chairs, tables and beds into the house. It was wonderful of them, and I spent the whole day in a stupor looking at this amazing, real, live house. The visitors all slept there that night and the next day I moved in myself. One very positive spin-off for me of the whole episode was that the Archbishop, having seen the conditions on the road, gave strong support to my request to CMS for a Land-Rover.

By then I had been in my little tin hut for eight months and it was marvellous to be able to start living with a little more space. I was able to unpack for the first time and delighted in having plenty of room for visitors. It was also a huge relief to be able to sit in the house through the middle of the day without getting roasted alive. A new era began as I could invite groups of people into the sitting room, and children gathered regularly on the veranda to gaze into the room and marvel at the strange sights they saw – there was a permanent line of small nose prints across the window.

Food was still very short, despite the rain, as so many people had already lost their cattle. So there was still a constant flow of people begging for food, which I did find difficult to handle. One old lady was particularly persistent and she used to sit across the doorway so that I had to step over her every time I went in or out. I usually ended up giving her something, not out of Christian charity but simply to get rid of her. A few months later, when most people had milk again, I heard her voice at the door and went out ready to tell her to go away. Mercifully something made me wait, and she started to untie a little bundle from inside her cloth. Then she handed me a small package of beans. 'When I was hungry you gave me food' she said, 'and now we have food so I can give something to you.'

Another visitor who came at that time was the wife of a medicine man. I had met her the week before when visiting her village; she had invited me into her house and started to prepare tea. As the flames from the fire lit up the inside of the hut I noticed some curious objects hanging on the wall. She explained that her husband was an *oloiboni* (medicine man), and that most of the objects were horns containing medicinal powders. When she arrived at my door the next week she was carrying a gourdful of milk that she had brought as a present all the way from her village, a good three hours' walk away. I was constantly amazed by the resilience of Maasai women and their cheerfulness and generosity in their hard lives.

Arrival of the girls

The Isinya Board met at Meto on 15 March and decided that the Girls VP should open in May. This was much earlier than I had expected, and it became a huge scramble to get ready in time. I went to Isinya the following week to interview fifty girls (primary school leavers) who wanted to come, and Ole Kipury, the chairman of the Meto committee, and myself selected thirty girls from across Kajiado District. Ole Kipury asked them all questions in Maasai and we only took those who could respond. The opening date was set for 3 May, by which time the rains were at their height.

Because of the continuing rain the Isinya truck was not able to get to Meto for ten weeks, so everything (building materials, furniture, etc) had to come in on the trailer, pulled by the tractor. Even with a Land-Rover the normal journey meant filling the vehicle with strong men, piling spades, jembes (hoes) and towrope into the back and then spending anything up to five hours pushing, digging, towing, wading, and skidding the thirty miles to the main road. I was frequently called out to help the tractor across the Lesongoyo, the nearest and most troublesome of the river crossings, and whenever it got stuck somewhere on the road in the rain everything got very wet. We lost one complete load of cement that way. It was something of a nightmare trying to get the VP site habitable before the girls arrived, but we did finally open with all the roofs on, most (but not all) of the doors and windows in place, and the beds made it just a day ahead of the girls. Luxuries like pipes and a chimney for the stove arrived the following week and tables three weeks later. We started with a dormitory, a kitchen, and a classroom, and a sea of mud.

Francis visited Kenya at the end of April and was with me in Meto when the girls arrived, and it was good to have him there at that time.

The girls should have come in the Isinya truck but that still could not get in, so we met the truck at the main road with my Land-Rover and the tractor and trailer, and one of the Isinya Land-Rovers helped us to ferry the girls on to Meto. It must have been one of the weirdest school openings that Maasailand has ever seen. We crammed as many of the girls as we could into the two Land-Rovers, and the rest had to sit on their boxes on the trailer. The procession set off into the bush and we slithered our way back to Meto. It was an extraordinary experience for the girls but they recovered remarkably quickly and spent most of the next few days digging drains, painting walls, and clearing the bush, all of which they did very willingly. There was a very good spirit amongst them from the start.

Robin tried to get to Meto the day after the girls arrived, but even in his Landcruiser he couldn't get through as all the rivers were up. He had to stop on the banks of a river that was flowing about ten feet deep and Teraia, who had driven the Isinya Land-Rover in and was trying to get out again, had to stop on the opposite bank of the same river. The water was making such a noise that they couldn't even communicate by shouting to each other, so they were hurling Coca-Cola bottles with notes inside across the river to try and exchange news. At Meto the tractor got stuck yet again in the Lesongoyo and a very tired runner arrived on my doorstep asking for help. So I picked up as many strong men as I could find, plus spades and a towrope, and went to investigate. The tractor had dug itself down into deep, damp sand in the river-bed, but we finally managed to pull it out.

When Francis left I took him into Nairobi to catch his flight home and then returned to Meto. After that the rains eased off and we had no more really heavy storms. Two weeks later I drove to Kajiado and reached the main road in an hour and a half – a welcome contrast to the four or five hours the journey had been taking. I did not have to get out of the Land-Rover once to prospect the road ahead, I did not have to go into four-wheel drive much, and only had to go into low ratio twice. After that it was dry.

Once the girls had done the initial work needed to make the VP habitable, we tried to make a start on the courses. The idea was to have courses in agriculture, tailoring and home economics, and I supplemented the official courses by a little teaching of scripture and English. It took us a while to get the agriculture course started, as the first instructor, Rufus Kibuika, was so horrified by the remoteness of Meto that he only stayed three hours. When he arrived I went out to greet him and found him furiously puffing at a cigarette, refusing to take his things out of the Land-Rover. He asked me where the nearest telephone was, and when I told him it was in Kajiado he said he couldn't possibly live at Meto. We couldn't persuade him to change his mind, so he went back in the Land-Rover that day. Zecharia, a cheerful agriculturalist from Kalema, helped us out for a few weeks, and then George Kamau came. He got everything going on an excellent footing and stayed for some years. Jackson Okinda was with us from the start to establish the tailoring course, and he too did a first-rate job and stayed even longer than George. It took us a few months to find a home economics instructor, but eventually Mrs Ayieko arrived and transformed the culinary habits of the whole village.

We had a Maasai cook called Julius who was quite competent but a bit temperamental. The first night he was upset because we produced a goat for the girls' supper and the fellow who slaughtered the goat simply gave him an entire goat carcase. Julius didn't reckon it was a cook's job to chop up meat but only to cook it, and the slaughterer didn't reckon it was a slaughterer's job to cut up the goat but only to kill it. Eventually I managed to extract the slaughterer from where he was sorting out the skin and get him to come back and hack the carcase into about four pieces, by which time Julius felt it was reduced to an acceptable size for a cook to deal with. I'm not sure whether the problem was his union, tribal custom, or just first night nerves.

Elish Marrinka joined us for the first few weeks as matron. She was the wife of one of the primary school teachers and slept in the dormitory with the girls. One night at about 10 p.m. some of the girls came over to say that Elish had threatened one of them with an axe and they were frightened so please could I come over. Poor Elish, she was the gentlest, shyest soul imaginable, so I couldn't really make out what was going on. Anyway, I went over and got them all into bed and saw Elish – she did have an axe beside her bed but didn't have the remotest intention of using it on the girls (it was probably for cutting fire-wood). They did get a bit hysterical sometimes in those early days but they quickly recovered. We later decided that there was no need to employ a matron, mainly because the girls themselves were so sensible that they were perfectly well able to be responsible for one another. Although they were primary school leavers the average age was probably about seventeen.

The staff was completed by a splendid character, the night watchman Ole Nayiolo Ang. He had one tooth and was about five feet high, which is very short for a Maasai, so I gave him a hat that made him a few inches higher, and Francis's gumboots and an ex-British Army greatcoat. By the time he had donned all these and picked up his spear the whole effect was so incongruous it was enough to frighten anyone off. In fact we didn't really need a night watchman, but Gideon was upset at the thought of our starting without one so the Centre paid for him and, when the Dorper rams arrived, he spent most of his time making sure that the moran didn't steal the rams.

Abraham, one of the local shop keepers, supplied the VP with food. He had many cows and I had already had difficulties with him about water. The pipeline came to the Centre and VP first and then went on down the hill to his shop and the cattle dip. Whenever there was not enough water for the dip he came up and shouted at us and told us we were taking all the water. In fact we were as careful as we could be, and sometimes there simply was not enough water coming through to anyone. Other times someone would let a tap run freely at the dip and then we would find the storage tank on the hill was empty. So water was a constant source of friction and I was a little nervous about being dependent on Abraham for the food for the girls. In fact I think he did his best, but his ancient vehicle broke down so often that eventually we switched our custom to the Somali trader in the village.

Abraham was licensed to preach in the church and on Sundays we would have to endure anything up to an hour of Abraham's rambling warnings against the evils of drink, the only subject he ever preached about. I was sorry to have to expose the girls to this, but one day in church an alarm clock suddenly went off after he had been preaching for under half an hour. He was so surprised that he stopped. Later I asked the girls about it. They looked rather embarrassed and said uncertainly: 'Was it bad?' I could only laugh in response and from then on the ringing of the alarm clock became an accepted part of the liturgy.

It was wonderful having the girls to transform the worship in the church. We met every morning for prayers and they loved singing. They used to arrive early and sit there singing away until I arrived. They sang instinctively in harmony and as their repertoire increased they were much in demand as a choir. Some of them also started up a lively Sunday School. They used to go out early in the morning to the largest of the local settlements and gather together as many children as they could find. They then led them singing along the bush paths back to the Centre. The children thoroughly enjoyed these sessions, so the girls made a very valuable contribution to the life of the little church at Meto. There was only a handful of Maasai Christians at Meto at that time, though a few women had been baptised recently and were very faithful. The oldest of them, and the most respected, was Nambulong.

The courses started well. In a link letter of November 1977 I reported on the progress that George had made. 'George has been fighting a valiant battle against wandering donkeys, goats, squirrels, buck and birds, and has had constant difficulty in getting enough water. However, the soil here is rich in minerals and there is plenty of cattle manure available so the results have been encouraging. We supplied the kitchen in September with maize, potatoes, cabbages and onions and a second planting is now almost ready to be harvested. We have bought a hundred day-old chicks and are hoping to start producing eggs in due course. The chief hazards will probably be rats and snakes but George thinks he can outwit them.' The hens started laying the following May and egg production went up to ninety a day. The land that the girls had cleared and planted transformed the landscape of Meto, and it was interesting to see wandering elders watching the girls as they planted beans. Later that year beans started to appear all over the area. Had we offered to teach elders how to grow beans there would have been little response, but by copying what the girls were doing many of the elders and their families benefited from this new source of protein.

The girls all chose to do either agriculture or tailoring, and Jackson helped the girls on the tailoring course to start producing some remarkably professional-looking garments. Soon anyone who was anyone was walking round Meto with a VP-produced outfit. The group produced their first man's suit to the order of Julius the cook. Julius was as pleased as punch, in spite of the fact that it cost him a month's salary, and I had to take a photograph of him wearing it, flanked by the seamstresses. Samuel, who chopped the wood, bought a denim suit which he was delighted with, and Joseph the dispenser bought a shirt that he was very pleased with and walked round in all the time. I ordered a blouse and Elish the matron got all her children wearing dresses that the girls had made. When the chairman of the Meto Committee came, he was so impressed by all this that he had himself measured up for a suit. Then the girls started to get orders from primary schools for uniforms which was a good income-spinner. The hope was that each girl would be able to earn enough money at Meto to buy a machine to take home with her when she left.

All the girls did home economics, and although Mrs Ayieko came from Western Kenya she made a real effort to get to know the local

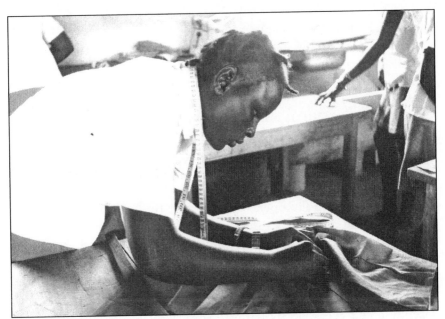

Tailoring class

Maasai so that she could do thing with the girls that would be appropriate in a Maasai context. One of the things she noticed was the number of small children who fall into fires in the huts and get burnt, so she designed a fireplace with a low protective mud–wall that stopped children rolling onto the embers. The girls made a number of these fireplaces in the homes of women round about who were all delighted with them. Mrs Ayieko taught cookery, hygiene, nutrition and childcare, and Joseph the dispenser came in to help with the health education. He was very supportive of all that was happening and was a great help when the girls were ill.

The VP offered no paper qualifications but aimed to help the girls to lead fuller lives in their villages, so we tried to make sure that everything we taught the girls was something they could continue to do in their own homes. In order to test this out we asked the girls to put into practice some of the things they had learnt at Meto when they went home during the holidays. The first time they went away each girl was given a eucalyptus tree to plant and all reported that their trees were all alive and well when they returned. Some of the girls planted vegetables and showed their families what they were doing, others did sewing projects and taught their younger sisters, others did Sunday school teaching and a few helped in their local dispensaries. During the next

Christmas holiday I took George and Jackson to visit as many of the girls as we could in their homes. We managed to see twenty of them and visited all the girls doing agriculture. It was a very worthwhile time; we learnt so much from meeting their parents and seeing their homes, and we were able to have some very useful talks about the future of the girls when they left the VP. It was encouraging to find that the courses they were following at Meto did seem to be opening up practical opportunities for them in their own home areas. We examined marketing possibilities in each area for eggs, vegetables and clothes, and George had a good look at the agricultural potential in each place.

The VP was officially opened in October (long after it had actually started) by the Deputy Commissioner for Social Services. As the Commissioner stepped forward to unveil a plaque commemorating the event, the heavens opened – the short rains chose that precise moment to announce their arrival. A tropical downpour drenched the assembled crowd and the Commissioner's smart suit was ruined. As soon as they decently could everyone rushed for cover and then jumped into their vehicles to get away before the rivers started to rise. I thought it was all a disaster at first, and then realised it was the best thing that could have happened. Rain is such a sign of blessing that everyone was delighted and saw the event as a singular sign of God's blessing on the whole enterprise. By this time I had acquired the Maasai name Ngoto Ntoyie, meaning 'the mother of the girls.'

One day we took all the girls on an outing to visit the cloth mills and agricultural research station at Thika. It was their first such outing and there was great excitement all round. But when the girls started going round the cloth mill, many of them fainted from shock at the sight and sound of the machinery. I think the noise and heat were too much for them, and I had never stopped to think what the effect of it all might be on Maasai girls straight from the bush. As one of the girls put it later 'From the time we were born we have never seen such big machines.' It was obviously a shattering experience for those coming from the silence of the bush to be subjected to the level of noise emitted by heavy machinery, and some of them suffered real pain in their ear-drums. They finally recovered enough to go on to the horticultural station where three more collapsed with a delayed reaction, much to the surprise and concern of the men who were showing us their peaceful and totally silent plants. Most of the girls recovered when we were safely back in Maasailand, but several heads were still spinning three days later. On Sunday afternoons I often took the girls to explore the Meto Hills, and

Enjoying the Meto Hills

69

once they had adjusted to the novel idea of walking for no useful purpose, they throughly enjoyed these outings.

Julius continued to be a rather temperamental cook and one afternoon he lost his temper when quarrelling with George and launched a potentially lethal attack on him with a kitchen knife. Some of the girls and myself were standing near and we all threw ourselves at Julius and managed to get the knife away from him before it had done any damage. Julius himself was in fact the only casualty, as George hit him over the head with a piece of wood that he had picked up in self-defence. From then on a wild-eyed Julius promised me that he was going to murder George. I tried to enlist the help of the police in Kajiado but they were too far away to be of any practical help. In the end the local Maasai elders sorted it all out and restored the peace. At a five-hour meeting of elders it was decided that Julius's blood had been shed by George (no one seemed to be interested in who had been the aggressor) and that the blood price should be 200 shillings. In the presence of the elders George then handed the money to Julius and the two men shook hands. Everyone assured me that would put an end to the whole affair. George was a Kikuyu, which was why they had decided on cash for the blood price. Had he been a Maasai, he would have been asked for a sheep, and the sheep would have been slaughtered. The two men would then have shed the blood of the sheep and eaten the meat in the presence of the elders, and that would have restored peace between them. It all seemed an amazingly vivid parallel to the Christian theology of atonement.

In June 1978 we had a second intake of girls, twenty this time, having again had a real scramble to get the extra buildings needed ready in time. By the time there were fifty girls Meto was starting to feel like a real metropolis. By then ongoing support had been secured from the Ministry of Social Services who agreed to pay the salaries of all the instructors, so by the end of that year the VP had basically been established.

Water was a continuing problem throughout my time at Meto, and over the three years I joined a number of expeditions up the pipeline to see what was happening when water failed to appear. A miscellaneous collection of elders and moran usually gathered, clutching jembes (hoes), spades, spanners and spears, and disappeared up the hill led by Gideon. A visiting anthropologist once remarked that it looked more like a lion hunt than a plumbing party; I thought it looked as though we were part of a peasant revolution. In fact when we came to the place where the pipe was blocked everyone sorted it out with remarkable efficiency. It was an amicable sort of work party and Gideon organised everyone in a leisurely but effective way. By evening a great deal of indescribably dirty water was usually rushing into the tank and everyone had had a thoroughly sociable day.

In June 1978 rather more serious problems arose, and as there were fifty girls at the VP by then we decided to offer the girls as a workforce to help deal with the various problems. First of all the second spring had to be dug out again and then connected with the old pipeline at a lower level. We took the girls up to the spring as far as possible on the trailer. This proved to be a somewhat hazardous journey as the access track was completely overgrown and low-lying branches of thorn trees swept the trailer at intervals, forcing everyone to dive for cover. I was foolishly sitting in a particularly exposed position at the front but escaped unscathed, thanks to the efforts of a roguish-looking elder who hurled himself protectively in front of me every time. This exhibition of chivalry was as welcome as it was unexpected. Maasai thorns are no joke. The girls spent the day carrying pipes, mixing cement, building support posts and digging the trench. It was hard work, but they were well rewarded when the water finally came flowing through at the end of the second day.

The disappointment that followed was to discover that out of a total of 18,000 gallons a day flowing into the pipe from the spring only about 3,000 gallons were reaching the storage tank at the bottom of the hill. Piero, a visiting Italian water-engineer, discovered that the effective diameter of the pipe had been reduced to half an inch because of an accumulation of silt, and decided it would be necessary to clean out the last mile of pipe. No easy operation as the pipe was buried for most of the way, but with the help of the girls the job was done in a week. They dug up the pipes, took them apart and then hammered on every section with pickaxes and jembes. This realeased quantities of filthy water that was spilt out onto the hillside. By the end of the week the tank was totally empty, so the population of Meto was getting a bit desperate. Piero and the girls were on the final stretch leading to the tank by then so they worked on, racing against the sun, and when the sun set there were still some dozen pipe lengths to go. Undeterred by darkness they carried on by moonlight, and by 10 p.m. all the pipes were reconnected. For a few days the water was still very dirty, but eventually it settled down and a revitalised flow of water reached the people.

The girls did a great deal of heavy work that week to get the water flowing, and from then on there were fewer grumbles about the amount of water the girls were using. On the whole the local Maasai were remarkably accepting of the strange idea of educating girls, though I noticed with interest that the tactics that Abraham employed when he wanted to stop things happening were very similar to those used by the housemasters at Gordonstoun, so my experience there came in useful.

Every now and again we had problems when we discovered that a girl at the VP had been promised in marriage to an elder and that cows had already been paid to her father. Spear-carrying Maasai once rushed through the dormitory in search of a promised bride, and we had to enter into negotiations with the girl's family, but generally girls only came to the VP if their family was in support of the idea. On one occasion a very excited group of elders came to see me, demanding to know where 'she' was. When I finally disentangled the story, I discovered they were looking for Mary, the twelve-year-old daughter of our matron, who had just finished at primary school and applied to come to the VP later that year. A man had arrived to take her away in marriage and she had promptly disappeared. The elders all thought she was hiding in the VP and did not believe my protestations that we had no idea where she was, so they reappeared in the afternoon and marched through the dormitory before I could stop them. They were all waving their sticks and spears about and the father was threatening to beat up his wife unless she produced the girl. I finally managed to get them all off the VP site, and as soon as the man had left Meto, Mary reappeared – from inside a cupboard where she had been hiding in her father's own house.

A small group of Maasai Christians who lived in and around Meto gathered for worship in the church every Sunday, but there were almost no Christians in the wider area around the Centre. A young Maasai evangelist called Jonathan was working at Meto when I first arrived and he used to visit outlying settlements to share his faith with those who had never heard of the Christian Gospel. His work was just starting to bear fruit when he was moved from Meto, which was a real shame.

During the second year someone gave me a film-strip projector that could be run off the battery of the Land-Rover. So I started giving regular film shows in the church at Meto, and sometimes went out to one of the nearby villages where we improvised a screen by hanging a sheet from the nearest thorn tree. I had a number of *Jungle Doctor* films which were enormously popular. The Maasai got very excited with the animals that appeared on the screen and the comments from the audience were hilarious. How much anyone really understood of the message of these films I never knew, but the enterprise generated a huge amount of interest.

I very much wanted to be able to have more contact with those in the more outlying settlements, and thought that if I had a donkey it could carry a tent and sleeping bag for me and I could go off with a Maasai companion and stay in the villages. So one day I bought a donkey called Kunoti. When we were first introduced he about-turned and kicked me smartly on the shin. Everyone assured me that once he got used to me it would be all right, and people tried to teach me a few vital words of command that Maasai donkeys understand. I found it impossible to make the clicking noises that were needed, and was mortified when Ole Seita's youngest son (who was about two feet high) clicked the donkey into totally submissive obedience. I kept Kunoti for a few weeks, putting him in an enclosure near the house during the night and tethering him to a tree during the day. When other donkeys came near he sometimes got restless and broke free and we then had to go on a donkey-chase which caused much hilarity. In fact I did not really need to chase him because everyone knew whose donkey he was and before the end of the day someone would always bring him back. But Kunoti continued to be what the girls called 'epe', and when I looked the word up in my dictionary I found it meant 'wild, troublesome, jittery' which was an apt description. So eventually I gave him to Ngoto Tipape, Ole Seita's wife, who was highly delighted. She used Kunoti to carry water for her every day, and Tipape used to write and give me an update on Kunoti's carrying capacity for many years after I had left Meto.

In June 1977 an *eunoto* was held on the plains below Ol Doinyo Orok. This is a ceremony that only happens every seven years, and the date is always very uncertain as the positions of certain stars, the phase of the moon and the presence of rain have to be just right. Everyone waited for months for the elders to decide on the auspicious date, and then a great gathering took place. Five hundred moran from all around the district came together for a week, together with their families, to celebrate the graduation from being warriors to becoming elders. In Maasai society all the men belong to an age group that spans seven years, so every seven years the members of one age group go through the transition together. Becoming a warrior and ceasing to be a warrior are the two most important days of their lives. At an *eunoto* the warriors have to cut off their red pigtails, so their mothers shave their heads and it is a time of great stress. Then they all come together and the sight of five hundred warriors marching, singing and jumping in the middle of the bush was stunning. Many bulls were slaughtered and much beer was drunk. It was the most colourful and dramatic sight.

The Maasai still practise female circumcision, despite pressures for it to cease. The practice makes for all sorts of complications for the women at childbirth, and the operation itself often gives rise to serious infection. Around Meto some of the families used to take both boys and girls to the local dispenser so that it could be done under hygienic conditions. However the operation was done, a party had to be given afterwards and I used to be invited to such gatherings, where there was always a lot of amazing jumping and singing. I often saw the results of circumcision when I gave Joseph a lift to help women who were in very painful and extended childbirth. More than once the woman concerned died. But there was little we could do to change this long-established tradition.

Maasai normally co-exist fairly comfortably with wild life, and I was always told very firmly that Maasai never eat game meat. Killing game animals was anyway against the law. One day I was wandering through the bush and came to a group of men who were roasting meat over a fire. They offered me a piece of the meat and as the taste was new to me I asked them what it was. They then told me it was giraffe meat. When I asked them how they had got hold of the meat, they explained with wide-eyed innocence that a passing giraffe had suddenly fallen down dead. I did not ask what it was that had caused the giraffe to fall down dead as it was fairly obvious.

During the three years at Meto I did have several breaks and both Christmases I spent with Jenny and Fred Burgess and Catherine (my god-daughter) on their farm at Rongai. I also had a stream of visitors when the road was dry, and in October 1978 my cousin Lucy Holder and her friend Lavinia came to stay for a week. They were both nurses so they launched in and taught health education to the girls, which was an interesting experience for them as well as for the girls.

In August that year I went up to northern Kenya with Pat and Derek, Chris and Rosemary Carey, and Rosaleen Bryson. Derek and I both took our Land-Rovers and we spent a marvellous ten days travelling up to Lake Turkana and then east across the Chalbi desert to Marsabit. I had long wanted to see the east shore of Lake Turkana – the rocky desert to the east of the lake is one of the most spectacular sights in Kenya. We camped four nights beside the lake where it was so windy that we gave up trying to pitch tents and slept under the stars. Rosaleen and I slept out on cliffs overlooking the lake and it was quite out of this world, watching the stars wheeling overhead and then waking to the dawn light over the lake and listening to the lapping of the water along the shore.

By December 1978 the second year of girls were well settled in and the VP was basically established. So I felt that my part in it all had been completed, and arranged to hand over the post of VP Manager to Gideon. But in many ways I was very sorry to leave Meto. It had all been an amazingly rich experience, and I had so much enjoyed the girls as well as the local Maasai. The whole community gave me a tremendous farewell party. Mrs Ayieko organised a feast the like of which Meto had never seen before, the girls sang, staff, girls and Nambulong speechified, and even Abraham said he was sorry I was going. I had never had such a send-off, and when I got back to the house afterwards I burst into tears. But as I drove out the next day and crossed the Lesongoyo for the last time I must confess that my heart lifted at the thought of not having to cross it again. By then every mile of that road held memories for me of getting bogged down in the mud or camping beside rivers waiting for the water to fall. So I knew it was the right time to leave, but at the same time I was filled with gratitude to God for the gift of being able to live for those three years amongst my Maasai friends.

CHAPTER 7

Exploring Zaire

T HERE WAS A WHITE CHRISTMAS THAT YEAR in the Cotswolds, so I came straight from the heat and dust of the Maasai bush to an Upper Slaughter enveloped in snow. We sang carols around the village in traditional style, holding lanterns to read the words from the song sheets as snow flakes fell on the paper and our fingers froze, and then being welcomed into warm houses and thawing out beside roaring log fires with the help of mince pies and generous glasses of port. It was good to be back with the family, and I wandered round in something of a daze marvelling at the abundance of taps, telephones, and tarmac roads. I maddened everyone by washing up in half an inch of water as I still couldn't quite believe that water could be used freely.

On Christmas Eve I had a phone call from CMS asking if I would be willing to help out at Crowther Hall for the spring and summer terms. A tutor was needed to fill in until a permanent appointment could be made in September. This was a quite unexpected development as I had hoped to have a break and then start visiting my link parishes, but as I had enjoyed my earlier time at Crowther I agreed to go. It was good to be back in the international environment of Selly Oak and I fitted in visits to my link churches in the Cotswolds over the weekends. The Selly Oak colleges ran an excellent course in Development Studies so in the summer term I seized the chance to take this course. Many of the issues that we discussed were ones that had come up during my time at Meto and it was very helpful to reflect on them with others.

At the end of June CMS held a conference for mission partners and there I had a talk with Jesse Hillman, the Africa Secretary, to discuss my next location. I had assumed CMS would want me to go back to Kenya, but to my surprise Jesse started talking about Zaire. He was puzzled about the situation in Zaire, as Anglican Churches were suddenly sprouting up all over the country and no one in London quite knew how to respond to the multiplicity of requests for help that were coming in. So Jesse asked if I would be willing to go out for six months to carry out a survey of the possibilities for rural development in the dioceses of Boga and Bukavu. All I knew about Boga at that stage was that it was

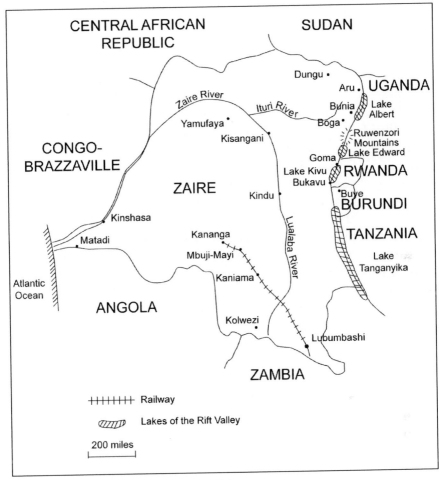

Zaire

very remote and that the roads in Zaire were terrible. Having only just recovered from struggling with the Meto road, the suggestion had little immediate appeal, but Jesse assured me that I need make no ongoing commitment to Zaire. I prayed hard about it that night and the next day agreed to do the survey. In order to recover some of my long-forgotten French I did a crash language course in Boulogne in August.

After what had been a fairly busy ten months in Britain I packed up again and left for Zaire in October. Derek and Pat Wilks hosted me in Nairobi and put me on a little Africa Inland Mission (AIM) plane to fly to Bunia in NE Zaire. I made that flight many times over the years and never tired of it. First the plane went westwards across the plains of the

Rift Valley, then flew over the massive wheat fields of the Mau escarpment and across the densely populated areas of Western Kenya before reaching the great watery expanse of Lake Victoria. The Ugandan shoreline appeared at the Owen Falls at Jinja, the plane then followed the Nile northwards across the Ugandan bush until a more westerly course took us to the shores of Lake Albert (or Lac Mobutu as it is known in Zaire). Finally the green, rolling hills of Zaire would rise to meet us and on a clear day we could see the snows on the Ruwenzori Mountains.

Zaire has one of the most bizarre histories of colonialism on the continent. This huge chunk of central Africa first emerged as one country in 1885 when the Congo Free State was established under the personal sovereignty of King Leopold II of Belgium. During this time the King amassed a huge personal fortune by allowing exploitative and cruel practices to be used against the local population, such as the use of hand-chopping as a penalty for workers who failed to meet rubber quotas. In 1908 the country came under the control of the Belgium government and was known as the Belgian Congo until independence in 1960. President Mobutu came to power in 1965 and changed the name of the country to Zaire. When he was ousted by Laurent Kabila in 1996 the name was changed again, this time to the Democratic Republic of Congo. Throughout this memoir the name used is Zaire.

In terms of natural resources Zaire is one of the richest countries in Africa, second only to South Africa in terms of mineral resources that include gold and diamonds. Massive potential sources of hydro-power can be found along the length of the Lualaba and Congo rivers, yet only the Inga dam below Kinshasa has so far been effectively exploited. The government of Zaire has long been predatory in relation to its own population (a habit first learnt from the Belgians), and economists had to coin a new word, 'kleptocracy', to describe the mode of government. President Mobutu systematically creamed off the profits generated in every sector of the economy for the benefit of his own family and friends and became one of the most spectacularly rich leaders of his time. By contrast the general population of Zaire was reduced to desperate poverty and hundreds of thousands of people died over the years of his misrule as a result of starvation and disease.

Most countries in sub-Saharan Africa are labelled as 'developing' countries: in Zaire 'undeveloping' would be a more apt description. A lack of normal infastructures of government had led to the collapse of transport and communication systems and to the disastrous running

A main road in Zaire

down of educational and medical services. The Belgians left Zaire with 100,000 miles of all-weather roads, but twenty years later only some 20,000 miles of that road system were still usable. As bridges collapsed from lack of maintenance they had not been replaced and the associated road networks had fallen into disuse. Thus distances between places by road were constantly increasing. The roads that were still passable were mud-surfaced and filled with such massive potholes that they were only usable by four-wheel drive vehicles. In schools none of the students and few of the teachers had text books, so the teachers were mainly using the notes they had taken themselves at school, i.e. the whole education system was effectively reverting to oral tradition. Even at university level the situation was not much better. When the Belgians left the country at independence only six Zaireans had completed their education to degree level, so it was not surprising that the country fell into such chaos at that time. Government-run hospitals and health centres mostly consisted of decaying, empty buildings, staffed by doctors and dispensers who were appointed and occasionally paid, but who had no drugs, so there were no patients. The drug distribution system had broken down and many of the drugs found their way into markets where injectable penicillin was on sale alongside pineapples and bananas. The only health centres that delivered a meaningful service were those run by the Churches.

A sociologist whom I met in Kisangani once commented that as far as he could see every public organisation set up by the Zaire government succeeded in achieving the diametrically opposite result from that which it was set up to achieve. Air Zaire (commonly known as 'Air Peut-être') succeeded in preventing people from flying, banks effectively prevented the circulation of money, the 'Bureau des Routes' prevented the maintenance of roads, and so on. Corruption was endemic and local officials, who rarely received a salary, lived off the imposition of illegal taxes. It was so difficult to meet government rules and regulations that people simply ignored official systems and found ingenious ways of operating what was known as the 'alternative' economy.

All this provided the context in which the rapidly growing Anglican Church was set. Why, people asked me from time to time, was there an Anglican Church in Zaire at all? The Anglican churches in Africa are mainly (though not exclusively) to be found in countries where there has been some past British influence. In Zaire the birth of the Anglican Church was the direct result of a border change. Originally the border between Zaire and Uganda was drawn along the Ituri River which meant that Boga lay in Uganda and was first evangelised by Apolo Kivebulaya and others from the Church of Uganda. In 1905 the border was redrawn along the Semliki River which put Boga and its Anglican church into the Belgian Congo. Since then Christians from Boga had moved to other parts of the country, particularly to Kisangani where students from Boga went to university, thus starting the spread of Anglicanism.

The dominant churches in Zaire were the hugely powerful Roman Catholic Church and the Kimbanguist Church, an indigenous Zairean religion started by the charismatic prophet Simon Kimbangu in 1921. A large number of Protestant missions had come into the country over the years, resulting in the setting up of numerous different churches and sects. President Mobutu decided in 1971 that there could only be four churches in Zaire, Roman Catholic, Kimbanguist, Protestant and Orthodox, and in order to effect this tidy scenario the Eglise du Christ au Zaire (ECZ) was set up as a single Protestant church. An arbitrary fifty-seven of the numerous Protestant groups were allowed to become part of the ECZ, so the many groups that were not offered membership found themselves in a dilemma. Basically they had three options: to close down, to go underground and continue operating illegally, or to join forces with one of the groups that had been allowed in. Many such groups turned to the Anglican Church, which was a bona fide member of the ECZ, and asked to become Anglicans, most of them without having any idea what Anglicanism was all about. The Anglicans had responded to these requests with a spirit of hospitality, hence the growth of the church at that time. One of my tasks was to try to get some clearer picture of what was going on and how the huge training needs that this situation presented might be met.

It was typical of the difficulties of communication at that time that I unknowingly arrived in Zaire just as Bishop Philip Ridsdale and his wife Lucy were about to go away for two weeks to attend the consecration of the new Bishop of Buye in Burundi. They turned up in Nyankunde (a large medical centre near Bunia) as soon as I arrived, together with the Reverend Ben Bataaga, and decided to sweep me up and take me with them on their two-thousand-mile journey to Buye. So I had an interesting detour that took me through north-eastern Zaire, Rwanda and Burundi, before first setting eyes on Boga itself.

Our progress was complicated by the state of disrepair of the ancient Land-Rover that represented the only form of diocesan transport. The handbrake had long collapsed, the footbrake only started to become effective after vigorous pumping, the headlights lit up a few bushes at the side of the road but illuminated little of the road ahead, and the self-starter did not work. The back door did not close properly, so every now and then the door burst open and an assortment of buckets, pots and pans, pineapples and so on tumbled out of the door and bounced merrily down the road behind us. Ben and I then chased down the road to retrieve as much as possible before this manna from heaven had been appropriated by needy passers-by and disappeared into the forest.

The journey took us through some amazingly beautiful country, starting with the mountains of eastern Zaire. From the misty Zairean highlands we descended the escarpment to the Virunga National Park, restocked at that time with game that had fled the guns of hungry soldiers in the game parks of Uganda. We wound our way through the Virunga volcanoes, driving over a huge lava flow from Nyamlagavo that had erupted dramatically only the year before, nearly engulfing the lakeside town of Goma. From Goma we drove round the west side of Lake Kivu to Bukavu and thence through the orderly environments of Rwanda and Burundi where the hills were terraced and petrol stations still operated. At the gathering in Buye, Bezaleri Ndahura, Bishop of Bukavu, was chosen to be the first Archbishop of the new Francophone Province of Burundi, Rwanda and Zaire.

Two weeks and two thousand miles after leaving Bunia we were back there again and finally set off along the road to Boga. We bumped and slid our way down the road in the rain, passing a plaque on the way that marked the final encampment of Stanley before he dropped down to the lakeshore to rescue Emin Pasha in 1888. Then we passed another plaque marking the Nile/Congo watershed. After eight hours on the road we reached Boga well after dark. Amongst all the horror stories that I had heard about Zaire I had quite failed to register that Boga is in one of the most beautiful corners of Africa. The village sits up on the escarpment of the western wall of the Rift Valley, overlooking the Semliki Plains and commanding a grandstand view of the Ruwenzori Mountains. I woke that first morning to see the snow on the glaciers as the dawn light touched the peaks, and to the north I could just see the glittering waters of Lake Albert.

After only a week in Boga we set off once again to visit Kisangani. At that time Kisangani was still within the Diocese of Boga-Zaire, and Philip had an extensive confirmation tour planned for that area. It took us five days of hard driving to get there, much of the way driving through mile upon mile of the giant trees of the Ituri Forest. On the last day we found several lorries that were bogged down in the middle of the road and queues of vehicles were forming on the road in both directions. The roads in the forest are all so narrow that it is very difficult to get round another vehicle that is stuck, but mercifully the Land-Rover was just able to pass the lorries by slithering off the track and scraping the bark off the nearest trees. We felt sorry for the passengers who were riding on the top of the loads on the lorries, as they would clearly be there for some days and there was no food, water or shelter in the area. One of the lorries was carrying a load of Coca-Cola and already the driver was selling off bottles at outrageously inflated prices.

Kisangani was hot and humid and full of dilapidated buildings, but it was an enormous relief to be beside the river after our days in the forest. The Zaire River is about half a mile wide there and is the last place that can be reached by steamers from Kinshasa before the Stanley Falls. There was much activity at the landing stages, and we crossed the river on a canoe, carved from a single tree, that held sixty people. Few Zaireans can swim, so if a canoe overturns there is much loss of life.

We were welcomed in Kisangani by Archdeacon and Mrs Tibafa and by Margaret Pooley of CMS. Life in Kisangani was not easy as it was impossible to get fresh milk and meat, other than small animals from the forest, and there were few fresh vegetables. The staple food was rice or cassava, with fish as a luxury, and malnutrition was endemic. Having seen around Kisangani we set off to visit churches in the forest villages to the west. For three weeks we were on the road, taking the Land-Rover over endless narrow sandy tracks and negotiating innumerable wet, slippery log bridges over the network of waterways that criss-crossed the area. We crossed the major rivers on ancient, dilapidated ferries that were often on the other side of the river, half a mile away, when we arrived at the crossing point. Messages would then be sent via speaking drums to establish that we wanted to cross and that we had enough diesel for the ferry, as the ferries themselves rarely had any fuel. We coaxed the Land-Rover over hundreds of miles of rutted forest tracks by day, and slept in the villages by night. Philip held confirmation services in the churches, and we visited ill-equipped schools and decaying health centres.

Christmas itself we spent at Yamufaya, a small village inhabited by a most engaging people called the Topokei. The older generation all had ferociously filed teeth and their grandparents were probably cannibals, but they gave us a tremendously warm welcome. The mud-walled, palm-thatched church was filled to bursting for the Christmas service and the rows of bamboo seats creaked ominously under the weight of the congregation. From time to time one of the bamboo poles broke and deposited a row of worshippers on the ground which provided an entertaining diversion. Monkey meat, the greatest delicacy in the forest, appeared for our Christmas lunch, and the most honoured guest was given the head. The little skull sat on a plate with its empty eye sockets reproaching the eater. Luckily Philip was the principal guest so I did not have to cope with that. No turkeys were available but a great feast was provided for our Christmas fare. Yamufaya is in the heart of the forest and has few links with the outside world. When I threw away an empty packet of Daz one day, the local boys fought over it as it was the first fresh reading matter to arrive in the village for some months.

From Yamufaya we returned to Kisangani where we walked into a major currency crisis. No shops were accepting existing banknotes, as the government had announced that all old notes had to be changed in a bank before the end of the year. As we arrived on 29 December, which was a Saturday, this meant spending the next two days struggling unsuccessfully to change money. Some of the banks in the city were burnt down as people realised that there was no new money to be distributed, and rioting spread. After a few days of keeping our heads down and living on rice, Philip eventually managed to find enough new money for the fuel to get us home, so off we set on the long drive back to Boga.

There was still no money available when we returned to Boga, and we heard afterwards that of all the five and ten zaire notes that had been in circulation only ten per cent were replaced by new ones, so the majority of Zaireans woke up on 1 January having lost all their money. In any other country such robbery of its citizens on the part of the government would have been met by widespread protest and civil disobedience. But in Zaire this did not happen; it was almost as though the population was inured to oppression. For a while most places reverted to a barter economy and then gradually normal trade resumed. In Komanda Bridget Lane, who was working with Scripture Union, continued to live with her three Zairean companions in a grass hut and paid her way by getting up early each morning and working with them in the fields before starting her own day's work. At Boga people were able to keep alive on the food they grew and the milk and meat from the cattle. But there was no question of travelling as no fuel could be bought.

Eve Vause, the CMS nurse at Boga, ran monthly child and mother clinics in many of the villages in the area and was concerned about not being able to get out to her clinics. So we decided that we would see if we could get to some of the nearer places by bicycle. The diocesan treasurer produced two rather ancient but serviceable machines, and off we set, with a runner going ahead with the medical supplies to let people know we were coming. The roads in that area are not exactly built for bicycles, the narrow tracks were rocky, muddy and sandy in turns and we had to walk down most of the hills as well as up them because the brakes did not work properly. In some of the stretches of forest we had to lift the machines over fallen tree trunks and carry them through streams. But it was good exercise and provided a great deal of entertainment all round. We managed a trip of about ninety kilometres in four days, visiting the clinics at Zunguluka, Kainama and Bwakadi. Eve saw a large number of mothers and children and I learnt much about the local health problems.

Our host at Bwakadi was the cheerful pastor, Robeni Mukulungani, who became a great friend over the years. On that trip he took me on a visit to the little village of Tondoli which lies on the plains below the escarpment. Two small boys led the way, one of them carrying my bundle on his head, followed by Robeni walking jauntily down with a straw boater on his head and wearing a dog-collar. Tondoli lies on a fertile, open spur above the Semliki river and when we arrived, in the heat of the day, we found that the entire population had gathered outside the church to welcome us. When travelling in that whole area I was delighted to find that I could talk freely with everyone in Swahili. We spent the night at Tondoli and then climbed back up the escarpment in the cool of the day. Life is hard for people in such isolated villages, but they fed us a huge meal that night and the next day produced gifts of a pineapple, two dozen eggs, a large bowl of rice and a hen. A runner was despatched to Boga and there it all was on my doorstep when we got back. I never failed to marvel at the generosity of those who have so little.

A few weeks later I visited Bwakadi again and Pastor Robeni took me into the forest to meet two of the Bambuti (Pygmy) congregations. We visited Makoka the first day, then the following day went to Vukaka which lay deeper in the forest. The Bambuti gave us a warm welcome but had no Swahili so communication was more difficult. After we had worshipped together at Vukaka everyone disappeared into the trees and then re-emerged carrying freshly-cut reed pipes. The adults had long pipes and the children had short ones, so between them they had a complete orchestra. They then danced round in a wide circle, playing intricate harmonies on their pipes. It was magical listening to them. Each time we visited a group we took a gift of salt, the equivalent of gold dust to a Bambuti, and one of the few essentials of life that they need the outside world to provide.

Robeni Mukulungani with community health workers

During the month that I had at Boga I visited as many of the churches in the area as I could, went to the local cattle market, talked with the local chief, visited some of the schools and health centres, taught the students in the Bible school and met with the women. It all helped to build up a picture of the problems faced by the local people. One of the factors that affected life in the area at that time was the insecurity in Uganda. Supplies from outside normally reached north-eastern Zaire through the port of Mombasa, but as trucks had to travel through Kenya and Uganda very few were coming through. This was one reason why there was so little fuel about.

I spent some time in Bunia, hosted by Archdeacon Munige Kabarole and his wife. I realised that life in Bunia was very much harder than life in Boga and never really understood how people in towns managed to survive at all. One day Munige and I went down to Kasenye, the fishing port on the shores of Lake Albert. We travelled on a fish lorry that wound its way down a number of dramatic hairpin bends to reach the lakeshore some four thousand feet below the Bunia hills. The once thriving port was in a state of dilapidation and decay, no ferries were crossing at all, and only a handful of dugout canoes represented the fishing fleet.

Having had a good look at Boga Diocese I then went on to Bukavu Diocese and this time was relieved to be able to fly to Bukavu. Archdeacon Kolini Mbona and Richard Menees (from the Episcopal Church of the USA) met me in the diocesan Land-Rover and told me that Bishop Bezaleri had left just the day before to attend Robert Runcie's consecration as Archbishop of Canterbury. That was quite frustrating news as I could have come down earlier had I known that he was about to leave. However, everyone expected him back in a couple of weeks. In the event he flew on to the States from London and it was six weeks before he finally returned to Bukavu. I could not really complete my report without talking with him, so I spent the time finding out as much as I could about what was going on in Bukavu and starting to write up my report. Richard Menees was extremely kind in offering hospitality all that time, and luckily there was a spare room at the diocesan centre.

Bukavu is beautifully situated beside the shores of Lake Kivu and in Belgian times it was a popular holiday resort. The hills of North Kivu rise up behind the lake and much of the city itself is perched on these slopes. People used to compare Bukavu to the towns of the Italian Lakes. But like everywhere else in Zaire everything was in a chronic state of dilapidation, with buildings falling down and cratered roads where there were once beautifully surfaced boulevards. Despite all the dilapidation the waters of the lake were still a magnificent, sparkling green, and peaceful places could be found were one could walk along the lakeshore. There were few fish in the lake because of the volcanic gases that permeate the water, but the students at the Bible school assured me that mermaids lived in the lake. When I asked about swimming I was told it would be too dangerous as the mermaids would drag me down under the water and suck out my brains. (Believe it or not they were not joking.)

Bukavu is at the centre of what was once a very fertile area, but agricultural productivity fell dramatically following independence. Government-appointed agricultural officers worked in the rural areas, but most of them had no transport and no funds for travelling so they simply sat in empty offices all day. I once met an agricultural officer who told me that he did visit the farmers in his area, so I asked him what he did. He said that if he saw the farmers were not looking after their land well, he arrested them and put them in prison. Putting people in prison was an occupational activity in Zaire as officials invented regulations and arrested innocent citizens for transgressing rules they had never heard of. Money was then demanded for their release which helped the officials whose salaries were rarely paid. Richard's cook was regularly arrested as the local police knew that Richard could be relied on to bail him out.

I finally left Bukavu a few days after Bezaleri had returned and a few days before the inauguration of the Province of Burundi, Rwanda and Zaire and the enthronement of Bezaleri as Archbishop. The Archbishop of Canterbury came to Bukavu for the inauguration, together with Richard Chartres and Terry Waite, so there was quite a gathering. But by that time I had already spent much longer in Bukavu than planned and needed to fly back to Nairobi.

Derek and Pat Wilks welcomed me in Nairobi and Derek's secretary, Yolanda, kindly typed my fifty-page report so that I had it all ready for duplication when I got back to London. While she was doing that Derek took me out to Meto for a night and it was marvellous to meet so many old friends and to see how the VP was developing. The three original instructors, Mrs Ayieko, George Kamau and Jackson Okinda, were still there, working hard, and the trees we had planted three years earlier were flourishing. As word went round that we had arrived, the women started to bring gourdfuls of milk to welcome us. Nambulong arrived with a gift of honey and Tipape appeared as alert as ever and a few inches higher. Ole Seita turned up, on the scrounge as usual, but grinning from ear to ear as he proudly produced Kunoti (the untameable donkey) complete with water tins on his back. Then back I went to London, after six full and memorable months in Zaire.

The Mission Operations Committee of CMS discussed the findings of my Zaire report, together with Dr Peter Green's report on the medical services at Boga, at a series of meetings in London in May. Following those meetings it was agreed that CMS should concentrate for the time being on fresh development initiatives in the Boga area where the church had a well enough established infrastructure of its own to support such work. The Society agreed to try to recruit a doctor, two nurses, an agriculturalist, a water engineer, an administrator and a theologian. I was asked to visit Crowther Hall to meet Tim Rous, an engineer who was very interested in rural development and the use of appropriate technology for the provision of clean water sources. Tim had an ideal background for the work needed as well as the commitment to handle the problems presented by the Zaire situation. So that was a most encouraging start, and it was agreed that Tim should be located to Boga.

In June the Revd Patrice Njojo, who had been elected to become the new Bishop of Boga, visited the CMS offices and it was lovely to meet him. I was then asked to become further involved in the out-working of the recommendations of the report, and spent much of the autumn in the CMS offices. During that time I saw something of a nurse, Pat Nickson, who was also helping out in the regional offices as she recovered after a long period of sick leave. Pat and I had lunch together one day so that Pat could quiz me about the medical scenario at Boga. She was interested professionally, but as she had been working in Asia for some years no one had thought of Pat herself as being available for Zaire. Halfway through the conversation we suddenly stopped talking and looked at each other as the same thought dawned; we had a shared conviction that God was calling Pat to Boga. This overthrew all the plans of the Asia desk, but her own sense of calling grew and it was finally agreed that Pat, once she had fully recovered, would be located to Zaire. This was another hugely encouraging development as Pat had wide experience in primary health care and had already worked in many remote parts of the world.

Based in Nairobi
In 1981 the CMS Kenya office in Nairobi was closed as work was handed over to the Kenyan Church, but it was recognised that CMS

mission partners in Uganda and Zaire still needed a support base in Kenya. So after much discussion it was agreed that I would be posted to Nairobi for two years as Assistant Regional Secretary, with responsibility for relating to the Churches and CMS personnel in Uganda and Zaire and for helping to shape the new developments in Zaire. In February I arrived in Nairobi and throughout the two years made regular visits to Uganda and Zaire as well as hosting a flow of visitors who came through Kenya from those countries.

At the end of February I flew to Zaire, primarily to discuss development proposals for Boga with Bishop Njojo and to find out what his own thoughts were before writing a project proposal to put to outside donors. He convened a meeting of representatives of the local community, including the chief, teachers and pastors, so the plan was widely discussed. The chief was very supportive, and a clear shape for the proposals emerged. When I returned to Nairobi I wrote a project proposal to ICCO, the Dutch church-related development agency, asking for a grant of £100,000 to help to get an integrated community health programme established at Boga. The proposal covered agricultural activities and the establishing of clean water sources, as well as a development of the existing primary health care programme and an upgrading of the little hospital at Boga. ICCO eventually agreed to fund the programme which made it possible to start implementing the various proposals. As the work developed Tim later put in a proposal for a much more ambitious scheme, but that initial grant was vital to get things going.

During 1981 I made four visits to Uganda and will write about the Uganda journeys in a separate chapter. In relation to Zaire, we heard in July that ICCO had agreed funding for the community health programme, and Tim Rous arrived in Nairobi to study Swahili at the language school through August. We also heard that Pat Nickson had been given a clean bill of health and would be arriving the following February, so things were really starting to move. In December I went back to Boga again to see how Tim was getting on, this time travelling with Peter Batchelor, a rural development consultant.

Tim had slotted marvellously into life at Boga, his French was already fluent and his Swahili was rapidly coming on. He took the difficulties of life in Boga in his stride and was quite unperturbed by the fact that all his tools were still sitting at Wilson Airport in Nairobi due to the disappearance of some vital piece of paper. He was full of ideas about what to do, and already planning to start courses in carpentry and vehicle maintenance. He was concerned about the airstrip as the existing one was short, bumpy and wrongly aligned for the prevailing wind. A plane had recently run off the end of the strip into a clump of beer bananas, and pilots were becoming reluctant to fly into Boga. So Tim walked me over a possible new alignment for the airstrip, and when I got back to Nairobi I put in another request to ICCO for the improvement of Boga airstrip. I carried a chainsaw with me on my next visit to Boga to help Tim to clear the new alignment of trees.

At the end of the year we heard the sad news that Bezaleri Ndahura had died in Bukavu on Christmas Day, only eighteen months after becoming Archbishop of the new Francophone Province. The news came as great shock to many people and his sudden death affected the church in both Bukavu and Boga Dioceses. His body was brought back to Boga for burial.

Early the next year Pat Nickson arrived in Nairobi and on 15 February I took her to Wilson Airport and waved her off to Boga. As the little plane disappeared into the sky, there was a lump in my throat as I knew that Pat's arrival in Boga would mark the start of a new era in health care, and thanked God for all the gifts and experience that she was taking with her to that needy situation. But she had only recently overcome severe health problems of her own and I knew that many demands would be placed on her by the expectant community.

Following Archbishop Bezaleri Ndahura's death, the Revd Diropka Bafaluga had been elected to succeed him as Bishop of Bukavu, and his consecration and enthronement were planned for 21 February. The Bishops of the Francophone Province were due to meet the following day to elect a new Archbishop, so there was clearly going to be a significant gathering in Bukavu which I joined. At the meetings I was asked to go to Kinshasa to help Archdeacon Ben Bataaga put in an application to the United Thank Offering (UTO) fund in the States to buy a much needed base for the Anglican Church in Kinshasa. The deadline was drawing near and someone was needed to finalise the application and identify a suitable property, so I made plans to visit Kinshasa two weeks later. Bishop Kolini Mbona extended a warm invitation for me to visit Shaba, so we agreed to meet in Lubumbashi three weeks later.

From Bukavu John Hayward and I travelled with Bishop and Mrs Tibafa by road to Kisangani. John travelled regularly to Zaire to help the church leaders with their finances and later, when I had left Nairobi, he and his wife Kathleen took over the CMS flat and offered a marvellous support base for people working in Zaire. We spent the next five and a half days on an epic crawl, humping down the road in a Land-Rover that was even more ancient than the Boga vehicle. We left at 4 a.m. each day, groping about in the dark to pack the Land-Rover, spent the next sixteen hours climbing in and out of pot-holes, and arrived a couple of hours after dark to stay in little 'chambres' (high quality) beside the road. We would sit on the bed in one of our bare rooms eating the cheese we had brought from Bukavu by the light of a candle and drinking hot tea miraculously produced by Mrs Tibafa. On the final day through the forest the driver managed to get into top gear for a few miles and we arrived in Kisangani just in time for the Sunday morning service, having already been on the road for five hours. We later heard that those who came by lake and air had had an even worse journey. A terrific storm blew up as they were crossing Lake Kivu and the eleven pastors on board were all quite sure that they were going to drown.

We spent a week in Kisangani visiting the various churches and projects in the area, then I booked a flight with Air Zaire to go to Kinshasa. It was the first time I had flown with 'Air Peut-être' and the experience was every bit as bad as I had feared. The flight eventually took off thirty-six hours after the scheduled time and Ben Bataaga spent several hours waiting for me at the airport on the advertised day without being able to gather any flight information from Air Zaire. There was a huge struggle to get on the plane, but I hung onto the coat tails of a portly Roman Catholic Bishop and managed to squeeze onto the plane in his wake just before the doors were shut behind us. Inside the plane a free fight was going on as people fought for seats. It was more like a Saturday night pub brawl than an aeroplane. The plane eventually landed in Kinshasa just before midnight and there was a huge crowd at the airport. There was no sign of Ben and I had no idea where he lived. I was finally rescued by one Madame Tambaki whose husband had failed to get onto the plane, but in the mêlée at Kisangani airport he had told me that his wife would know where to find Ben. She kindly put me up for the night and Ben turned up the next day.

Ben then took me out to one of the affluent suburbs where he had arranged for me to stay with Colonel and Mrs Miller. Colonel Miller was US Military Adviser to the Zaire Government, and a member of Ben's international congregation, and I spent the next two days living a life of luxury, dropping into the swimming pool and enjoying the cool spaciousness of the house which was full of young Americans – quite a culture shock after my normal life in Zaire. But Colonel Miller had some interesting insights to share, both about the Anglican Church and US/Zaire relations. The US was giving a huge amount of aid to Zaire at that time in the misguided belief that Zaire offered the western world a base in Africa from which to fight the forces of Communism. Ben had many members of the diplomatic community in his congregation and I moved on from the Millers to stay with Robert and Phyllis Oakley (the US Ambassador and his wife) in their spacious residence beside the river. The surroundings were even more luxurious and they were very kind and gracious. I came down to earth again at the end of the week and spent my final nights with Ben and his family in a very noisy, crowded cité area some fifteen kilometres from the city centre.

Having spent a week in Kinshasa I could understand more clearly the need of the Anglicans to have a proper base in the city, and spent some time exploring the property market so that a realistic figure could be put in the UTO funding application. Within the city centre, buildings were almost all well-appointed and spacious or cramped and dilapidated. There was very little in between these two extremes. So we looked at one or two properties in the new housing developments that were being built in the suburbs and saw some possible houses. Ben was reluctant to go for anything so far out of town, so in the end I put in an application for a grant of $60,000 (which I gathered would be the top limit) and left Ben to sort it out from there with Bishop Njojo.

The Air Zaire flight to Lubumbashi was surprisingly straightforward, greatly to my relief. Colonel Miller kindly took me to the airport for 4 a.m. and we took off at midday without having to do any fighting. I congratulated myself on getting to Lubumbashi the day that I had agreed with Bishop Kolini when we were in Bukavu, only to discover that Kolini himself had still not managed to get back. He had been stuck for two weeks in Goma and still no flight was expected. He finally appeared three days later which gave me time to finish the UTO application and to recover from the travelling of the previous month. Kolini Mbona had been made Assistant Bishop within the Diocese of Bukavu and sent to Lubumbashi in order to develop the work of the Anglican Church in Shaba. The expectation was that Shaba would become a diocese the following year despite an almost total lack of resources. Kolini and Freda and the family had only arrived in Lubumbashi six months earlier, so it was early days for them, and Kolini was still working out how to approach the difficult job he had been given.

Lubumbashi is a sprawling city that was built on the profits of the copper mines. As in Kinshasa there are two classes of housing: the smart houses that used to belong to the Belgians and the huge, overcrowded areas of slums where the Zairean population still live. Shaba is rich in mineral and agricultural resources and would be able to function much more easily without having to be linked to Kinshasa. Having travelled around Shaba for three weeks I could see why the independence movement was still alive in that part of Zaire. Anglicanism came over the border from Zambia, and there had been a small English-speaking congregation in Lubumbashi since 1950. In more recent years Anglican churches sprang into existence along the railway line, largely through the activity of one Mulumba Kalongi, who had no theological training but who encouraged dissident groups from other churches to adopt an Anglican label. Bishop Kolini was faced with the formidable task of trying to gather these fifty-six congregations together into something resembling an organised church, and had the help of only one other priest.

I spent three weeks travelling round Shaba with Kolini and we visited all the main centres of worship. Everywhere we were given a warm welcome and we attended some very lively, though not always very orthodox, worship. Kolini had no transport of his own so we were dependent on overcrowded buses on the roads and on an antique train when we ventured up the railway line to Kananga. The Belgians had built this line to link the towns of the copper belt with the gold and diamond-mining centres of Kasai. Kolini had heard of several Anglican churches in and around Kaniama, 450 miles up the line, and wanted to visit them. Rivers traditionally provided the main transport routes in Zaire so Kolini had never travelled by train before and we set off woefully ill prepared.

The train left six hours late and as we got into it we found that everything removable had been looted from the carriages including the upholstery that covered the seats. There was no glass left in any of the windows, all the light fittings had been torn out, there was no water anywhere on the train, and no food was available. We were due to spend forty hours on the train and we had no food or water with us. We perched uncomfortably on the bare springs, and later in the day cold air rushed in through the open windows and neither of us had any warm clothing. At one stage rain poured in through the windows and we had to put an umbrella up inside the carriage. Despite being billed as the 'rapide' we travelled very slowly, with frequent stops in the middle of nowhere. The slow train apparently took a week to reach Kaniama. We finally reached there at 4 a.m. on the third day and fell out of the train into a muddy bog that everyone assured us was Kaniama station. It was pitch dark and pouring with rain, so it was some time before our wet and tired reception committee managed to find us. We were then very warmly welcomed by the Anglican churches in the area where we stayed for three days.

A few days after getting back to Lubumbashi we set off again for Kolwezi, taking all day to get there as our bus managed to slip off the narrow tarmac road into a ditch. We drove through miles of an extraordinary landscape of open-cast copper and cobalt mines to reach the house of one of the mine-workers who hosted us, and were mobbed by a crowd of singing, chanting and ululating people as we entered the huge housing area for the mine-workers. On Sunday morning we attended a lively service where choirs sang with tremendous vitality and joy, drums beating, shakers shaking, and everyone hand-clapping and swaying to the rhythm.

When we got back to Lubumbashi we heard the news of Lord Carrington's resignation after the invasion of the Falklands by Argentina, and we also heard that the Zaire/Zambia border was open. That was a great relief as it had been closed in recent weeks and I was hoping to fly back to Nairobi from Lusaka. The next day Kolini kindly escorted me to the Zambian border and handed me over to Joseph Mabula, the bishop of Northern Zambia, who lived close to the border. Bishop and Mrs Mabula gave me a wonderfully warm welcome for the night and after a further night in Lusaka I flew to Nairobi. I arrived back tired after seven weeks of worthwhile but constantly demanding and uncertain travel.

Later in the year I went back to Boga for a month to see how the community health work was developing. Pat was a gifted enabler and the medical team blossomed under her encouragement and teaching. Eve had run mother and child clinics in the area for some years, but there had been no qualified leadership in the dispensary at Boga and the poor quality of medical care offered there had resulted in a loss of credibility amongst the local people. Now word was spreading that the situation had changed and the number of in-patients admitted monthly had already risen from three to seventy, which placed an unaccustomed load on all the resources of the centre.

The staff responded well to this challenge and were finding fresh fulfilment in caring for the patients after years of relative inactivity. The senior midwife, Evalina, had already learnt to do symphysiotomies, a life-saving operation in that part of the world, and Susanna, a traditional birth-attendant, handled night-time deliveries on her own that would have frightened many a fully trained nurse in Britain. Most of the emergencies were obstetric ones and a couple of times I went out with Pat on a night call. We would pick our way across the grass by torchlight, hoping to spot any wandering snakes, and then Pat would work by the light of a single paraffin lamp, perched on the rawhide straps of the patient's bed. Tim came to the rescue more than once by fashioning essential instruments in his workshop. Pat said that Tim's instruments, made to order, were better than the real thing.

A newly-shaped system of primary health care was slowly coming into being in the outlying areas around Boga through the establishment of village health committees who chose one or two 'animateurs' or village health-workers from their own community, and ten such people had already had their first training session. Pat was longing to get down to the isolated villages on the plains, but was not strong enough to walk back up the escarpment because of her ill health. She spoke nostalgically of the days when she was nursing in Afghanistan and rode over the mountains on horseback and lamented the fact that there were no pack animals in Zaire. A few weeks later two South African university students appeared in Boga on horseback. They had planned to ride from Sudan to Cape Town, but had run out of time and needed to leave the horses behind and fly home. They arrived saying 'Do you know anywhere we could leave our horses?' Pat immediately enlisted both horses as members of the community health team, and all the members of the team had lessons in horse-riding. The horses really opened up the accessibility of the villages on the plains and they became quite a tourist attraction as most of the local people had never seen a horse before.

Tim had achieved a remarkable amount despite innumerable practical difficulties. Amongst many other initiatives he had built a small dam across the stream above Boga, and fed the water from the stream down the hill to the dispensary. He organised a clean water supply for the local chief's house, together with a small hand-pump, so he was very popular with the chief. He was also starting to work with the village health committees and helping them to establish clean water sources in their villages, a crucial part of the health programme. As an equally crucial contribution to the transport possibilities he had organised the clearing of the new airstrip.

In January 1983 Bishop Dirokpa invited Pat and myself to come to Bukavu, to discuss the health needs in the diocese and to attend the first diocesan synod. In particular he wanted us to visit Kisehe, on the island of Idjwi in Lake Kivu. Idjwi is the largest island in the lake, over fifty miles long, and there were virtually no health facilities for the 70,000 people who lived there. There was not even a maternity centre and obstetric emergencies had to be taken to the nearest clinic on the mainland, a five-hour journey by canoe. The Anglican Church had opened two dispensaries in an effort to make some response, but both had to be closed because of lack of qualified staff. After our visit Pat advised the diocese to start a community health programme and Boga Diocese offered to help with the training of village health workers.

Idjwi is the most beautiful place and we were given a great welcome there. There are no roads on the island but most of the villages are on the lakeshore so a cheerful team of chanting paddlers ferried us (rather precariously) up and down the coast in a dug-out canoe. We spent a couple of days there, staying with our gracious hosts, Emil and Deodata, who lived in a house beautifully situated by the lakeshore. We then retraced our steps to the little port at Kisehe to catch the weekly ferry back to Bukavu. We had been warned that getting onto the ferry might not be easy, and as soon as the boat arrived everyone got so excited that the crew could not lower the gangway. We suddenly realised the boat was about to leave and that we needed to climb the vertical hull of the boat if we wanted to get away that week. The deck rail was some ten feet above our heads so I jumped for an old tyre that was swinging from the deck rail and was seized from above by half a dozen pairs of hands and unceremoniously heaved over the rail and dropped onto the deck. I picked myself up in time to see Pat following and landing in a pile of pineapples with her skirt over her head. Luckily no one on the quayside had a camera. It was quite rough on the three-hour crossing and everyone kept rushing from one side of the boat to the other, which did nothing to help the stability of the vessel.

When the Bukavu meetings were over Pat and I flew to Boga, a spectacular flight over Lake Kivu, the Virunga volcanoes, the western shore of Lake Edward, the foothills of the Ruwenzori (the glaciers were in cloud) and the Semliki Plains. We finally approached the western wall of the Rift Valley and there was Boga, perched on the edge of the escarpment. As we circled in to land we could see the new airstrip below us, miraculously completed by Tim Rous and his team in only a few months. It was a wonderful sight, and so good to know that pilots could land safely in any wind conditions and take off with a full load. The medical team were there to greet us, complete with the horses, so we disappeared into the long grass to change into jeans and then rode into Boga, a marvellous way to arrive.

We attended the official opening of the first village health post at the small village of Malaya where an official flag was raised amidst much drumming, singing and feasting. When I finally left to return to Nairobi, Pat and I rode back to the airstrip, but we were a little late and heard the plane coming as we were still on our way. We galloped up the length of the airstrip just ahead of the plane, trying to get the horses into the long grass at the top of the hill before the plane landed. The pilot expressed his views on such antics when he arrived, and I scrambled contritely onto the plane clutching a live chicken that someone had just given me. I then remembered I was still wearing a riding hat and just managed to open the window and throw it out onto the grass before we took off.

CHAPTER 8

Visits to Uganda

I VISITED UGANDA REGULARLY DURING THE TIME I was based in Nairobi, fitting in Uganda trips between the visits to Zaire that have been described in Chapter 7. It was a very difficult time for everyone in Uganda, and the hope was that I would be able to keep in touch with Ugandan Church leaders and CMS personnel through regular visits, and provide a support base for visitors from Uganda in Nairobi. My neighbour Doris Rowney, who had worked in Uganda for many years, was always ready to supply extra beds when my own flat was full, as well as offering hospitality to her own friends from Uganda. Nairobi was full of Ugandan refugees and a constant stream of them came to the door asking for help. Doris was invaluable in sorting out the reality behind the stories they told, and eventually the Kenyan Church opened an office for refugees so we were able to direct them there, which was a huge help.

It was two years since Idi Amin had been overthrown, but Uganda was still a place of violence and instability. Dr Milton Obote had become President (for the second time) in December 1980, and most of the army and police came from the northern part of the country, his own home area. The influential Baganda and others from western Uganda had little confidence in this continuing dominance by northerners, and a guerrilla movement had started under the leadership of Yoweri Museveni. Obote's government resorted to terror tactics, and the arbitrary killings and imprisonment that had started under Idi Amin continued unabated. Many observers assessed that there was even more violence in Uganda during the second Obote regime than during the leadership of Idi Amin.

Travelling in Uganda was easier than in Zaire, mainly because Uganda was a much smaller country and one could reach most places by road in a saloon car. However, little maintenance had been done on the roads for years and there were long patches of broken-up tarmac that made driving very slow. The main road into Kampala from Kenya was full of potholes, as was the main road out of Kampala to the west. Around Masaka there were still craters in the road from the shelling that took place during the Tanzanian invasion. The worst roads in the whole country were in Kampala itself where vehicles took tortuous routes, circling round the jagged edges of deep potholes. A popular joke in Kampala was that you could tell when drivers were drunk because they drove in straight lines. There were chronic fuel shortages, so fuel prices were extortionate and queues outside petrol stations were usually several blocks long, with drivers often having to spend the night sleeping in their cars. But the greatest hazard of driving in Uganda came from the ubiquitous roadblocks that were manned by drunk, trigger-happy soldiers. Ugandans were systematically robbed at these roadblocks, and those who offered any resistance, or who simply could not pay enough, were often shot. Stories of people who had been killed or wounded at roadblocks were rife.

Soldiers and armed police made systematic raids on villages in many areas, and the infamous Luwero Triangle to the west of Kampala was under assault at that time. Thousands of people were killed and others simply fled from such areas, which then became virtually depopulated. In Kampala robbery with violence was rife and every night one could hear the noise of gunfire. When the sound came close people gathered together and prayed, and each night families committed their lives into God's hands and prayed for protection before going to sleep. The first prayer in the morning was always one of thankfulness to God for still being alive. I used to stay in Kampala with Cynthia Mackay and Penny Carlisle and marvelled at the way they managed to keep serene and cheerful in an extraordinarily difficult, and at times dangerous, situation. They and most of their neighbours had been attacked with physical violence more than once, and no one knew what each night would bring. Added to this, there was no water on Namirembe Hill. Every drop had to be fetched from a tap about half a mile away, so that meant taking the car with a load of plastic water containers. But often there was no fuel, so then a night had to be spent queueing for petrol before the water supply could be replenished.

During those years of violence in Uganda CMS mission partners continued to stay and work all over the country. A basic principle of the Society is that danger alone is not a reason for withdrawing personnel, and at times of difficulty it is important to stay in order to share the danger and offer support. All over Uganda I found a real appreciation of the fact that CMS had stayed through those years when many other organisations had withdrawn their people. A relationship of deep trust seemed to have been forged and deepened between CMS and Ugandan Christians. Everywhere I went I was incredibly warmly welcomed, and was embarrassed by the generosity of the hospitality at a time when food was so short for everyone. In Kenya the idea of 'moratorium' was still being discussed, so one did sometimes feel that expatriate personnel were 'needed but not wanted'. There was no vestige of this dynamic in Uganda – I was quite struck by the difference. But of course the whole history of the two countries had been different, and Uganda had not shared the extensive Kenyan experience of settler-farmers on their land.

The Ugandan economy had long collapsed, following the expulsion of the Asian community, and many ordinary goods were either impossible or very difficult to find. There was no soap or salt in the country, even at black market prices, and Kenya prohibited the export of many goods, including food, across her boarders. I had hoped to be able to open some kind of supply line to Uganda from Nairobi, but it was not possible to take spare parts for vehicles (badly needed by everyone) across the border unless they had been made in Kenya and one had an export licence. The only things that were being manufactured in Kenya at the time were tyres and batteries. The sugar shortage was ironic as miles of abandoned sugar-cane plantations lined the roads into Kampala.

The Church of Uganda has truly sprung from the blood of martyrs, from the boy martyrs of Namugongo and the murdered Bishop Hannington to the more recent death of Archbishop Janani Luwum, and every time I visited Uganda I was humbled and inspired by the depth of faith of so many Ugandan Christians. At Namirembe I was always welcomed with great warmth by Bishop Misaeri and Geraldine Kauma, and marvelled at the loving and peaceful way in which they ministered to their people in such a stressful and difficult situation. I was continually challenged, too, by the way that ordinary Christians so open-handedly shared their meagre resources with one another. Yet the Ugandan story was not only of deepened spirituality. When prices have sky-rocketed so that a man's monthly earnings will only buy food that will feed his family for two days, what is he to do? The temptations to resort to dishonest means were great and church leaders spoke of the need for moral rehabilitation.

Chris Carey, then the CMS Regional Secretary for Kenya, Uganda and Zaire, came out from London from time to time and in May 1981 we travelled together to Karamoja. There had been a serious drought in this north-eastern part of the country the previous year, so CMS and Christian Aid co-operated in the resuscitation of government medical centres in the area, working alongside Ugandan colleagues. CMS found personnel for three medical teams and Christian Aid provided the financial support needed. We found the teams were all doing well and by then food was coming into the area. The wild plains of Karamoja are home to nomadic herdsmen and cattle-raiding is a time-honoured occupation in that part of the world. The raiders were traditionally armed with spears, but these days they have kalashnikovs and anti-tank weapons, so part of the work of the medical teams was to patch up the survivors of the cattle battles.

In Namirembe we met Christina de Wind, a Dutch surgeon who was working as a CMS volunteer at Mengo Hospital. Christina was the only surgeon at Mengo at the time and she regularly had to deal with bullet wounds – in a hospital where there was no X-ray machine. Christina was undeterred by having to search for bullets without being able to see where they were, but there was no water at the hospital so she could only operate when the patient's relatives provided water. Security men often came into the hospital to take off any patients who they thought had been involved in a shooting incident, so on the notes at the foot of the patients' beds Christina was careful never to make mention of bullet wounds. Christina thrived in such situations and later went on to work in a number of different war zones around the world.

I arrived back in Kampala just in time to attend a Provincial Assembly at Mukono, the first meeting the Church of Uganda had been able to have for some years. Bishops had gathered from all over the country and Lord Coggan led a retreat in which he challenged the bishops in a very forthright way about the nature of their episcopal ministry. 'Bishops are not chosen to be financiers, they are not chosen to be big chiefs, they are not chosen to be world travellers.' As he said this he looked at the bishops and everyone knew that half of them had spent the previous year chasing funds in the States. No one but a retired Archbishop of Canterbury could have got away with such schoolmasterly scolding, but the message was well heard. He ended by talking inspirationally of the hard years still ahead: 'Be strong in the grace that is yours in Christ. God reigns, God loves, God cares. When you have grasped that you will be strong to recreate Uganda.'

By the end of 1981 a few small signs of hope were appearing in Uganda. Some of the potholes were being filled in with asphalt and essential goods such as sugar, salt, and soap were back in the shops, albeit at inflated prices. But schools and colleges were still in difficulty as many professional Ugandans had left the country, including a third of the graduate teachers. People were still living in fear and I heard many stories from relatives of those who had been imprisoned or shot or simply disappeared.

The next time that I visited Uganda was in 1992 when Beverley Jones (from Christian Aid) and I found ourselves landing unexpectedly at Entebbe after a visit to Southern Sudan. I could not believe my eyes as we drove into Kampala along smooth tarmac roads and passed busy markets overflowing with fresh fruit and vegetables. Kampala had changed completely since 1982, and it was wonderful to see at least one African country that had dramatically changed for the better during those years.

CHAPTER 9

Theological Education by Extension

B Y EARLY 1983 I HAD COMPLETED TWO YEARS in Nairobi, and the particular job that I had been invited to do in relation to Zaire was no longer needed as the development work in Boga was well-established. So John and Kathleen Hayward, who already knew Zaire well, took over the Nairobi office and were a marvellous support to us all. I had six months' leave in UK, including some more French study in Belgium, and in October went to Boga where Bishop Njojo had invited me to initiate a basic-level programme of Theological Education by Extension (TEE).

All the rapidly growing churches in Africa were struggling at that time with the crucial question of how to train leaders for their new and expanding congregations. Residential theological colleges could only serve limited numbers and were very costly to run, so some churches had started programmes of TEE to complement the work of the residential centres. In TEE programmes the students studied at home, working through prepared material each day, and then met once a week with other students nearby to discuss the material, together with the help of a trained group leader. The members of the group were expected to take practical action together as they related what they were learning to the life of their own community. This method of teaching made it possible to involve large numbers of students at a relatively low cost, and there was no danger of the theology they learnt being divorced from the reality of their everyday lives.

The logistical problems of running a TEE programme in Zaire were a little daunting as I knew it would not be easy to get hold of the books, to get the books to students, to bring group leaders together for training, or to keep in touch with the groups once they were up and running. In the event we were able to get materials translated into Zaire-Swahili from the Protestant Press in Bukavu, and every now and then MAF (Missionary Aviation Fellowship) would fly a load in to Boga. SPCK provided much of the funding to buy the books which was a huge help, and SECA (the Africa Inland Church in Zaire) held a three-day course in training TEE group leaders that enabled Buleta Katara and myself to see what needed to be done.

Buleta was the principal of the Bible school at Boga and he became very interested in TEE after the SECA course and asked to be involved in the ongoing work. So that was an encouraging start, as it was good to have a Zairean colleague to work with. In January 1984 we held our own training course for group leaders to which we invited six pastors who had already expressed interest. Buleta and I together ran the course, which everyone seemed to enjoy, and afterwards the pastors went back to their villages to get their groups going. After a few weeks Buleta and I started to visit the groups to see how they were getting on. In some places we found the students were still meekly waiting for their leader to give them all the answers, so at the next training session we spent more time trying to help the leaders to understand that they were not expected to preach or even to teach (the book was there to give the basic teaching input), but to enable the members of the group to share their ideas with one another. We tried to stop the leaders from answering all the questions and encouraged them to help the group members to participate fully in the discussions. It was wonderful to see how a group came to life when everyone realised that they had their own unique experience of God that they could share with the rest of the group.

By mid 1984 some 270 pastors, catechists and church teachers were involved in the programme and we had already reached our limit for being able to provide books and for keeping in touch with the scattered groups. Travel was never easy, but we were eventually able to find a motor cycle for Buleta, who could then travel more freely in the Boga area. For going further afield we sometimes joined medical safaris and did TEE business alongside the community health team.

Francis visited Boga before Christmas and Tim orchestrated an expedition through the forest from Zunguluka to Mafifi. The idea was to explore a possible route for a short cut that would link Boga with the main road from Bunia to Beni and shorten the distance to Beni by 170 miles. So Francis and I went with him, escorted by Pastor Robeni Mukulungani who had moved from Bwakadi to Zunguluka. It was a round trip of fifty miles which Tim did in two days, but Francis and I took a more leisurely three days, sleeping in the forest village of Makanga on the way back. We went deep into the forest, passing under the giant trees, saw fresh elephant tracks and met scattered groups of pygmies. We had some interesting river crossings, navigating rotten log bridges and wading through fast-flowing rivers. Francis was amused to see Pastor Robeni taking his dog-collar off to wash it in one of the

Bishop Patrice Njojo by the Semliki River

rivers. As we sat under the stars around a log fire in the heart of the forest at Makanga Francis looked relaxed. His bank could not reach him – there was no telex in the Ituri Forest.

In March Bishop Njojo invited me to travel with him on his annual confirmation safari to the north of the diocese, the areas around Mahagi and Aru. Aru is just across the border from Arua in northern Uganda whence many Ugandans had fled into Zaire to escape the violence in the West Nile area of Uganda. The UNHCR had settled thousands of these refugees into camps to the west and north of Aru, and there were many members of the Church of Uganda amongst them. This greatly increased the number of Anglicans in the north of Boga diocese and Bishop Njojo responded by sending pastors from Boga to minister in the camps and by bringing some of the Ugandan lay leaders in the camps down to Boga for training. We went to some of the camps and had a wonderfully warm reception from the Ugandan Christians. Each church had a superb orchestra of home-made stringed instruments, and we heard some marvellously rhythmic singing and playing. Most of the Ugandans were able to go home a few years later as security in Uganda improved, but their faith was such that they left behind them a renewed Zairean church.

Towards the end of July I flew to Britain to recover from a bout of typhoid and was then interviewed for the post of CMS Regional

Secretary for West Africa, Sudan and Zaire, and offered the job. This was a change from what had originally been planned, as I had been in Zaire for less than a year. But Bishop Njojo was very gracious about releasing me, and I was confident that Buleta would be able to take over the TEE work and continue to develop the programme. I was excited at the thought of the new work, as the shape of the Region had been changed at that time and Zaire had been placed with West Africa and Sudan. I had only visited Sudan once, very briefly, and had never set foot in West Africa, but at least I knew Zaire well.

I returned to Boga in November for six weeks to hand over the TEE work to Buleta. We ran two seminars during that time, arranged by Buleta, and I was delighted to find that he had been visiting many of the groups while I had been away.

The previous year Judy Somerville had arrived in Boga to teach at the Bible School and to handle Bishop Njojo's international correspondence. Tim and Judy soon became engaged, to everyone's delight, and they were married in England. They arrived back in Boga while I was there to find Tim's carpentry students had made them a magnificent bed. Their first child was born in Boga, which was a real vote of confidence in the newly upgraded medical services.

I was sad to leave many friends in Boga, but cheered to know that there was no need to say 'goodbye', only 'au revoir' as I would be back.

CHAPTER 10

Life in London

MOVING FROM BOGA TO LONDON was quite a shock to the system. It was a move from a remote village on the edge of the Rift Valley to the heart of a busy city. In Boga the air was clean, the views were magnificent, and the only sounds to break the silence were the voices of people, animals and birds. Admittedly we had no running water or electricity and communications with the outside world were slow and uncertain, but the quality of the environment was superb. By contrast London seemed polluted and crowded and the cost of living was astronomical by Boga standards.

For the first three years I lived in a treeless road in North London and then bought a flat of my own in Kew, just across the road from the Royal Botanical Gardens. My spirit revived once more in the abundance of grass and trees in the area. I joined St Luke's Church and discovered that Tim Beaumont, the vicar, was an old boy of Gordonstoun and father of Hubert, who had been a great ally of mine as he was the Guardian (head boy) the first year that the girls arrived. Tim later persuaded me to embark on a Reader's course in Southwark Diocese, and I had a regular preaching ministry after being licensed in 1991.

I started work in the CMS regional office in February 1985. For the next ten years I was under constant pressure, juggling the many different responsibilities of the job. I constantly had to switch my mind from one country to another, but in order to make life simpler for readers of this book I have presented the account of this decade by countries rather than chronologically. There was so much to do that the time available for friends and family was constantly squeezed out, but whenever I did manage to have a break I regularly headed for the hills of Britain where kind friends offered hospitality. Despite the constant demands of the job I enjoyed the work enormously and found it very fulfilling. It was a great privilege to be able to travel everywhere as a guest of the local church and I was always given a warmly generous welcome. During that decade I spent a total of nearly two years in Africa.

All the countries in the region were marked by varying degrees of political instability, and responding to coups d'état became something of a routine. During the next few years crises in Sudan and Zaire resulted in an expulsion or major exodus of CMS mission partners, and, later on, Sudanese affairs alone almost swamped the work of the regional desk. It was from this experience particularly, as I moved amongst the suffering yet vibrant churches of southern Sudan, that the title for this book emerged.

Life at the office was so busy that I felt a great need of space for reflection and prayer, and I tried to spend one day each month in the convent at Ham Common and to go on a week's retreat each year. I made a first visit to St Beuno's in North Wales in May 1990 and the following year CMS kindly gave me a three-month sabbatical break, which I spent a St Beuno's, taking part in their course on Apostolic Spirituality. The course incorporated the thirty days of prayer of the Spiritual Exercises so it was a powerful experience, and enriching to undertake it with others who had come from many different parts of the world. As I settled in to the room that would be my home for the next three months, I realised that I had rarely slept in the same bed for more than five consecutive nights in the last seven years. The time there provided a much needed opportunity to be still.

Kenya was not in my area of responsibility, but I regularly passed through Nairobi en route to eastern Zaire and southern Sudan, and in August 1989 I managed to have a weekend at Meto, the first time I had been there for nearly ten years. It was heart-warming when the first Maasai that we saw on the Meto road broke into a huge grin and shouted 'Diyana!' Many old friends were still there, and Sarah, one of the first women to be baptised in Meto, took me back to her village, plied me with Maasai milk and chatted about the new congregations that were gathering in the villages further into the hills. Tipape, a diminutive schoolboy when I last saw him, strode into the village having walked twenty miles from Namanga, and we had a great reunion. The village polytechnic was still going strong and I was delighted to meet several of the old girls, all married and with large families.

On Monday, 23 July 1990 a phone call came from The Dingle to say that my mother had been taken to the Radcliffe Hospital in Oxford for emergency surgery. The whole family was gathered by Thursday, and she died during the night. It was a very sad time, yet we were thankful that she had had an active and independent life at The Dingle right up until the time that she went into hospital, and that she had been spared any protracted time of pain and disability. She was 87 years old. Her funeral was held at St Peter's Church, Upper Slaughter on 1 August,

Francis's birthday, and it was a great gathering, the little church filled to bursting with all those who had known her gracious, loving and gentle presence. In Witts tradition the bells rang out unmuffled as she was buried beside my father.

Sometimes I was able to fit in a visit to friends in Central Africa after leaving Southern Zaire, and in August 1991 I came home from Lubumbashi via Malawi and had ten days' holiday with Rosaleen Bryson and Eric Jager. Eric was tied up with his work at Zomba University but Rosaleen and I had a marvellous four days on Mount Mulanje, an extensive mountain massif with numerous rocky peaks rising from a highland plateau. Mountain huts have been built at convenient places on the plateau and we walked from hut to hut through cool pine forests, across icy mountain streams, over open moorland and up rocky outcrops commanding magnificent views. Thick cloud, rain and a gale thwarted our attempt to climb the highest point, Sapitwa, and we had an interesting night at its foot when the precarious little shelter half collapsed in the wind. I slept out that night and revelled in lying watching the stars, feeling the wind on my face, and finally watching the sun rise over the peaks. It was the kind of mountain experience that I had not had for many years and it brought back a host of rich memories.

During 1991 Francis took early retirement from his bank and was asked to do a temporary, part-time job at Lambeth Palace as advisor to the Archbishop of Canterbury on Middle East Affairs, the main purpose of the job being to continue the hunt for Terry Waite. Terry was freed later that year and Francis was involved in the events of Terry's release and the immediate aftermath. News of the release came through when I was at St Beuno's and I caught a fleeting glimpse of Francis on the television news, arriving with the welcoming party. Francis then went to ground for several weeks, in a very cloak and dagger way, and eventually reappeared at The Dingle on Christmas Eve.

In the autumn of 1992 I became the 'focal person' for the Africa Forum of the Churches' Commission on Mission. This forum was a gathering point for Africa specialists from the Churches in Britain and Ireland and provided an important and stimulating meeting ground. I was very interested in it all, but setting up the forum involved a great deal of work and I was already overstretched with my CMS responsibilities. After two years I was able to hand it on to a successor, but I enjoyed the ecumenical working together that flowed from the forum.

In July 1994 the Archbishop of Canterbury held his regular garden party for those working for the wider Anglican Communion around the

world, and that year he invited me to preach at the service following the
tea. It was somewhat daunting to preach in the chapel at Lambeth
Palace, with all its historic connections, but I was helped by having
plenty of friends in the congregation, including Francis who by then was
working for the St Andrew's Trust. In October I found myself in the
chapel once more, this time to receive an award of the Cross of St
Augustine from the Archbishop. I was allowed to invite ten visitors and
the greatest triumph of the day was getting my godmother Aunt Edie
to the service. Cousin Hannah spied out the territory and found a route
that made it possible to get Edie to the chapel in a wheelchair. She was
thrilled to bits, dear Edie, especially when the Archbishop went out of
his way to talk with her after the service.

During the ten years I picked up a number of tropical diseases,
including cerebral malaria and typhoid, but on the whole was blessed
with the health and strength to maintain a physically demanding
programme of travel. By the end of the ten years I was well, but
chronically tired, and fully intended to retire at sixty, i.e. in 1996. Events
in fact turned out rather differently, as will be revealed later.

CHAPTER 11

West Africa

THE PROVINCE OF WEST AFRICA comprises the Anglican Churches in Cameroon, Gambia, Guinea, Ghana, Liberia, Senegal and Sierra Leone. These countries are from both Francophone and Anglophone Africa, so there is no common language across the Province. They emerged from three different experiences of colonial influence (American, British and French) and the churches were founded by three different mission agencies, two from Britain and one from the USA, so different patterns of churchmanship have been inherited across the Province. The countries are not contiguous, communication between and within them is slow and unreliable, and in 1985 the Archbishop lived in Liberia, the Provincial Secretary in Ghana and the Provincial Treasurer in Sierra Leone. In some ways it was surprising that the Province was able to hold together at all.

A Partners in Mission meeting in Accra in 1987 provided my first opportunity to attend a Provincial gathering. All the churches seemed to be struggling with inadequate financial resources and many reported a drift of young people away from Anglicanism to the rapidly growing Pentecostal churches in the region. One of the diocesan speakers presenting a report on health work described the need for a clinic in a certain area because of 'the many deaths through child-birth, snake bites and other minor ailments.' Our minds spun at the thought of what major ailment might be. There was little discussion of the central issues faced by the churches but the time was immensely valuable for the chance it gave to talk with delegates from across the Province. Archbishop George Browne from Liberia chaired the meetings and handled the mix of languages with sensitivity but without losing too much time. It was the last time I saw him before Liberia descended into the anarchy of civil war.

The first CMS missionaries to be sent overseas were three German Lutherans who arrived in Freetown in 1805 to start work among the growing population of freed slaves. **Sierra Leone** had been designated by the British Government to be a haven for freed slaves from many parts of the world following the abolition of the slave trade. The west coast of Africa soon became known as the 'the white man's grave' and the majority of the early missionaries in Sierra Leone died of disease within their first year. However, churches were slowly established, particularly amongst the new population of returned slaves living on the Freetown Peninsula. It thus seemed appropriate that my first visit to West Africa should be to Sierra Leone, and in August 1985 I flew to Freetown. On arrival at Lungi Airport I climbed off the plane into a bath of air that was hot and humid even in the relative cool of the morning. Freetown is only a few miles from Lungi across a wide estuary, but all the ferries had broken down and we had to make a seventy-mile drive on muddy, pot-holed roads to get there. We later heard stories of people who had seen visitors off from Lungi on flights to London. The visitors had arrived at Heathrow before they themselves had managed to get back to Freetown.

The heat and humidity of West Africa reminded me very much of the forest areas of Zaire, and the sprawling growth of banana plantations, oil palms, and forest vegetation seemed very familiar. There were other similarities such as fuel shortages, rising prices, dilapidated buildings, and rusty machinery that had broken down for lack of spare parts and maintenance. In Freetown the city was regularly plunged into darkness as the electricity supply failed, and water was often cut off. Telephone and postal services were spectacularly inefficient, but did sometimes work, so people were constantly frustrated when these services broke down. In Zaire such services had long since ceased to function, so people had found other ways of coping.

The majority of Christians in Sierra Leone are Creoles (descendants of returned slaves) living on the Freetown Peninsula. I spent the first few days in Freetown Diocese visiting some of the fifty-two churches in this area, the medical work at Port Loko, and Fourah Bay College, the oldest university in West Africa, that sits high above the town and commands superb views of the great sweep of Freetown Bay. Freetown is full of narrow, congested streets lined by old, wooden, balconied buildings. The town is squeezed between the mountains and the sea so the traffic moves slowly, vehicles and pedestrians competing for space. The church bookshop in the centre of town has a sign celebrating the centenary of CMS in 1899, an amazing reminder that CMS had already been working in Sierra Leone for nearly a hundred years at a time when Nairobi was still an uninhabited swamp.

At the main service in the cathedral on Sunday morning all the women wore smart dresses and even smarter hats and the men turned up in black serge suits and bowlers. The cathedral had stained glass windows, ornate wooden pews and an organ, and the worship was very formal, following the 1662 prayer book. I was assured that this was all a genuine expression of Creole culture, and it became clear that Christianity was strongly identified with the Creole community. For this reason few of the indigenous people of Sierra Leone, living in 'the hinterland', had responded to the gospel.

The Anglican Church made a brave move to change this by establishing the missionary diocese of Bo, an inland area where there were only five churches, and CMS had put considerable resources into supporting the new diocese and its first bishop, Michael Keili. I travelled to Bo and stayed with the bishop and his wife Agnes, who were both Mende-speaking, and they had a real vision for bringing the gospel to their own people. CMS mission partners working in the area were helping with teaching ministries and rural development. In a country that had once exported rice to Britain, people were queuing for expensive imported rice.

When Bishop Michael visited Freetown he used to stay with his sister-in-law who was a Muslim. She had a small mosque in one corner of the garden where she said her prayers, and she was quite happy for Michael to have a chapel in another part of the compound. Christian/Muslim marriages seemed to be quite relaxed in Sierra Leone generally, and there were many mixed marriages. In the mayhem that later engulfed the country religious differences were never cited as a cause of violence.

I next visited Sierra Leone in August 1987 before travelling on to Accra for the PIM meetings. By then the economy had deteriorated yet further and the currency fell from an exchange rate of six to fifty leones to the US dollar while I was there. There had recently been a failed coup and treason trials were going on in Freetown. Vehicles were in as sad a state of disrepair as ever, and several buses that we passed had *God save the travellers* painted in cheerful colours on the side.

A disaster had overtaken Theological Hall, the main theological training centre, just a few weeks earlier when the ancient cotton tree that over-arched it collapsed in a storm one night, destroying one end of the building and killing the night watchman. The huge trunk and branches still lay across the smashed roof and the inside of the building was open to the sky. It was a sad sight, and seen as a very bad omen by those who lived in the area. Theological Hall had been one of the earliest buildings in Freetown and was a fine example of a three-storied, balconied, wooden house. The cotton tree itself was probably a century older than the building.

In October 1990 I made a final visit to Sierra Leone where the whole situation was affected by the chaos in Liberia. Some 500,000 refugees had streamed over land borders into neighbouring Sierra Leone, Guinea and Ivory Coast to escape the violence, and Sierra Leone was ill-equipped to respond to the needs of the terrified refugees who had fled without warning from appalling atrocities. In Bo Diocese people were offering hospitality as best they could, but there were all kinds of cultural and linguistic problems that added to the difficulties of assimilating such a sudden influx of people. Freetown was full of activity as naval vessels of the West African peace-keeping force used the harbour as a base. A gunboat was berthed just below the old CMS house and ships were leaving the harbour with relief supplies and returning with loads of yet more refugees. A jet fighter screamed overhead as I was visiting Fourah Bay College, almost taking the top off the ten-storey lecture block.

The new Diocese of **Guinea** was inaugurated on 1 August 1985 and I was invited to join the final synod of the old diocese (Gambia and Guinea) and the inaugural celebrations for the new one. The synod was held in the main conference hall of the Palais du Peuple in Conakry, an enormous building put up by the Marxist regime of Sekou Toure who had been deposed the previous year. Huge murals covered the walls – pictures of men carrying guns and muscular women brandishing agricultural implements and sheaves of corn. It was a somewhat bizarre setting for a church meeting, especially as we were all guests of a Muslim government. Guinea is 99 per cent Muslim, but the government were so desperate to rebuild the country after the disastrous years of Sekou Toure that they were looking to the churches for help with the re-establishment of educational and medical services.

Few of the Guinean delegates to the synod knew any English, and none of the Gambian delegates knew any French, so every document had to be produced in both languages and every contribution to the lengthy debates had to be interpreted. When we came to the sensitive question of how the assets of the diocese should be shared out between Gambia and Guinea, the excitement reached fever pitch and the translators could not keep up. The whole thing came within a whisker of pitched battle. There was a midnight curfew in Conakry, but no one noticed that and the discussions kept going till 1 a.m. when there was a power cut and the lights went out. I thought that signalled a chance to get to bed, but no such luck; two candles were lit and the discussion went on. Everyone was very bleary-eyed the next day.

The service of inauguration of the Diocese of Guinea lasted four hours and was most colourful and lively. Local instruments took over when the organ died in the next power cut and the excellent choir, dressed in an extraordinary combination of blue silk dresses and dull green pudding-basin felt hats, sang splendidly. Afterwards everyone embraced everyone else and kissed each other, French style, on both cheeks. After the service we were all invited back to the Palais du Peuple where we had a hilarious evening. There was a lively band, the choir was still with us, and the Archbishop's wife (an ex-dancer) led us in an African style hokey-cokey round the floor of the conference hall. Bishop Rigal and George Browne, the Archbishop of West Africa, took to the floor, whirling portly Gambian matrons round the hall, and when my turn came I reckoned it was all in the cause of building relationships with our partner churches. At midnight we toasted the new diocese with champagne and the choir did a really sexy turn to the refrain 'Jesus sanctify me'. It all came to an end several hours after the curfew and we finished the evening with a lusty rendering of 'Auld Lang Syne' in French.

I made a second visit to Guinea in October 1990. Guinea, like Zaire, suffers from being a Francophone country in a largely Anglophone Anglican Communion and I had many conversations while I was there about how to find appropriate Christian teaching materials in French. Justice McCarthy, Chancellor of the diocese, had recently been travelling in the States and told me of his frustration in continually having to explain that he did not come from *New* Guinea, nor from *Equatorial* Guinea, nor from Guinea *Bissau*, but from just plain *Guinea*.

When I visited Conakry in 1985 a pressing invitation was extended for CMS to send missionary personnel. It took us five years to find appropriate people to go, but in 1990 the Revd Tim and Dr Joanna Wiersum and their two small boys arrived in Conakry. Tim was appointed priest in charge of All Saints' Cathedral and Joanna helped to set up a small clinic in the cathedral offices. One day we hired a motorised dug-out canoe and visited Fotoba Island, home to the oldest parish in Guinea. We skirted reefs and mango swamps and the Wiersum boys had a wonderful time imagining Barbary pirates at every turn. On arrival the local Christians welcomed us warmly with a service and a feast. The Anglican Church in Guinea is very small, just six congregations in the whole country, but the people maintain a significant Christian witness in a predominantly Muslim community.

Gambia started life as a British Protectorate and its borders are defined by the area that could be protected by a British gunboat from the Gambia River. The borders run either side of the river at the range of a cannon shot, and go up to the highest point where the river is navigable for a gunboat, about two hundred miles upriver from Banjul. So the country is a very odd shape and is surrounded by Senegal apart from the port at Banjul. The country is 95 per cent Muslim and the Anglican Church there is very small, but like Guinea the church has good relations with the Government and represents a significant Christian presence in a largely Muslim community.

Most of the centres of the Anglican Church are in the Banjul area, but in recent years a vocational training centre has been established at Farafenni, about halfway up the Gambia River. I made three visits to Gambia in all and each time went up to Farafenni where people tend to feel a bit isolated. Some two hundred young people were being trained in skills that would enable them to earn a living in their home areas. Most of the students were Muslims though there was a handful of Christians and a tiny church had been started.

Michael Nazir-Ali and I had originally hoped to visit **Liberia** in 1990, but civil war broke out there during the course of the year and by the summer there was no possibility of being able to get to Monrovia. Archbishop George Browne had extended a warm invitation to visit his diocese and I was sorry that I never managed to get there before such terrible violence overtook the country.

By October 1990 nothing had been heard of the Archbishop for several months and at one stage it was feared that he and all his family had been killed. In fact they had fled to a remote rural area where they stayed in hiding, living in constant insecurity and fear, and with very little to eat, for the next year. The Archbishop kept in touch with his clergy as best he could and exhorted them to read the 23rd Psalm slowly, three times, morning, noon and night, every day that they were still alive. When he visited London at the end of the year, a visibly shrunken man, we gathered in the Partnership House chapel and he told us about that time. He then read the 23rd Psalm to us with extraordinary power. It was clear that the words had helped to sustain many people in their faith as they walked through the darkness of those terrible days. He died a few years later of an illness that must have been exacerbated by the extreme physical privations he had suffered.

At the Fulani meetings in Jos in 1992 the chairman was Ronald Diggs, the Lutheran Bishop of Liberia, who arrived straight from Monrovia and gave us a vivid up-date on the situation there. Charles Taylor's forces included many young boys who were given guns and drugs and lured into attacks on Monrovia by false radio reports that the city was already under rebel control. This posed a real problem for the defending forces who were reluctant to kill children and tried to disarm them, sometimes at the cost of their own lives. He also described how Christians and Muslims were working together on an inter-faith mediation committee, a very encouraging development.

Province of Nigeria

My first visit to Nigeria was in February 1986. We left Heathrow in a blizzard, from a runway only just cleared of snow, in a plane with freshly de-iced wings. We landed five hours later in Kano airport, where the temperature was 40°C, and queued up on the sun-baked tarmac before being allowed into the shade of the terminal buildings. The Nigerian government had launched a 'War Against Indiscipline' which meant that people had to queue at every possible opportunity. This was a profoundly un-Nigerian way to behave, so officials enforced the policy with some vigour and I nearly got roasted alive in the unaccustomed heat. Discipline had broken down by the time we reached immigration desks and it was a relief when I finally retrieved my passport from the mêlée of the arrivals hall. The next three weeks were spent travelling round the three northern dioceses of the Church of Nigeria: Kano, Kaduna and Jos. CMS then had over twenty mission partners working in the north, as that was the part of the country where the church most needed support. I managed to meet many of the church leaders and visited all the CMS personnel.

Driving round the north I learnt about the roads in Nigeria. All the main roads were tarmac (amazing after Zaire) and people drove at a furious pace in vehicles with bald tyres and failing brakes, trying to cover huge distances in the minimum time. Fuel was easily available at that time and dirt cheap by UK standards so there was plenty of traffic around. The road from Kaduna to Zaria had entered the Guinness book of records as the most dangerous stretch of road in the world in terms of the number of deaths per mile per year, and we saw the wrecks of many cars lying beside the road. Everyone prayed fervently for 'journeying mercies' before driving anywhere.

We headed first for Jos, passing through a dry landscape where there were no crops, just occasional baobabs and thorn trees. Traffic appeared in the form of lorries, buses, cars, motor-cycles (their riders wearing flowing robes) and the odd donkey. As we approached Jos, rocky outcrops appeared and we gained height. The Jos Plateau is a few thousand feet higher than the rest of Nigeria so the climate is relatively cool and many Christian organisations have their headquarters there. I met an ecumenical range of people in Jos and was particularly interested to meet Panya Baba, General Secretary of the missionary arm of the Evangelical Church of West Africa. He told me of the 622 Nigerian missionaries that his church supported, mainly working in Northern Nigeria but also in Niger and Chad, and it was encouraging to hear of this Nigerian initiative.

Jeremy and Wendy Hinds welcomed me to their home in Bukuru where Jeremy was teaching Islamic studies. They had lived in northern Nigeria for many years and Jeremy spoke fluent Hausa and Arabic. He regaled me with stories of his encounters with Muslims and spoke of the many Muslims he knew who had come to faith in Christ by studying the references to Jesus in the Koran. He had a beard and wore local dress, and was known throughout Northern Nigeria as 'Alhaji Hinds', a term of respect normally reserved for those who had completed the pilgrimage to Mecca. He had also done much work amongst the 'Issawa' (Jesus) groups, Hausa Muslims who already believed that Jesus was a greater prophet than Mohammed before the arrival of the first missionaries.

Islam in Nigeria had experienced a resurgence, due at least in part to the petro-dollar, and in January 1986 the government announced that Nigeria had become a member of the Conference of Islamic States. This horrified the Christian community and there was widespread protest. Hostility towards Islam was widespread in the north, though most church leaders were working hard to promote good relations between the two communities. Despite this, tension continued to grow and there were many outbreaks of violence in the years that followed.

After a warm welcome in Jos I left clutching numerous gifts and went on to Abuja. At that time the new capital was still only half-built and it was an extraordinary experience navigating the roads. One minute we would be driving on a mud track through the bush, passing herds of white cattle and straw-hatted Fulani herdsmen, then we would be on part of a six-carriage expressway passing the Hilton Hotel, then the next minute back to the mud and bush. The most developed area was dominated by the presidential palace and a huge, gold-domed mosque. The only government ministry that was open and functioning was the Ministry of Complaints. Peter Akinola, who later became Bishop of

Abuja, and then Primate of Nigeria, welcomed us and gave us a lightning tour of the city, and also took us out to see some local Gwari villages.

On the way back to Kaduna we visited Wusasa where most CMS work was based in the early days. St Francis Theological College is still a significant training centre for the church in the north and St Luke's Hospital continues the tradition of a ministry of healing. The church and some of the staff houses were built in the traditional style of the area with thick mud walls. Idwal Richards, an indomitable 80-year-old Welshman who had worked amongst the Fulani for many years, took us out to visit one of the nearby Fulani villages. We spent an hour chatting with women drawing water from a well and a group of men who were sitting on the ground weaving mats. Idwal talked with them about Jesus as the prophet revealed in the Koran and as the Son of God revealed in the Bible. It was all very friendly and at the end they asked Idwal to pray. Our vehicle sank up to its axles on the way back, just as it was getting dark, but there were plenty of strong Fulani around to get us back on the road.

We met Idwal setting off the next morning, stick in hand and pack on back, for a round trip of ten miles on foot. He went off like this every day to visit the Fulani villages, but in recent years he often got lost. Someone would always bring him back to Wusasa and the taxi-drivers never accepted a fare. Two years later he set out as usual in the morning but never returned. Despite the efforts of a search party it was a week before his body was found in thick undergrowth at the base of Wusasa Rock. He was buried where he lay in the place where his heart had been for so many years.

On the return journey through Kano, Garba Jibo, who had taken over the Issawa work from Jeremy Hinds, took me out to three of the Issawa villages which was a fascinating experience. At Bici na Bardo we sat with the local mallam (teacher) and several of the elders in a small mud-walled room, sitting barefoot on rush mats, while Garba discussed Genesis 1 with them, reading from a Hausa Bible in Arabic script. At the next village a lively discussion followed Garba's teaching, and afterwards I was surprised to discover that they had been reading the genealogy at the start of St Matthew's gospel. In Britain we tend to skip over this passage fairly rapidly, but for a people who have such respect for their ancestors it was clearly an important subject. On the way back Garba pointed out the numerous Koranic schools along the road, little clusters of corn-stalk huts where the students live with their mallams for the five months of the dry season.

In May I visited Southern Nigeria, making a whistle-stop tour that covered twelve dioceses in fourteen days. I was welcomed very warmly everywhere and came home staggering under a pile of gifts. Provincial officials rescued me from the milling crowds at Lagos Airport and Sunday, the provincial driver, swept us back to the church guesthouse along the amazing sequence of expressways that cross the city. That evening I was royally entertained by Joseph Adetiloye, the Bishop of Lagos.

In Lagos I started to experience something of the reality behind the statistics about Nigeria: one in every three Africans south of the Sahara is a Nigerian and the Church of Nigeria, with over ten million members then (the number is still higher now), is the largest church in the Anglican Communion outside Britain. In fact many more Anglicans are actually at church on Sunday mornings in Nigeria than in England. The size and vitality of the Nigerian congregations was something amazing to see, and almost everywhere I went we worshipped in a church that was already bursting at the seams and saw the foundations of an even bigger church being dug next door. It was clear that the churches were growing apace.

Sunday drove me to Ibadan where Archbishop Timothy Olofusoye welcomed me with many speeches about all that the Church of Nigeria owed to CMS, and sent me on a round of every institution that CMS had founded in the Ibadan area — I became quite dizzy with all the schools, clinics and churches involved. Then he kindly lent me his air-conditioned car, together with Sunday, who took me to many of the other western dioceses on our way to the east. At Onitsha, where we crossed the Niger River, Sunday handed me over to Bishop Jonathan Onyemelukwe and returned to Lagos. Sunday had been a wonderful companion, and very safe driver, and three months later I was dismayed to hear that he had been killed in a car accident.

During the Biafran war most CMS missionaries had stayed in post, even though there was real danger and deprivation and the British government had strongly advised everyone to leave. The fact that CMS stayed with the people to share the difficulties and dangers of that time was remembered throughout the churches in that part of Nigeria, and I was given a particularly warm welcome by all the bishops in the east. One of the last places I went to was Owerri where Bishop Ben Nwankiti asked me what my impressions of Nigeria had been. I made some comment to the effect that I had met so many able and committed Nigerian Christians that CMS was surely no longer needed in southern

Nigeria. When he heard this he said with some passion: 'But we need people from other cultures to help us to see ourselves as we are.' That was a compelling insight, and it articulated for me one of the most important reasons why Christians in Britain need those from other cultures to work in Britain.

Over the next few years it became more and more difficult to get work permits for expatriates to work in Nigeria, so the numbers of CMS mission partners in the country steadily dropped, but at the same time an increasing number of Nigerian Christians came and worked in the churches in Britain, some on short-term visits and others as full mission partners who stayed for several years. Thus the Church of Nigeria played an important part in helping to establish the CMS programme for mission in Britain.

During March 1987 there was great tension between the Christian and Muslim communities in northern Nigeria where riots in Kaduna State resulted in many deaths and the destruction of 150 Christian places of worship. St Francis of Assisi College at Wusasa was attacked one evening by a group of young men and the Jeavons family had a terrifying experience when their house was surrounded and set on fire. They were able to escape onto the flat roof, and when the rest of the college community came to help they threw the children down to safety. Their lives were undoubtedly saved by the thick mud walls of the house that did not burn, even though everything inside the house was in flames. The following February I visited St Francis College and saw the damage done by the fire; most of the buildings had been affected and some of the staff houses were totally gutted. But the library was miraculously still intact and the college community was making a great effort to make all the buildings habitable again. St Luke's Hospital next door was untouched.

Later I was taken round Zaria, where we toured the Sabon Gari area and saw the burnt-out shells of churches and the destroyed business premises of Christian traders from the south. It was a sad sight and reactions amongst Christians were very mixed. Some people expressed militant feelings against Muslims but on the whole the approach of the church leadership was more irenic. Having seen the charred-out shell of St Michael's church, open to the sky, we went to evensong at St George's where a lay reader, preaching on the text 'Be ye perfect' said, 'We must love our Muslim neighbours.' Congregations continued to worship in the charred remains of their churches, and the attacks had the effect of strengthening the church, partly because Christians of all denominations were brought together by a shared experience of loss.

Economically Nigeria was in difficulties at the time as a Structural Adjustment Programme (SAP) had been introduced at the insistence of the World Bank. For many years Nigeria had been using oil revenues to indulge in a huge spending spree, and the agricultural and other sectors of the economy had been largely neglected. So one of the purposes of SAP was to reduce imports, especially the import of food, in order to revitalise home industries. The immediate effect of SAP was to devalue the naira by a factor of five, and everywhere people were lamenting the 'SAPping effect' all this was having on the economy. The last weekend of that trip I spent with Ken and Ngozi Okeke in Lagos. They had recently returned home after Ken's years as Nigerian chaplain in London so the family were still readjusting to life in Nigeria and it was very good to be with them.

In November 1988 I returned to Northern Nigeria to attend the Joint Christian Ministry for West Africa (JCMWA) Assembly. This was a biennial gathering of people from all over West Africa who were involved in Christian ministries amongst the Fulani. I always found it a valuable opportunity to meet people from many different countries across the Sahel, and that year there were delegates from Benin, Burkina Faso, Cameroon, Central African Republic, Chad, Niger Liberia, Mali, Niger, Nigeria, Senegal and Sierra Leone. The Fulani are the largest cattle-owning, nomadic group in West Africa, over a million of them are spread across thirteen countries of the Sahel, and most of them come from a Muslim background. An outreach ministry to the Fulani therefore presents Christians with the challenge of communicating the gospel in a society which is both nomadic and Islamic. One year a Maasai bishop from Tanzania was brought over as one of the speakers and the Fulani were fascinated to hear all that he had to say about their East African cousins. He rather unwisely told the Maasai creation story about God giving all the cattle in the world as a personal gift to the Maasai. I was sitting amongst a group of Fulani as he got to this point and could feel their bodies stiffen. One of them sprang to his feet and furiously told the bishop that this was quite wrong because when God created the world he gave all the cattle to the Fulani. It was a fascinating meeting of cultures.

After the meetings I visited Zaria and Wusasa and it was most encouraging to see how many of the burnt-out churches were already being rebuilt. In Kano I stayed with Marie Bray, who was involved in health education. She had recently added another dimension to the building of Christian/Muslim relations in Kano by agreeing to run a Brownie pack in the Emir's palace.

In 1990 the Anglican Communion launched a Decade of Evangelism and the Church of Nigeria led the way through the inauguration of eight new missionary dioceses in the predominantly Muslim north of the country. So in April I went to Nigeria for the service of consecration of the eight new missionary bishops in Kaduna. A few days before the consecration there was an unsuccessful coup attempt and government officials were still very jittery. In the aftermath several prominent Christians were among the civilians arrested, which meant that Christian/Muslim relations were very tense and the security forces advised the church not to hold the service in the stadium in the centre of Kaduna as originally planned. Archbishop Adetiloye was very reluctant to accept this advice, but in the early hours of the Sunday morning agreed to change the venue to the cathedral.

As the cathedral in Kaduna could hold only about a third of the congregation, thousands of people gathered outside the building in the hot sun. For those inside, the temperature and humidity rose steadily. The service lasted five and a half hours and as Kaduna was brewing up for the first rain of the season, humidity was at its peak. The air in the cathedral became increasingly humid, heavy and hot. The bishops sweltered in their heavy robes and perspiration streamed down the faces of the diocesan chancellors who were wearing woollen wigs. One of the bishops afterwards wrote to me expressing the hope that I had recovered from 'our ordeal by suffocation'. I did survive it, just, and was glad to be there for such an historic event, but it was not an experience I would want to repeat.

After the service the congregation poured out of the cathedral and merged with a crowd of Christians who were demonstrating against the arrest of one of their leaders in the round-up following the aborted coup. The atmosphere was extremely tense and riot police were at the ready to come in with tear gas. A violent sand-storm blew up as we came out, followed by the first rain of the season; water fell from the sky in a tropical deluge that dispersed the crowds in a matter of minutes as everyone ran wildly for cover. The rain not only defused the tension but was seen, as always in Africa, as a sign of God's blessing on the whole enterprise. The creation of the missionary dioceses was a very bold initiative and, ten years on, the church had grown significantly throughout the north. Before the inauguration of the new dioceses most of the Christians living in the north had been southerners who had moved up there for work, but the creation of the new dioceses stimulated growth amongst the indigenous peoples of the north, which was a very significant development for the church.

In November 1990 I spent a week in Sokoto Diocese before going to the JCMWA assembly. Sue Essam and I then travelled to Abuja where Bishop Peter Akinola gave us a great welcome and put us up in VIP accommodation at the Hilton Hotel. It was five years since my last visit to Abuja and much building had been done despite the economic difficulties. The network of highways had been completed and five ministries had moved from Lagos. An enormous mosque, the largest on the continent outside Cairo, dominated the skyline with its gold-covered dome. The mosque had been built with the help of government funding and the Christian community was negotiating to receive similar government help with the building of an ecumenical place of worship that would hold ten thousand people.

The first Niger expedition landed on the Nigerian coast in 1842, so on All Saints' Day in 1992 a service was held in Onitsha Cathedral to celebrate the 150th anniversary of the founding of the Anglican Church in Nigeria. The newly-completed cathedral building was consecrated by the Archbishop who arrived from Lagos, and it was a great occasion. The cathedral itself was packed and thousands more stood outside. A multiplicity of choirs sang throughout the service, which lasted four and a half hours, and warm tribute was paid to CMS. Following the service I travelled to Jos for the next JCMWA meeting where Father Jarlash Walsh presented an analysis of the recent outbreaks of violence in Northern Nigeria. His scholarly findings disentangled the complex political, economic, ethnic, and religious causes of the violence. It was a most helpful analysis and did much to counter the dangerous assumption that all the antagonism stemmed from religious differences.

In May 1997 I was delighted to be invited to meetings in Ibadan of the newly formed Church of Nigeria Missionary Society. It was exciting to see this new mission structure emerging from the Church of Nigeria as the birth of the Society clearly held the potential to release large resources for mission around the world. All three provinces of the national church were being mobilised for mission and it was great to see the enthusiasm of the delegates we met. A huge service was held in Ibadan Cathedral on the Sunday, where hundreds of magnificently dressed worshippers committed themselves to the new work.

CHAPTER 12

Growth and instability in Zaire

M<small>Y INVOLVEMENT WITH ZAIRE CONTINUED</small> until taking over the Southern Africa brief, and for the first few years the numbers of mission partners steadily rose as many new opportunities emerged. By 1988 CMS had mission partners all over Zaire from Lubumbashi in the south near the Zambian border to Aru in the north, two thousand kilometres away and almost into Sudan. There were twenty-one CMS mission partners from the UK in Zaire by then, and another twenty-two Anglican mission personnel from Australia, New Zealand, Ireland and the USA had arrived in Zaire. This meant that the total number of expatriate personnel working with the church had leapt from six to forty-three in only eight years. The church was growing so fast that help was needed, but it was important not to inhibit Zaireans themselves from taking on positions of leadership by having too many outsiders around. Most of the expatriates were involved in training of one kind or another, and aimed to hand over to a Zairean successor as soon as was feasible.

In Boga Tim Rous and Pat Nickson did just this with Nyakato and Nyangoma Kabarole, identical twins and two of the most remarkable people in Boga. Tim worked closely from the start with Nyakato and, when he left Boga, she took over leadership of the diocesan development office. By then the office had a large team of mainly male workers who accepted her leadership happily, even though it ran very much against local culture for men to be subordinate to a woman. Pat worked equally closely with Nyangoma, who was similarly able and dedicated to the work. Pat arranged for her to do a course at the Liverpool School of Tropical Medicine and, when Pat left, Nyangoma took on responsibility for the community health work of the Anglican Church throughout Zaire. Nyakato and Nyangoma were both very gifted people and deeply committed Christians. Their hospitable home, which they shared with their mother and numerous small children, was always open to friends, and the only way I could ever tell them apart was by the slight gap that Nyangoma had between two of her front teeth. Very sadly, and greatly to Boga's loss, they both died young as the result of an inherited blood disorder.

Nyakato Kabarole and Tim Rous

As the number of different locations for CMS people increased, I was faced with longer and more complicated journeys to get round them all. Mercifully fuel became more freely available as Uganda settled down, and Scibe Airlift (a private airline) had been given a franchise to operate internally in Zaire which transformed the possibilities for getting about the country. On one trip I made nine flights and everything went like clockwork, which was most amazing for Zaire. But sometimes there were still shortages of aviation fuel and I was caught in this way one time when trying to reach Goma from Lubumbashi, a two-hour flight. All internal flights were cancelled and it took me five days to get to Goma, travelling outside Zaire via Lusaka and Nairobi.

In February 1989 I flew up to Aru in the far north-eastern corner of Zaire to visit Sally Barton and Ian Tarrant. The family had settled in very quickly and as well as rattling away in Swahili they were starting to learn the local language, *Lugbara*. The only hospital in the area was across the border at Culuva in Uganda but this did not seem to worry them, even though they had two small children. Sally and Ian took me across the border into Uganda one day to attend a confirmation service at Vurra in the Diocese of West Nile. CMS had never worked in this part of Uganda, but some 20,000 Sudanese refugees were living in the diocese so I wanted to talk with the bishop, Ephraim Adrale, about the needs of the refugees and to see whether or not any CMS involvement would be welcome. He responded very positively, and said how difficult it was for Ugandans in the area to help Sudanese as they were only just resettling in Uganda after being refugees themselves in Zaire and Sudan. In the years that followed CMS placed a number of mission partners in the Diocese, mainly in order to help with theological training for the Sudanese community in exile. Later still Aru was used as a base for mission partners who travelled regularly into Sudan.

When I was last up in Aru there were eleven churches in the area. By 1989, only five years later, there were 114 churches in the same area, and this rapid growth had undoubtedly been stimulated by the influx of Ugandan refugees. Although the refugees had almost all returned to Uganda by then, they had injected fresh life into the Zairean congregations. New churches were being opened all the time and one day Ian was asked what form of service he used when he was opening a new church at home. Ian had to admit that he had never needed such a liturgy in Britain.

There was a good deal of political unrest in the country during 1990, with rioting breaking out in many places and teachers on strike; university campuses across the country were closed after security forces shot a number of students in the halls of residence in Lubumbashi. The root cause of the discontent was continuing deterioration in the economy and a collapse in the currency. In 1979, when I first visited Zaire, the unit of currency, the zaire, changed at 4Z to the pound. When I arrived in February 1991 the rate of exchange was 5,000Z, and by the time I finally made it to Lubumbashi in August the rate had soared to 20,000Z to the pound. Salaried workers found that their monthly wages would barely buy one small bottle of paraffin and the salaries of Anglican pastors were worth less than £2 a month. In rural areas people could grow their own food, but even there hunger was becoming a real problem and in the cities the situation was very much worse.

In the north of Boga Diocese Sudanese refugees were arriving in large numbers, so I flew up to Ade, where I was met by Ian Tarrant and David Sharland, to see something of the work that the church was doing amongst the refugees. Thousands of Sudanese from Yei and Maridi had streamed across the border in recent months because of increased SPLA activity in their home areas, and most of them were living in settlement areas. David had become increasingly involved in community development work with the refugees and was trying to get in supplies of seeds and hoes before the next rains. Schools for the children were springing up in the bush but the Zairean authorities insisted that French should be used as the medium of teaching. None of the Sudanese teachers knew any French so this was bureaucracy gone mad, and David and Ian were trying to persuade the local officials to relax the rules. Ian had recently been in touch with Bishop Seme Solomona who made regular pastoral visits to his people in Zaire. It was very good to know that Bishop Seme was safe, as we had totally lost touch with him in London.

Louise Wright and Judith Wilson (who were amongst the last six expatriates to leave Juba in November 1988) had both relocated to Zaire. Louise went to Bukavu were I found her happily settled in and already speaking fluent Swahili. Judith, having married Clive Main, went to Kisangani Diocese. After the wedding Judith and Clive spent the first six months of their married life in Yamufaya, a Topokei village deep in the heart of the forest and a two-day journey from Kisangani. There were many Anglican churches in this area, and the Christians had long been asking for help. Judith and Clive were the first Europeans to live in Topokei country since the Simba rebellion and their presence was enormously appreciated by the local people. Clive had a teaching ministry and Judith helped the nurse in charge of the little health centre with encouragement and advice. They lived very simply, eating local food and living in a house built for them by the local Christians. They had bicycles so they were able to ride the ten miles to Lingungu once a week and keep in touch with Kisangani, using a radio belonging to the Baptists. By the time I visited Kisangani they were back there, so I heard much about their unique honeymoon experience.

During the autumn of 1991 violence erupted in many parts of Zaire. President Mobutu's term of office was due to expire in December so he announced the introduction of a multi-party democracy. Over a hundred political parties were formed overnight and when a constitutional conference opened in Kinshasa some 3,500 participants turned up. This chaotic situation led to the collapse of the conference and on 20 September rioting and pillaging broke out in Kinshasa and quickly spread to other parts of the country. The pillaging was mainly led by long-unpaid soldiers. There was huge unrest already because of the disastrous economic situation, and a further downward plunge in the economy had been triggered by a massive reduction in overseas aid, especially from the USA. Following the collapse of Communism in

Eastern Europe the USA was no longer interested in supporting Zaire as a geographical buffer against Communism in Africa. The violence in Kinshasa was stopped by the arrival of French and Belgian paratroopers who evacuated foreigners from the most affected centres of population.

All CMS mission partners in Zaire were affected by these events. In Kisangani there were several days of violent looting in the city and then the French Air Force arrived and, at an hour's notice, gathered up all the expatriates at the airport and flew them to Bangui in the Central African Republic. The speed at which this happened added to the trauma experienced by the Main and Jennings families, as there was no time for discussion with the bishop or farewells with friends and colleagues. In Lubumbashi the Naish family was rushed out of the country by the Belgian army who drove them to the Zambian border in convoy, so they too had no time for packing up or farewells. The Pitt family, who were based at Rutshuru in North Kivu, moved over the border to Uganda, and all mission partners in Bukavu moved across the border to Cyangugu in Rwanda for a period at night, but returned to Bukavu each day to work.

In Boga the Rous, Crooks and Montgomery families left when a radio message arrived from Bunia advising everyone to leave and Bishop Njojo made sure that all the families flew out to Kenya. The two single men, Nigel Pearson and Philip Bingham, stayed in Boga. There was considerable tension in Bunia, where a drunken military presence led to unpredictable violence, but Judy Acheson stayed put and David Peppiatt, a young short-term mission partner, flew in to Bunia just as most other expatriates were flying out. Pat Nickson also ignored the exodus and stayed put at Nyankunde. The only area that was relatively unaffected by the violence was Aru where the Tarrant family and David Sharland continued their work.

All this had happened while I was at St Beuno's, and by the time I got back to the office some of the displaced families had been able to return. But there was still a lot to sort out, and in May I visited Zaire to find out what was happening and to explore new locations for the mission partners who could not return to Kisangani. By then the violence had calmed down, though the economic plight of the people was as desperate as ever. The exchange rate had risen to 300,000 Z to the pound and money had become almost meaningless. 'Pesa ni bure' (money is useless) was a constant refrain. Millions of zaires were needed for the most trivial purchases, and large cases were needed to carry the notes. The quality of life of most Zaireans had reached such a low ebb (malnourishment and ill-health were endemic and infant mortality rates were rising) that outbreaks of violence in the community were not surprising.

The Province of Zaire was inaugurated in May 1992. It was a great occasion, but we were all aware of the precarious situation into which the new province was born. The Anglican Church in Zaire started its independent life in a situation of heavy financial dependency on its overseas friends, and it was hard to see how the church could move towards a greater degree of self-sufficiency, given the general economic situation in Zaire and the level of insecurity that pervaded the country. Somehow the province has held together since then, despite the problems of communication and the terrible violence that swept through the country only a few years later.

At Boga the presence of soldiers caused much fear amongst the local people as atrocities were committed against the civilian population in many places. Commandos typically walked around with a revolver over one hip, a hand-grenade dangling from the other, and an AK 47 over their shoulder. They were often high on drink or drugs, and within the first week of being at Boga their commander blew himself up in his own house by tripping over a hand-grenade. One day some of the men went off into the forest looking for 'rebels' and on their way back to Boga they saw a monkey and decided it would be good to eat. Some five hundred rounds of ammunition were enthusiastically let off into the trees, but history does not relate whether anyone actually hit the monkey. Meanwhile the rest of the commandos, hearing the racket, assumed they were being attacked and started firing back in the direction of the shots. It was a couple of hours before a trader driving down the road crossed the firing line and told them they were firing on their own men. Miraculously none of the local population were hurt in this exchange. Nyakato Kabarole played an amazingly courageous part in controlling the soldiers, who held her in the greatest respect.

When Bishop Joseph Marona and his people were driven from their homes in Maridi in Southern Sudan they fled across the border into Zaire and many of them gathered in refugee camps around Dungu. Dungu is geographically within the Diocese of Boga, so Bishop Njojo then agreed to send Tim and Judy Rous, with their two small boys Jonathan and Daniel, to live at Dungu for a period to help Bishop Joseph. I flew up to Dungu on this visit and spent five nights with Bishop Joseph and his family, seeing something of the work being done amongst the 60,000 Sudanese refugees. We visited two of the nearest camps, where people were struggling to re-establish their lives. The refugees had been given small plots of land and inadequate supplies of seeds and tools, and it was a real struggle for the weakened families to start cultivating and harvest the first crops before the initial handouts of food were stopped. Those who had been there longest had achieved a remarkable degree of self-sufficiency for food but new arrivals were still destitute. Schools had been started with no outside help, so children built their own classrooms and teachers taught without salaries. Many people were suffering from water-borne diseases so Tim's skill in helping to produce clean water sources was greatly needed. The refugees had horrific stories to tell about their journeys through the bush from Sudan to Dungu, and many families had been dispersed and were still trying to find one another in Zaire.

Tim and Judy and the boys lived in one room in the compound of the bishop's house, and had settled in remarkably happily to their cramped quarters despite the isolation, heat and humidity. When violence erupted in Dungu a few months later the compound was attacked and they lost many of their already meagre possessions. So they decided to move out to one of the refugee camps for security. The refugees were delighted and immediately built a house for them. This move brought them even more closely into the life of the refugees and Jonathan and Daniel were adopted by the whole community. Despite the very real physical demands of living in a refugee camp the family felt more secure there than amongst the soldiers in the town. Tim told me at one stage that if Zairean soldiers came anywhere near the camp the family would have the immediate protection of fifty stalwart Sudanese bowmen.

CHAPTER 13

Southern Africa

EARLY IN 1993 MICHAEL NAZIR-ALI received a letter from Archbishop Desmond Tutu inviting CMS to become partners with the Church of the Province of Southern Africa (CPSA). In April I was asked to take on responsibility for this new relationship, and in order to give me time to do this Chris Carey was asked to take over responsibility for Burundi, Rwanda and Zaire. I was a little sad to lose links with Zaire, but I was grateful to Chris for taking over the heavy volume of personnel work there, and very interested in the thought of engaging with Southern Africa. In June Archbishop Desmond Tutu came through London, so Bishop Michael took me to meet him and the Archbishop invited me to attend the next meeting of the Provincial Standing Committee of the CPSA that was due to be held in South Africa in September. I thus flew to Johannesburg three months later, and went to Modderpoort, high up in hills near the border with Lesotho, where the five days of meetings were held. This gave me an ideal opportunity to start getting to know some of the church leaders.

24 April 1994 had been set as the date for South Africa's first democratic elections, so it was a very interesting time to arrive. Everyone was talking about the democratic process, hoping and praying for a peaceful transition of power, but violence in parts of the country was giving rise to serious fears that the elections might not be able to take place. Chief Buthelezi had declared that the Inkatha Freedom Party would not take part in the elections, and the Afrikaner Volksfront, the right-wing white party, was also threatening to boycott the electoral process. We heard much about horrific violence in East Rand and Natal, and the Archbishop left the meetings one day to lead a day of prayer in one of the most badly affected townships. But on the whole there was a spirit of hope abroad and it was recognised that the churches would have a key role to play in the task of reconstruction and reconciliation that lay ahead. The Archbishop wore a jersey bearing the slogan 'Peace is Possible'.

The Province covers six countries: Angola, Lesotho, Mozambique, Namibia, South Africa and Swaziland. Mozambique was just starting to recover from a civil war that had ravaged the country and shattered the economy; the people of Mozambique currently had the lowest per capita income in Africa and millions of refugees were still living in neighbouring countries. But peace did seem to be holding and the church, which had grown during years of terrible suffering, was deeply committed to working for the reconstruction of society. Bishop Dinis Sengulane spoke movingly about the need for reconciliation, and described the 'swords into ploughshares' scheme whereby hoes and seeds were given out in return for weapons handed in. Bishop Dinis also had episcopal oversight of the Anglican congregations in Angola, a country that was still being torn apart by civil war. Tensions in the wider community were reflected in the meetings, and there were many difficult moments in the discussions. But Archbishop Desmond held the whole gathering together by the uniquely creative way in which he chaired the meetings. One minute he would defuse the tension by getting everyone roaring with laughter, and the next minute the entire assembly would be called to still, silent prayer.

The spirituality of the CPSA springs from a church that has engaged in a costly struggle for justice in the search for reconciliation, and the presence in the meetings of the youth chaplain, Michael Lapsley, provided a constant reminder of the context of political violence. Michael, a supporter of the African National Congress, had been the victim of a letter-bomb attack a few years earlier when he lost both his hands and nearly lost his sight. At the final eucharist he stood in front of the altar holding the paten in his callipers, inviting each of us to take our own bread. He wore a beautifully embroidered stole that had been worked by mothers of the Disappeared in Chile, a moving symbol of fellowship in suffering across the world.

Every day we gathered in small groups for Bible study and the materials included some searching questions. Each member of the group was given time to contribute their own response and people spoke very freely and honestly as they shared their thoughts. Catholic and Evangelical traditions were woven together in the corporate worship during the meetings, and every act of worship included periods of silence. A wonderful variety of languages was used in the singing, praying, and readings from Scripture, and at the consecration service of two suffragan bishops in Bloemfontein Cathedral we heard some wonderfully rich and rythmic singing, unique to that part of the world. The spirituality of the province clearly has something very precious to offer the world church.

CMS had been invited to partner the CPSA in the specific areas of evangelism, interchange and inter-faith concerns. Varied levels of interest in CMS were expressed by the different dioceses, and everyone went out of their way to make it clear that the partnership needed to be one of mutuality. Woe betide anyone who approached the CPSA with paternalistic ideas. The remarkable and rich spirituality of the province, combined with the social and political awareness that had developed in recent years through the struggle for peace and justice, were clearly God-given gifts that could be shared with the wider world church. But in the areas of interchange and inter-faith concerns there were ways in which the CPSA could receive the gifts of others, and I had some interesting discussions about possible exchanges between South Africa and Nigeria, and between the Portugese-speaking churches of Mozambique and Brazil. The political isolation of South Africa for so many years meant that many people had little first-hand knowledge of even their own African neighbours.

The focus on issues of peace, justice and reconciliation in the province meant that inter-faith concerns had been relatively neglected, even though South Africa itself had become a thoroughly multi-faith community. Bishop Peter Lee, of the Diocese of Christ the King, later asked CMS if we could find someone, possibly an Indian, who could minister in a multi-faith community on the outskirts of Johannesburg. We were able to put him in touch with the Revd Arun John, working on the staff of the cathedral in Delhi, who later moved to South Africa and played a very significant role in helping the clergy of the diocese to relate to their Hindu and Muslim neighbours. Arun brought with him years of experience of working with Hindus and Muslims, and was able to speak the same language as the thousands of people of Indian origin living around Johannesburg.

In May the following year I returned to South Africa to attend another provincial gathering at Modderpoort, this time a Conference on Mission and Ministry. The CPSA had held a full-scale Partners in Mission conference in 1989, and this meeting was designed to have another look at the province, five years on, to formulate a fresh vision for the post-apartheid years. It was deliberately planned to happen soon after the elections and was indeed an appropriate moment for the new vision to emerge.

The elections had taken place only three few weeks earlier and everyone was still in euphoric mood. 'Yippee!' was the exuberant cry of Archbishop Desmond as he cast his vote on that historic day, expressing a widely shared feeling of amazement and immense relief. Fear had gripped many people as the election date drew near, especially when violence erupted in central Johannesberg. There was a realisation that violence could overtake the country and the long-prophesied bloodbath be at hand. The peaceful nature of the elections in the event, and the ensuing statesmanship of reconciliation amongst the elected leaders, was described as miraculous by everyone I met. The birth of democracy had happened in a way that no one, even a year earlier, would have thought possible.

Many of those who had attended the inauguration of the President mentioned the moment of the fly-past. As the helicopters clattered overhead people were gripped with a reflexive fear as memories of helicopter gunships flying over the township crowded in. By the time the jets were screaming past, dramatically trailing the colours of the New South African flag, realisation dawned that this was the South African Defence Forces saluting Nelson Mandela. Both men and women told me that tears came at that moment, as they realised that all they had been striving for, for so many long years, had at last become a reality.

Clearly the honeymoon could not last forever, and a daunting task faced the new government. Expectations about improved housing, employment opportunities, education and health services were bound-less and unrealisable. The patience of the electorate might not last as well as it did during the astonishing days of queuing outside the polling booths. It seemed, though, that something radical had changed during the voting process; everyone had to wait their turn together (sometimes for days), and during this shared experience conversations started up that opened fresh windows of understanding within the community.

The Churches in South Africa were determined to play their part in the challenges that lay ahead in the huge task of reconstruction and healing that faced society. Already the government had announced the setting up of a Truth Commission as a help towards the healing of past history, and the churches recognised that much trauma counselling would be needed, not only by those who had suffered but also by those who had inflicted suffering. The Anglican Church was already involved in the training of trauma counsellors and in the setting up of a network of counselling centres. Everyone was aware that attitudinal changes would take longer to achieve than structural changes and hoped that the churches would have a significant role to play in this. People were also aware that the deep wounds of the past would take many years to heal.

As well as recognising the need for trauma counselling in South Africa there was much talk about the situation in Mozambique where the churches had already embarked on a 'guns into ploughshares' initiative. A weapon-free society was the goal in both countries, but in South Africa it was recognised that the manufacture and export of arms was an economically attractive option for the new government that would be difficult to resist in the shaky economic situation.

After the conference I travelled with Bishop Philip Makuku to Lesotho where he and his wife Matsepo welcomed me to their home in Maseru. The mountain kingdom of Lesotho was in the throes of a constitutional crisis in which Bishop Philip was playing a central reconciliatory role. The police were on strike and the governor of the central bank had been abducted by armed police officers who wanted their pay. The Bishop managed to negotiate the governor's release, and then got caught up in problems at the prison where the warders were on strike. The prisoners were rioting as they had not been fed, and the Bishop went in to try to calm them down. His main fear was for the safety of the prisoners as he thought the army might be sent in and start shooting.

In between these unusual episcopal activities, which included talks with the King of Lesotho, Bishop Philip kindly drove me around the diocese, assuring me that I was helping him to relax by giving him a reason to get away from the telephone. We went over the God Help Me Pass and saw something of the very beautiful mountainous country surrounding Maseru. There was little traffic about on the roads, but we passed several magnificent horsemen, wrapped in colourful traditional blankets.

My final visit was to Cape Town where I stayed with Mike (the Provincial Co-ordinator for Evangelism) and Lorna McCoy. Mike took me to the Archbishop's residence, set in extensive grounds and commanding dramatic views of Table Mountain. He also took me to Cowley House in the centre of the city that used to act as a half-way house for people waiting to visit relatives in prison on Robben Island. The year before it had been transformed into a trauma centre to help victims of violence and torture. Michael Lapsley was very much involved in the work here and he told us more about the help that was available. The centre offered psychological, clinical, and spiritual services through a multi-disciplinary, multi-faith approach that included individual and group therapy, creative arts therapy, pastoral counselling, survivor support groups, and help for front-line workers. An enormously imaginative enterprise.

Mike took me on a scramble up the Lion's Head with his two agile sons, and we all rode the cable car to the top of Table Mountain. Cape

Town must be one of the most beautiful cities in the world, and to my great relief it was warm, even though there was still snow on the mountains to the north.

CHAPTER 14

Sudan: the gathering storm

SUDAN BECAME INDEPENDENT IN 1956 and only eight years later growing tensions between north and south led to civil war. From 1964 to 1972 conflict tore the country apart and resulted in huge destruction and loss of life. An agreement signed in Addis Ababa opened the way for peace but after only eleven years fighting broke out again in 1983. This second phase of the civil war was to continue for over twenty years and bring further devastation to the south. Over two million people were to die from violence and starvation, some five million were internally displaced within Sudan, and hundreds of thousands more were forced into exile as refugees around the world. There was widespread destruction of property and many people lost their cattle. It was a disaster on a massive scale.

Causes of the conflict were complex. Reasons of history included the legacy of the slave trade and underdevelopment of the south during the Anglo-Egyptian Condominium. Sudan, the largest country in Africa, straddles both Arab and African areas of the continent so there are many ethnic differences. Politically, power had for too long been concentrated in Khartoum. There were also religious tensions, exacerbated by the arrival of the National Front and its policy of Islamisation. Western journalists usually described the fighting as being between 'the Muslim north and the Christian and Animist south' but this oversimplified the reality. Christians and Muslims alike were slaughtered in ferocious attacks on villages in the Nuba Mountains and Amnesty International regularly published lists of moderate Muslims who were being held and tortured in the jails of Khartoum. Some Muslims joined the Sudan People's Liberation Army (SPLA). When Southerners talked about government forces, they generally referred to 'those Arabs', rather than 'those Muslims'.

In May 1983 the garrison at Bor, in the heart of Dinka country, mutinied, and in October the SPLA was established. When I went into Sudan in 1985 armed conflict was spreading across the south, but it was still possible to travel freely west of the Nile amongst the agriculturalists of Western Equatoria. The violence escalated seriously

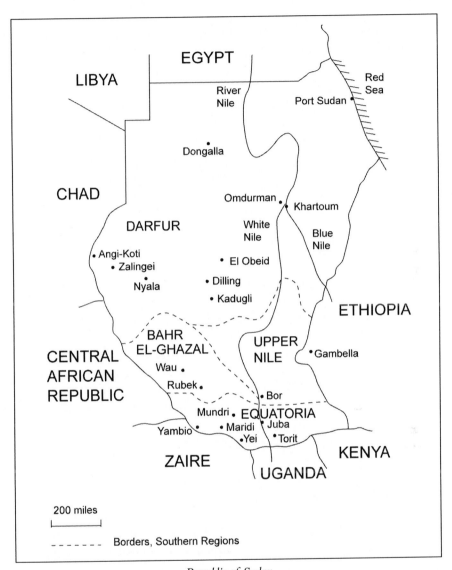

Republic of Sudan

some two years later, and in November 1988 the last CMS personnel had to leave Juba. For three years the chaos in the south made it almost impossible for outsiders to visit, but by February 1992, as the SPLA gained control of significant areas, the area started to open up again. The cattle people of Bahr el Ghazal and Upper Nile, especially the Dinka, were at the heart of the war-torn areas, and suffered death, displacement and the loss of cattle on a massive scale. Yet during this time the churches grew at an unprecedented rate, and when the south opened up I was able to see something of the extraordinary growth of these churches during their years of isolation. The ebb and flow of war dominated my experiences of those years, and it was a constant inspiration to see the courage and faith of so many Sudanese people.

Before flying into Sudan in 1985 I attended a meeting of the Association of Christian Resource Organisations Serving Sudan (ACROSS) in Nairobi. At that time the only way that CMS could get permission to work in Southern Sudan was through being a member of ACROSS but, because of our historic links with the Episcopal Church of Sudan (ECS), we regularly seconded some of our ACROSS mission partners to the ECS. On arrival in Juba I visited the ACROSS offices and the ECS offices, where I met Archbishop Elenana Ngalamu and the Provincial Secretary John Kanyikwa, and had time with CMS mission partners.

In order to travel outside Juba, ACROSS kindly lent Pauline Walker and me a Suzuki jeep complete with Augustino, a cheerful driver. Pauline had taught in Juba for some years and spoke Juba Arabic, so it was very helpful to have her as a companion. The road to Mundri was well graded, though heavily corrugated in places, and we passed through dry scrub and a succession of interesting rocky outcrops or 'jebels'. Bishop Eluzai Munda and Archdeacon Bullen hijacked us as we passed through Lui and gave us an unexpected meal and then we went on to Bishop Gwynne College, the provincial training centre for the ECS, where we met up with Benaiah Poggo (the principal) and staff members including Andy and Sue Wheeler and Marc Nikkel. Everyone was warmly welcoming, but something of a cloud hung over the college as one of the students had died the previous week and the college cook had died the day before after being bitten by a snake. There had been recent SPLA activity in the area and government soldiers had arrived in Mundri, which added to the general sense of fear.

Andy preached at the communion service the next morning from Daniel chapter 3. He focused on the response of Shadrach, Meshach and Abednego to King Nebuchadnezzar: 'If our God whom we serve is able to deliver us from the furnace of blazing fire and out of your hand, O king, let him deliver us. **But if not**, let it be known to you, O king, that we will not serve your gods and we will not worship the golden statue that you have set up.' It was a very powerful message, as everyone knew that Christians were already being tested in Sudan, and Andy concentrated on the words 'but if not'. Faith in God was no insurance policy against death – was the faith of the students strong enough to hold whatever the outcome might be? Many who were there that day did hold the faith with great courage through the horrendous years that followed, and many paid the ultimate price. Marc Nikkel painted images of the four figures in the fiery furnace on the walls on the new chapel when it was complete, and when Andy and I found our way to the abandoned chapel through the long grass eight years later the murals were still there. Through the anarchy and violence of years of civil war the paintings had been preserved.

Life was clearly dangerous on the east bank of the Nile and during the service the news came through that Janice Arensen, an AIM missionary who had been shot by bandits on the road near Torit two days before, had died. We prayed for Janice's family, and for all Sudanese who were already experiencing the fire of suffering. We also prayed for Bishop Nathaniel Garang of Bor who had not been heard of for several months. He had returned to Bor town after his consecration in Juba the previous year and then moved into the SPLA-held areas. Everyone hoped he was still alive, but he seemed to have disappeared into the vast bush of Southern Sudan.

From Mundri we drove on to Maridi where Bishop Joseph Marona was waiting for us at the police post on the edge of the town. He set off on his motor bicycle to lead the way and we followed him to the church where we were greeted by a great crowd of singing, dancing and ululating women, children, and all the church officials. It was a marvellous welcome, and we had to drive slowly as they waved flowers and ran beside us. The next day it took us five hours to reach Yei, passing through seven Ugandan refugee settlements. As long as we were travelling in an area looked after by the United Nations High Commission for Refugees (UNHCR) the road was extremely well graded, but whenever we reverted to a stretch of road that was the responsibility of the local Sudanese authorities, the surface deteriorated dramatically. One could understand the resentment that is generated when refugees are given more help than the local population. We passed through some beautifully open country that became progressively more fertile as we neared Yei. On arrival in Yei we found that both ACROSS and Bishop Seme Solomona were expecting us to stay with them, and each had invited the other to supper to meet us. We eventually negotiated to feast with Bishop Seme and stay the night with ACROSS.

Much of the ACROSS involvement at Yei was relief work with Ugandan refugees. Schools, clinics, access roads and boreholes were being built for sixteen settlement areas of about 2,500 refugees each. Most of the refugees had come across the border four years earlier when there was trouble in West Nile, so they were watching the situation in Uganda and waiting to go back as soon as things had settled down. In its work with the Ugandan refugees, ACROSS administered massive funding supplied by the UNHCR. At that time the country of Sudan hosted a total of 800,000 refugees from Ethiopia, Chad and Uganda. A country that already had massive problems of its own – drought, famine, floods, civil war, political confusion and economic bankruptcy – had to cope with the largest influx of refugees on the continent.

The next day we returned to Juba, and early the following morning I flew to Khartoum. Most of the next two days were taken up with ACROSS-related meetings, but on the Sunday I worshipped at All Saints' Cathedral and met Clement Janda, General Secretary of the Sudan Council of Churches. He later took me on a tour of the Three Towns (Khartoum, Khartoum North and Omdurman), crossing bridges over the Blue and White Niles and admiring the Mahdi's tomb from a distance. We came back past Gordon's palace and the gun emplacements facing across the confluence of the two rivers towards Omdurman.

My next priority was to visit Western Darfur. Drought and civil war in Chad had resulted in a massive flow of refugees into western Sudan and ACROSS had been asked to organise a medical team in the camp at Angi-Koti. CMS had recently sent ten short-term volunteers (two doctors, five nurses, an anthropologist and an agriculturalist) to help, so I needed to see how they were getting on. Dan Kelly, the director of ACROSS in northern Sudan, arranged for me to fly with him on a UN charter flight to Nyala and on to Angi-Koti. The ten-seater plane took three hours to reach Nyala flying over a totally empty landscape; there was nothing below us but boulder-strewn desert crossed periodically by dried up water courses. Only as we neared Nyala did we see any signs of cultivation or habitation, and round Nyala some trees appeared. After refuelling we flew on for another hour to reach Angi-Koti on the Chad border, and I shared a seat with the director of the Islamic Relief Agency. As we approached Angi-Koti we could see the neat layout of the camp, the beautiful green stretch of the wadi that runs between Angi-Koti and Foro Boranga, and the mountains across the border in Chad.

The medical team were in good spirits and had successfully coped with a major outbreak of cholera only two weeks after arriving. The camp held 25,000 refugees and everything seemed extremely well-

Refugee from Chad at Angi-Koti

organised. But it was a harsh, hot, and dusty environment for the team and there had been a good deal of sickness amongst them such as malaria, dysentery, and chest infections. I slept out under the stars and was woken the first morning by the sound of galloping hooves as a horseman headed at speed for the wadi and disappeared in a cloud of dust over the horizon. A procession of women with water jars on their heads then passed by on their way to the river, followed by a couple of small boys and a man leading a camel. Later on one of the team took me to visit some of the homes in the camp where everyone was warmly welcoming and we were offered many cups of tea. Each family had been allocated a small plot and given poles and grass mats as building materials, and when the rains started green tarpaulins were distributed for extra protection. A few camels, horses and donkeys were around, but most people had lost their livestock.

The weekly food distribution took place that day and it was a marvellously colourful event as everyone came to collect their supplies on camels. It was all very orderly and well-organised apart from the bellowing complaint of the camels when they were being loaded. The camels were loaded with bags of flour and multi-coloured piles of blankets and then left for the different 'blocks', some of which were several miles away. I wanted to see what happened when the loads arrived, so borrowed a bicycle and pedalled off through the soft sand. It was not a very efficient mode of transport and I abandoned it after getting a puncture, but it did enable me to follow one of the camel trains and watch the distribution process at the other end.

After two days in the camp I left by road for Nyala in a Land-Rover. It took five hours to reach Zalingei on a very sandy track and we crossed numerous dry water courses filled with deep loose sand. During the rains this stretch of road sometimes took three days for the trucks coming in with supplies. It was surprisingly green all the way and we passed some very healthy sorghum and millet and two large herds of well-fattened cattle. Other traffic on the road included colourful camel trains, horses, donkeys, and a couple of suk lorries with at least fifty passengers in flowing white jellabas clutching precariously to their seats on top of the loads. Then we hit an isolated 200 kilometres of tarmac road that took us swiftly to Nyala.

At Nyala I met up again with Dan Kelly and spent the night at the ACROSS guest-house. At that time an air-bridge had been established between Khartoum and Nyala and every day several Hercules transport planes flew in, each one carrying twenty tons of relief supplies for the camps along the border. The plan was that I would go back to Khartoum in one of the returning planes, and when we heard the roar of the first plane landing the next day I was taken out to the airstrip. The Hercules was sitting on the runway so I cautiously climbed the ladder leading up to the cockpit where a friendly American welcomed me on board. I was given a seat in the cockpit behind the pilot, and throughout the flight back was generously plied with coke, cookies and apples from California. Two hours later we were back in Khartoum. To have travelled from Nyala to Khartoum by land would have taken at least a week.

The situation in Sudan continued to deteriorate, and over the next ten years events constantly unfolded in unpredictable ways. In March 1986 the ACROSS team at Angi-Koti was expelled from Darfur. This was a shock to everyone, as the team had responded to a humanitarian crisis that was ongoing, and the work of the team had been much appreciated by local government officials. On 20 May we heard the tragic news that John Malau, Bishop of Rumbek, had been killed. He was travelling in a small plane from Wau to Rumbek, bringing relief supplies to the people of the stricken town, when the plane was accidentally shot down by the SPLA. He was an outstanding, spiritually gifted leader, and his death was a huge loss to the Dinka church.

At the ACROSS meetings in Nairobi in October the main issues of concern were the closure of many programmes in the south because of the fighting, and the difficulty of getting permission from the Sudan government to start new work in the north. The organisation had a much larger infrastructure than was actually needed to support the programmes still running, so some painful decisions about cutbacks were made. While in Nairobi I met Archbishop Elenana Ngalamu, who had been away from Sudan for nearly a year because of ill health. During his absence his ten-year term of office had come to completion, and the other Sudanese bishops had given Benjamina Yugusuk full archiepiscopal authority until a new archbishop could be elected. Elenana was trying to get back to Juba to stop this happening, and this marked the start of a schism that tore the ECS apart for several years.

In November 1987 the ACROSS board met again in Nairobi. Only a week before the meetings Daniel Bitrus had received a letter from the Sudanese Attorney General instructing ACROSS to liquidate all activities in Sudan within three weeks. In the event ACROSS lodged an appeal and the expulsion order was withdrawn, but clearly the position of ACROSS was becoming very precarious. Apart from the expulsion order ACROSS was already facing major difficulties as all their programmes in the south outside Juba had been closed because of the fighting. Increasing SPLA activity made it impossible to keep work going in many outlying areas and all ACROSS personnel had by then left the country or withdrawn to Juba. Only twenty-seven expatriate staff were left in Juba, of whom fourteen were CMS mission partners, so I badly needed to reach Juba to see them and to discuss the situation with the ECS. The Sudanese Embassy in London had refused my request for a visa, but I eventually succeeded in getting a visa from the embassy in Nairobi, thanks to the help of some influential members of the ECS who happened to be in Nairobi.

The next question was how to get to Juba. The only plane flying into Juba from Nairobi that had permission to carry civilians was a freight plane, a Boeing 707. It only flew once a week and the flight the week before had been cancelled as the government had commandeered the plane to fly horses to Saudi Arabia. We finally got away on a pre-dawn flight carrying thirty tons of grain into Juba, sitting on bags of American maize. I had been warned that the plane would stay as high as possible until the last moment and then corkscrew down into Juba, losing all

36,000 feet in the final five minutes in order to avoid SPLA rockets. It did not seem quite as bad as that, but I was a bit dizzy when we landed.

Juba was pleasantly cool and everything was lush and green as it was the tail-end of the rainy season. Central Juba had an unexpected air of normality and everyone seemed to be getting on with their lives as best they could. But the population of Juba and its immediate surroundings had increased dramatically in the previous few months, as there had been a huge influx of refugees from the surrounding countryside, and there was overcrowding everywhere. Every home housed three or four families and schools catered for up to three times their normal numbers of students, using a shift system to cope with multiple classes. On the outskirts of the town thousands of newly arrived refugees lived in tents that provided scant protection from sun and rain, and in some places seas of tents stretched to the horizon.

The ten days that I had in Juba were very full. I spent time with the CMS folk, individually and together, as everyone was living in a state of continuing uncertainty. Morale was good, and everyone was determined to stay in Sudan as long as possible, but people did find it claustrophobic not being able to move outside the town.

Within the ECS Bishop Benjamina Yugusuk had assumed a leadership role as acting archbishop, and most of the people I talked with were supportive of this. But there were those who had tribal loyalty for the retired archbishop, and a split in the church was fast developing between Morus and Dinkas who supported Elenana, and Baris and others who supported Benjamina. It was difficult to see how the church could be expected to go on living with a leadership vacuum, especially at such a time of crisis, and Benjamina was providing badly needed leadership.

John Kanyikwa orchestrated my flight to Khartoum on a plane that arrived with a hundred government troops, several tons of boxes of ammunition, drums of fuel and two live rams. It then loaded up with sacks of coffee from Yambio, some of it no doubt smuggled across the border from Zaire. Passengers were fork-lifted into the hold and I was given a seat in the cockpit with Bishop Michael Lugor. On arrival in Khartoum Bishop Michael took me straight to the Sahara Hotel and insisted on my staying there as a guest of the ECS. I then had a stream of visitors, who all came and talked at great length about the split in the church. At first I was prevented from meeting anyone who was not pro-Benjamina, so eventually I took myself off to the cathedral to see Provost Ephraim Natana and others who supported Elenana. It was sad to see all this going on, especially at a time of such crisis in the nation as a whole.

When passing through Nairobi en route to Boga in September 1988, I visited the ACROSS office and talked with Dan Kelly about the situation in Sudan. ACROSS was trying to offer logistical support to the churches in the south but communications were getting more difficult all the time. In recent weeks, flights had been getting to Juba only sporadically as the SPLA had gained control of Jebel Lado, a prominence offering a firing base from which planes approaching Juba Airport could be targeted. Road access to Juba had been totally cut since a convoy of food lorries from Kenya had been ambushed between Yei and Juba and fourteen of the Kenyan lorry drivers shot dead. ACROSS and other agencies were stockpiling food at Nairobi and Entebbe airports in the hope of eventually being able to establish an air-bridge into Juba where supplies of food were running very low. Six ACROSS people, including Carol Fallowes, Judith Wilson and Louise Wright of CMS, were the only expatriate ACROSS staff still working in Juba at that stage.

In November the last expatriate ACROSS staff left Juba. By that time Juba was being shelled and food was running very short so church leaders advised them to leave saying, 'Go home while you are still alive and tell people in Britain what is happening here.' It was a sad moment and we held a press conference in Partnership House for Carole, Judith and Louise to describe the situation in Juba. They all felt badly about the Sudanese friends they had left behind, even though none of them had left of their own choice.

The next meeting of the ACROSS Board was held in Sussex on 11 November when a decision was made to start working in the SPLA-controlled areas of the south. I pleaded hard for the decision to be delayed until we could consult our partner churches in Sudan, as I knew I could not agree to the decision without the blessing of the ECS. ECS leaders had to go on living and working with the Government of Sudan in Juba and Khartoum, and if ACROSS, of which CMS was known to be member, were to start working with the SPLA, this could become a difficulty. Some of the other members of the board were also cautious about such a move, but a majority agreed to the proposal. I went away angry about the decision and hurt by the insensitivity of others to the harm that this might do to the ECS.

When travelling through Nairobi the following February, I visited the ACROSS offices and met Dan Kelly who was already in the process of getting an agreement signed to start working in the SPLA-controlled areas around Pibor. John Kanyikwa from the ECS office in Juba was in Nairobi, so it was good to be able to talk it all through with him. He was very concerned that ACROSS had not consulted the churches, and agreed that it would be difficult for the ECS if CMS were to be part of such an initiative at that time. We talked together with Dan Kelly, but it was all too late. So I told Dan that CMS would cease to be a member of ACROSS the day that the agreement was signed. In fact the agreement was signed on 11 February, while I was in Zaire, so by the time I returned to Nairobi CMS had officially dissociated from ACROSS.

Khartoum and Cairo

For the next two years there was no possibility of visiting Southern Sudan, so each year I made a visit to Khartoum and spent a few days in Cairo on the way back. General Bashir had seized power in Khartoum in June 1989 and when I was there in February 1990 military security was still very tight; on the short drive from Khartoum airport to Omdurman we went through twelve road-blocks across streets that were almost deserted because of the curfew.

The situation amongst the ECS bishops was a sad one, as the division in the church between supporters of Elenana Ngalamu and of Benjamina Yugusuk was as unresolved as ever and there were no signs of any healing of the split. The Sudan Council of Churches (SCC) refused to recognise the legitimacy of either group, so this added to the confusion and placed the ECS in a very weak position in relation to the ecumenical aid agencies.

As violence had escalated in the south, many southerners had made the long trek north, and by 1990 over a million internally displaced Sudanese were living on the outskirts of Khartoum and Omdurman in temporary settlements or in refugee camps. The ECS had been given responsibility for food distribution in four camps holding 13,000 people and was also involved with water schemes (the provision of donkey carts) and income-generating activities, such as the running of grinding mills. I was taken out to see the nearest camp which was a depressing sight, sprawling out over the dusty plain and surrounded by rubbish-strewn wasteland. Families lived in igloo-shaped shelters made from a frame-work of sticks covered in sacking or cardboard that had been used to hold the relief food. For 3,000 people there was just one water collecting point, which often ran dry, hence the need for donkey carts.

We were invited into the home of a Nuer family who told us of their journey to the camp. They had trekked through the bush to Kadugli for a month, during which time many of the very young and the elderly died, and then reached Khartoum in a few days on a lorry. There was nothing inside their home except a fire, a few cooking utensils, and flour bags to sleep on. Some of the men in the camp were able to earn a little money through casual labour but there were not many opportunities for work in the area and there were often language problems. The UNHCR poured funds into the Ethiopian refugee camps, but did nothing for internally-displaced Sudanese.

On Sunday I was taken to a service in one of the camps on the outskirts of Omdurman where everything was the same dusty brown colour and rubbish was scattered all round. This scene was even more wretched as the camp was surrounded by ugly factory buildings; it had simply sprung up on waste ground within the city. The church was built of the same materials as the houses: sticks, sacking and cardboard. The sacking flapped about in the wind but the Christians had managed to enclose a space with room for over two hundred worshippers and everything had been arranged with the greatest care. The congregation sang vigorously, accompanied by drums and shakers, and joined in confidently with the liturgy, despite having no books. They were Dinkas from Aweil, and the church seemed to be the one place where they could recover their dignity and sense of community and maintain some continuity with their lost lives in Aweil. There was real joy in the worship and I marvelled at the sheer resilience of the people. It was a haunting scene.

Peter Yata had recently flown up from Juba and shared news of the situation there. Government forces were in control of Juba itself and up to six miles from the edge of the town. Beyond that the SPLA were in control of the villages, so the fighting was going on along that boundary rather than in the town itself and there had been no more shelling. The SPLA had been urging the civilian population over the radio to leave Juba, but the government forces were forcibly preventing anyone from leaving. Many of those who had tried to get out of Juba when the shelling first started had been forced to return because of foot mines on the paths. Relief food was being flown in again on a regular basis from Nairobi.

Peter also brought news of Bishop Seme Solomona from Yei. Yei was still under government control but the SPLA forced their way in for three hours and captured large numbers of civilians (including Bishop Seme and all his family) and took them back into the bush to an 'orientation' camp. The SPLA probably did this to empty Yei of civilians as far as possible before launching a full-scale attack. Peter thought

Bishop Seme might have been taken down to somewhere near the Uganda border.

During the week Bishop Michael Lugor arrived from Nairobi saying he had met Bishop Nathaniel Garang, which was wonderful news. It was the first time that he had been in touch with the outside world for six years so people had started to wonder if he was even still alive. Then the first rumours of his activities started to trickle through the bush and people heard that he was very much alive. It emerged that he had been walking through the bush teaching, baptising, and confirming that the church was growing fast. In Nairobi he spoke of six hundred new churches in the Bor area, a huge growth in the church there.

From Nairobi Bishop Nathaniel travelled with Bishop Paride Taban (the Roman Catholic Bishop of Torit) to visit the Vatican in Rome and to the World Council of Churches in Geneva. On return to London I managed to get in touch with him in Geneva and he agreed to take two days out of his time in Rome to visit London. When he arrived he spoke of God's providence during times of desperate physical need and of whole families and groups turning to Christ. He spoke of healing, of the breaking down of tribal and religious barriers, and of the emergence of wholly new indigenous forms of worship. From Rome he returned to Bor to continue his remarkable ministry, and the following year we invited him to Britain to visit churches around the country. As he spoke of the work of the Spirit amongst his people his face lit up with a rare radiance.

From Khartoum I flew to Cairo to visit Andy and Sue Wheeler. Andy was there to study Arabic, as the plan was that the family would eventually move to Khartoum. In fact that never happened, but while they were in Cairo Andy and Sue both had important ministries amongst the Sudanese refugee community. I arrived on Ash Wednesday and that evening we went to a service of ashes at Abu Sarga, the oldest church in Cairo. We wound our way in the dark through the narrow alleys of Coptic Cairo and climbed down a steep stone staircase to the crypt of the ancient church. By candlelight we made the traditional act of repentance as we received a cross of ashes on our foreheads and heard the words 'Remember you are dust and to dust you shall return.' Legend has it that the Holy Family slept in a cave below the church on their first night after arriving as refugees in Egypt. As we prayed that night my mind was full of the Sudanese I had seen so recently in the displaced camps around Khartoum and Omdur-man, and I found it deeply moving to be reminded so powerfully of Jesus' identification with the Sudanese in their refugee experience.

There were many Sudanese in Cairo at that time, some of whom had come for university studies and then been unable to return to their homes in Southern Sudan. Others had fled Sudan more recently and arrived with horrendous stories of their experiences on the way. Sudan and Egypt have an agreement that allows Sudanese to come to Egypt without needing a visa, and this means that in the eyes of the UNHCR the Sudanese in Cairo are not international refugees and only have the status of those who have been internally displaced. So the Sudanese we met were getting no help from the UNHCR. The cathedral in Cairo was just starting up a programme to help Sudanese to develop income-generating skills, a programme that grew steadily over the years as the numbers of Sudanese stranded in Cairo continued to rise.

I went to Cairo again the following year and was there on Maundy Thursday when a traditional foot-washing service was held for the refugees in the crypt of the cathedral. None of them had the money for bus fares so they had to walk long distances through the hot and dusty streets of Cairo to get there and it took buckets of hot water to clean their feet of sweat and dirt. It was a foot-washing service I shall always remember.

In June I was invited to visit the Sudan Council of Churches (SCC) in Khartoum as part of a small delegation from the World Council of Churches in Geneva. News came through during the week of events in the Gambella area of Ethiopia following the collapse of the Mengistu regime. Oromo rebels had started indiscriminate shooting in the Sudanese refugee camps along the border, which resulted in a massive movement of some 400,000 refugees streaming back across the border into Sudan. Once in Sudan the terrified refugees found themselves being bombed by the Sudanese Air Force. There were calls for the international community to do something to protect the refugees but little happened in response to this humanitarian crisis.

In October 1992 Chris Carey and I went to Harare for meetings of the Conference of the Anglican Provinces of Africa (CAPA). Representatives came from each province in Africa and a stir was caused by the arrival of Gabriel Roric Jur, Bishop of Rumbek. He had recently been appointed Minister of State for Foreign Affairs in the Khartoum government, so he was challenged about whether he was amongst us as a bishop of the church or as a minister of the Khartoum government. His Sudanese colleagues were nervous about saying anything in public, but the other delegates had no such scruples and the legitimacy of his dual role was challenged hard. I had a couple of days in Nairobi after this where I had non-stop meetings with Sudanese, trying to catch up on the latest news from Sudan. Everyone expressed a deep sense of anger and betrayal over Gabriel Roric Jur's appointment as a minister. The good news was that a service of reconciliation had taken place in Juba between Elenana and Benjamina supporters, and it did look as though the rift in the church was starting to be healed at last. Bishop Elenana died shortly after the service had taken place.

CHAPTER 15

The New Sudan

B Y 1992 THE SECOND PHASE OF THE CIVIL WAR in Sudan had lasted for nearly nine years and the Sudan People's Liberation Army (SPLA) had gained increasing control of Southern Sudan. Government forces still controlled the main towns of Juba, Wau, Rumbek and Yei, where there were large military garrisons, but those centres were all under close siege by SPLA forces who effectively controlled the rest of the south.

In these 'liberated' areas of the south, or in the language of the SPLA, the 'New Sudan', the civilian population included large numbers of Christians who found themselves cut off from their national church centres in Khartoum and Juba. Denominational differences were laid aside as Christians came together in a remarkable way to start reshaping their lives in this new situation. It was not possible for them to be in touch with the Sudan Council of Churches (SCC) in Khartoum, so under the leadership of the Roman Catholic Bishop of Torit, Paride Taban, and the Anglican Bishop of Bor, Nathaniel Garang, the churches in the liberated areas came together to form the New Sudan Council of Churches (NSCC) to represent the Christians living in that part of Sudan. When Bishops Paride Taban and Nathaniel Garang visited Geneva in 1990, the World Council of Churches approved the inauguration of the NSCC and Bishop Paride became chairman with Bishop Nathaniel as vice-chairman. Roger Schrock, of the Church of the Brethren in the USA, was appointed executive secretary.

These developments changed the situation for Christians in the liberated areas and opened up new possibilities for CMS and other organisations to be in touch with churches in these parts of Sudan. When Bishop Nathaniel Garang came to London in 1990 he warmly invited me to visit Bor Diocese, and when I was in Khartoum the next year I ascertained that Archbishop Benjamina would be happy for me to make such a visit. By then we were also in touch with Bishop Seme Solomona who was settled with his displaced people in Kaya, close to the Uganda border. He had sent a similarly warm invitation for me to visit Yei Diocese. So at the end of February 1992 I travelled with Beverley Jones of Christian Aid to make a first visit to the liberated areas.

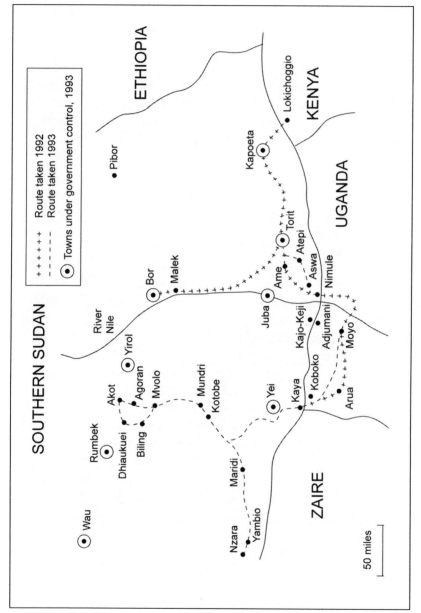

Southern Sudan

Roger Schrock kindly offered to expedite our travel, and we met up with his wife Carolyn in Nairobi.

We flew from Nairobi to Lokichoggio, the base in northern Kenya for relief agencies ferrying supplies into Sudan, and the next day Carolyn drove Beverley and myself into Sudan in an NSCC Land-Rover. It took us a full day of bumping in and out of dusty potholes to reach Torit, the first town of any size over the border. The road ran through the Imatong Mountains and was very rough in places as it had not been graded since the war began. An isolated signboard saying 'Welcome to the New Sudan' was the only thing that marked the border and it was many miles further on before we reached the first checkpoint. The only people we saw on the road for the first few hours were naked Taposa tribesmen carrying Kalashnikov rifles. Clothes were not easy to come by in that part of the world and we were warned before setting out that we should travel with a spare set of clothes hidden under the seat. Several vehicles passing that particular stretch of road in recent weeks had been stopped at gunpoint and the occupants relieved of all their possessions, including their clothes. There was little sign of life in the hot, dry bush. We passed the occasional herd of cattle and went through periodic checkpoints. Many of the roadside villages had been long abandoned as villagers had fled into the relative safety of the bush. After ten hours of driving we finally reached Torit.

In Torit we met Bishop Nathaniel and heard the latest news about the split within the SPLA, which had been encouraged by the government. The split led to inter-tribal fighting and the people of Bor had suffered a disastrous attack from Nuer tribesmen a few weeks earlier. An estimated 46,000 armed men had swept through the area killing over five thousand people and driving off all their cattle, leaving a complete trail of devastation behind. Many of the Bor Dinka who survived had moved up the road to emergency feeding centres, and others had found hospitality in an overcrowded Torit where Bishop Nathaniel's own family were staying.

In the evening we met with Bishop Taban Paride, the most respected civilian leader in the liberated areas. We met in his rather makeshift compound, for which he apologised, explaining that he had moved from his usual base, a few miles outside Torit, when the bombing increased. He had moved into the centre of town so that he could be with his people and share their danger. Bishop Taban was clearly a man of great spiritual stature who was providing inspired leadership. He told us that the churches held their services at first light on Sundays so that people could disperse before the first Antonov bombers could reach them from Khartoum. People had makeshift, shallow trenches but these offered little protection against a direct hit. Torit was being targeted at that time as it represented the gateway to the liberated areas on the east bank of the Nile from both Kenya and Uganda. The next morning I joined Bishop Nathaniel to travel on to Malek, his own home village, which lies a few miles south of the town of Bor. He was being driven in an ACROSS vehicle and the two ACROSS staff with him, Russ Noble and Paul Young, kindly agreed to give me a lift. It was an extraordinary day.

The drive took all day, and for the first eight hours the road held nothing but signs of death and destruction. All the bridges on the road had been destroyed and on either side of the road we saw a trail of burnt-out vehicles that had been blown up during successive periods of fighting in the area. Some of the wrecks were from the fighting of the Nimeiri days and were already half overgrown with vegetation. We passed several camps for displaced people who had fled from Bor following the recent massacre and saw relief food being distributed. As we came nearer to Bor we started to see more signs of the violence, passing burnt-out cattle camps and the contorted carcases of cattle that had been shot lying at the side of the road. At one point we saw the body of a child still lying on the verge. When I asked why no one had buried the body the Bishop explained patiently that after three weeks in the bush without food no one had the strength to bury the dead, so most of the bodies were still lying in the bush. Bodies found nearer the river were simply thrown into the water.

Towards the evening, when the light was already starting to go, we saw a large party of people on the road ahead. Through the fading light and the dust it was difficult to see what was happening, but vertical lines were visible which looked very like spears. For a moment or so it looked as though we were about to meet a raiding party on the warpath. The driver hesitated, but there was nowhere else to go so we drove on slowly. Then we saw that the mass of people coming towards us were carrying not spears but tall wooden crosses, and realised that they were Christians from Bor Diocese who were coming to welcome their Bishop. It was a quite extraordinary moment. They all swarmed around the vehicle, dancing and singing, then Bishop Nathaniel got out and everyone embraced him and he prayed with them. As we drove on down the road the cross-carrying welcomers ran behind us, chanting, and were joined by more groups as we neared Malek. By the time we

Bishop Nathaniel Garang at Malek

reached Malek some thousand people had gathered and we worshipped together under an ancient banyan tree beside the Nile.

All day on that long road we had seen nothing but signs of death and destruction – there was no human reason in that terrible place for anything but despair. Yet as we sang and prayed together that night I saw hope and joy lighting up the faces of those around me, and realised I was surrounded by people whose material securities had been utterly swept away and who had discovered what it means to trust in Christ alone. Many of the women embraced me afterwards, hugging me to themselves, and as I returned the embrace I could feel the skeletal thinness of their bodies. Yet still their faces shone with hope. It was a deeply moving, powerful, and humbling experience that has profoundly touched and enriched my own faith. I was hailed as the first person from CMS to visit Malek for nearly forty years and found myself being welcomed as a long-lost member of the family.

Bishop Nathaniel took us to see some of the newly-built churches in the area, including a huge cruciform church with a superbly woven grass roof that could hold over five hundred people. The construction work had been done by people who were still struggling to rebuild their own homes. As fast as churches were being burnt and destroyed others were being built. The growth of the church amongst the Bor Dinka in the previous few years had been quite astonishing. When Bishop Nathaniel came to Bor eight years earlier there were three churches still standing in the diocese. By 1992 there were 143 churches. Much of this growth was due to the ministry of Bishop Nathaniel himself, who had travelled tirelessly on foot over a huge area, teaching preaching, baptising, confirming and training up a new generation of pastors. The Dinka people had long been resistant to the gospel, but during those eight short years the Dinka as a community changed from being under 20 per cent to over 80 per cent Christian.

Bishop Nathaniel frequently referred to Archibald Shaw as the one who had planted the seed of the Gospel from which all this amazing growth had sprung. Shaw was the first missionary to live in Malek, in 1905, and after he had been there for ten years only two men had been baptised. The CMS committee in London decided he was wasting his time in Malek and wanted to move him further south where the churches were growing apace and help was needed. Shaw ignored all the letters that arrived, and eventually an official representative of CMS came up the Nile by boat to collect him and move him south. Shaw went off into the bush when he heard the boat was coming and only reappeared after it was out of sight. He continued to work at Malek for many years, even though he continued to see little fruit from his ministry. A wonderful story of God's hidden purposes.

Mark Gak, who had recently studied theology in Kenya on a CMS bursary, returned to Malek just before the raid to build a house for his family and described how he had run from the village with two friends on either side of him when the raiders came. They threw themselves onto the ground to avoid the bullets and when he got up to go on running neither of his companions moved; they had both been killed. Mark later returned to join his family, looking very emaciated after his time in the bush. When we left Malek, Mark was starting once more to build a house for his family.

The most fervent request that the people put to CMS was to send Dinka New Testaments for the growing congregations, and to provide fish hooks and mosquito nets so that people could start feeding themselves again. There was also a desperate cry to help with teaching materials so that schools could be reopened.

When we left Malek the women presented me with a cross. The long stem of the simple wooden cross was encircled by brass rings that were made from spent cartridge cases, bullets that had been used to kill and maim human beings. Dinka Christians had reshaped those instruments of death and destruction by threading through them that supreme symbol of life and healing, the cross of Christ. That bullet-encircled cross is now my most precious possession.

When we got back to Torit we found the only way to get to Kaya to visit Bishop Seme was to drive down to Nimule on the Uganda border, drive across northern Uganda to Arua, and then back into Sudan at Kaya. This represented another major drive so we were a little daunted and wondered what to do. However, a radio message came through from Bishop Seme saying, 'All the people of the diocese are waiting for you.' By then Roger Schrock had returned to Torit, and he nobly offered to drive us to Kaya. It took fourteen hours to get to Arua and the next morning we drove back into Sudan and arrived in Kaya where Bishop Seme and his wife Esther gave us a great welcome.

Bishop Seme led his people out of Yei in 1990 when a convoy of more than a hundred vehicles and about ten thousand people on foot made their way to this (then deserted) border town. They had been ordered to leave by the SPLA who were planning a major assault on the town. The SPLA escorted them through the bush for three days, travelling by night for fear of government attack, and then abandoned them. In Kaya Bishop Seme and Father Peter Dada of the Roman Catholic Church set up a community in displacement, working together to obtain and distribute relief food and emergency aid. Everyone had arrived in Kaya destitute but slowly the work of reconstruction began, and when we visited it was remarkable to see the relative normality of life in this church-run community. Bishop Seme took us to a health centre where courses were already being run for village health workers, and showed us where he was starting to build a diocesan Bible school to replace the centre he had been forced to abandon in Yei.

Bishop Seme travelled freely throughout his diocese, though he could not reach Yei town itself. He was the only ECS bishop living in the liberated areas of Western Equatoria and had visited all the neighbouring dioceses whose bishops were still in exile or in Khartoum. During that time he gave a remarkable lead to the ECS congregations in the area and had a widely appreciated pastoral ministry. As the area around Kaya had experienced fighting for a relatively short time, it had not been as devastated as the areas on the east bank of the Nile. We could hear the distant sounds of shells being fired into (or out of) Yei, but Kaya itself had not at that time been attacked. With 30,000 people crammed into a small village it was well protected from the air as all the houses were

Bishop Seme Solomona building a Bible School at Kaya

built on a slope and were not easily visible. But it was so close to the border that the last Antonov sent from Khartoum over-flew Kaya and dropped its bombs on Koboko in Uganda, which caused an international incident. The land was fertile and once some stability had been restored the people started planting and in many places were already self-sufficient for food. From Kaya we returned to Nairobi where I was swamped by Sudanese wanting to hear news of their home areas. I met two of the bishops from Western Equatoria and tried hard to encourage them to go back to their dioceses.

CMS invited both Bishop Nathaniel and Bishop Seme to visit Britain later that year in order to raise awareness about what was happening in Southern Sudan. They travelled widely and everyone who heard them speak was deeply moved by all that they had to say. We did all that we could to bring pressure to bear on the British government to take some more effective action in relation to the continuing crisis. The situation was discussed in the House of Lords, and I helped to brief a number of the speakers in the debate. We took both bishops to the Foreign Office where they made a moving plea for action. At one point Bishop Nathaniel said, 'We find it difficult to understand; in the world there are international laws against the killing of animals. We are human beings, and we are dying – but the world keeps quiet.'

Second journey to the New Sudan

In February 1993 a joint CMS/Diocese of Salisbury party visited the liberated areas of the south. Andy Wheeler (theological education co-ordinator for the New Sudan Council of Churches), Ian Smith (CMS Area Secretary) and myself represented CMS, and Peter Vaughan, Bishop of Ramsbury, represented Salisbury Diocese. We were not able to reach Bor as the main centres in Bor diocese had been recaptured by government forces since my visit the previous year, but we visited the displaced camps on the east bank of the Nile north of Nimule and then travelled widely on the west bank, starting at Kaya. In all the places that we visited beyond Kaya we were the first outside church visitors to arrive for many years, so our arrival everywhere was received with tumultuous acclaim. It was a deeply moving experience, and the scale of our welcome showed the deep sense of isolation that had been experienced before. We managed to reach six of the seven dioceses in the liberated areas, missing out only on Kajo-Keji for lack of time.

The visit was organised by Andy Wheeler, who successfully alerted the church leaders to the date of our arrival in each place, despite the difficulties of communication. The NSCC kindly provided our road transport plus Martin, our cheerful and indefatigable driver, who took us as gently as possible over nearly two thousand miles of dusty, bumpy, unsurfaced roads. We flew in and out of Sudan in a six-seater aircraft piloted by Heather, an enterprising freelance pilot. Our entry into Sudan was at Nimule where we landed on a small bush airstrip outside the town and were welcomed into the country by a choir from the nearest church. There was no sign of any immigration officials. The Revd Reuben Akurdit hosted us for the next two days us and took us to visit the three camps for displaced civilians in the Nimule corridor: Ame, Atepi and Aswa. Some people in the camps had come from the refugee camps at Itang in Ethiopia, thereby making a journey of some five hundred miles to return south, on top of the immense journeys they had all made to reach Itang in the first place. Many had been continuously on the move for the last two years.

Ame was only a few miles from Torit so it was the most vulnerable of the camps to the expected dry season offensive, and was within a day's drive of government tanks should they break out of Juba. The leaders of the camp, both civil and religious, spoke with almost tangible fear of what might unfold in the next few months and appealed desperately to the international community to halt the war before the government assault fell upon them. A few months later most of the 150,000 people in the camps fled south across the border into Uganda. Some food was reaching the camps but nothing came in adequate quantities. There were shortages of all basic commodities such as food, blankets and hoes, and the UN had discontinued any relief work on the east bank since the murder of four expatriate relief workers three months earlier. In each camp there were food stores: huge piles of sacks of grain covered by white tarpaulins. The white coverings were easily visible from the air so had been camouflaged with strips of sacking.

From Nimule we drove across northern Uganda, following the same route that I had travelled the year before, then came back into Sudan at Kaya. Kaya was a hive of activity and full of visitors, as a meeting of the NSCC was just finishing. So that gave us a useful opportunity to meet with a variety of people, including Bishop Nathaniel. Bishop Seme and his wife Esther were as warmly welcoming as ever and on that trip Bishop Seme acquired the nickname 'No Problem Seme'. Every time someone came to him with an awkward request he thought for a moment, then smiled broadly and said 'No problem.' He approached the difficulties that beset his people in the most robustly positive spirit, and very often problems did disappear under the assault of his confident love and practical common sense. He carried a huge load of responsibility at that time as there were still no other ECS bishops living on the west bank. Bishop Seme gave new meaning to the word 'roadblock'. We fully expected to be stopped at military roadblocks, which we did meet, but when travelling through Yei Diocese we were regularly stopped by large numbers of people who swarmed around the car and took us off into the bush for a feast. We could never work out how they knew we were coming, and how they were able to prepare a feast in the middle of the bush, but we were given some wonderfully warm welcomes in that way.

Everywhere we were confronted with the destruction caused by the war to social services, notably health and education. In a few places, outside help had started to come in, but the general picture was of local initiative as people constructed health centres and schools despite lacking the resources to run them. Yet the church was still growing. In his first service with Bishop Seme, Bishop Peter confirmed more people in one afternoon than he normally did in a year in Salisbury. We left Bishop Seme still busily confirming when we went up to Akot, and when we saw him in Yambio, five days later, he had confirmed over two thousand people since we last met.

From Kaya we drove through the bush on the roughly cleared bypass that avoided Yei, and then headed for Mundri. We were delayed by so many of Bishop Seme's wonderful 'roadblocks' that we arrived in Mundri several hours after dark. People had been waiting for us all day and when we finally appeared we were mobbed by such a huge crowd of ululating welcomers that our ear-drums were almost shattered by the noise. There was great excitement, particularly because Bishop Peter had arrived. They had not seen their own bishop for many years as he was in Khartoum.

After a night's sleep to recover, we visited the campus of Bishop Gwynne College, escorted by local officials. The college was deserted, though it had been inhabited by SPLA troops and by various waves of displaced people during the years since the college community had to evacuate to Juba in 1987. Doors and much of the woodwork had been removed for firewood, and the buildings had been stripped of all fittings, but otherwise they were in remarkably good condition. All the corrugated iron roofing sheets were still in place, which was remarkable – abandoned buildings generally lose their roofing sheets very quickly in Africa. Apparently the sheets had been left intact because the college campus was regarded as a holy place; no one would have dared to take them. The chapel was in good condition and Marc Nikkel's murals of the four figures in the fiery furnace were essentially intact. In the long grass house we came across a rusty bath tub that had acted as a font in the chapel for many years. Andy and Sue's daughter Clare had been baptised in it when they first arrived in Mundri.

Ten miles to the west of Mundri we visited a large camp at Kotobe for some 50,000 displaced people and were given a huge welcome. Many of the people in the camp were Dinka from the Bor area and when they realised I was the same person who had visited them in Bor the year before the women embraced me almost to the point of suffocation. They spoke of the events since we last met and told me that many of their sisters who had been in Bor at that time were now dead. When the government forces came, many people had died trying to cross the Nile; others had simply collapsed of hunger and exhaustion in the bush. Those who survived the crossing of the river gathered in Akot and then walked the long road south to Mundri (some eight hours' driving) in search of food. As we drove north on that road the next day we regularly passed little circles of ash on the road that marked the places where the exhausted people had camped for the night and lit fires. Each day some of the weaker members of the group collapsed in the bush, but it was not until the evening that people knew who was missing. They spoke of how lonely those deaths had been, and commented that the world only helps those who die in front of television cameras.

From Mundri we drove north to Akot, in the Diocese of Rumbek and Wau, where Bishop Nathaniel was acting as caretaker bishop in the absence of Bishop Gabriel Roric Jur. Bishop Nathaniel had gone ahead of us to make preparations for a welcome that started some twenty miles south of Akot at Agoran. First a massive roadblock of singing, dancing, cross-carrying Christians barred our way and then ran behind the vehicle as we drove slowly on. The next minute we saw an even larger crowd approaching, with Bishop Nathaniel in his flowing episcopal robes at its head. Behind him were hundreds more Christians carrying multi-coloured banners, flourishing flags flying high in the air, waving their crosses, playing their drums, singing, dancing and for all the world looking like a celebratory medieval army on the move. The drama of our meeting was meticulously planned. As we approached the church compound at Akot, the entire church community was lining the route. Bishop Nathaniel led the way with his hand on my shoulder – clearly the arrival of CMS was seen as being of historic significance.

We slept at Akot in a beautifully built house that had been specially prepared for us, and the next morning moved on to Dhiaukuei. Our arrival at Dhiaukuei was even more spectacular than our reception the day before. As we approached Dhiaukuei the bush opened out and we could see the open grazing plains beyond a small river, the River Naam. We then began a ceremonial drive with crowds lining the route on both sides for a mile and a half, singing, dancing, drumming and waving their crosses, an exuberant concourse of people that must have represented the entire population for miles around. It was all quite breathtaking and we finally emerged from the vehicles at a podium on the riverbank that was surmounted by a huge standing cross. There Bishop Nathaniel once more presented us to the people and prayed his thanksgiving.

From the podium we moved to the site of the Bible School, where some five thousand people had gathered in the 'conference hall', a clearing under the trees overlooking the plains. The local SPLA commander and all his retinue, together with the church people, were waiting to greet us. After the songs and speeches, we were shown to our rooms and discovered that an entire village had been especially built for us. Preparations for our visit must have started months earlier.

We were extremely thirsty by then and longing for a drink, but were disconcerted to be offered what looked like dirty brown river water. The first person who was brave enough to taste it discovered it was the most delicious honey water. Salted nuts were also produced, so our hosts had produced a perfect rehydration regime.

At Dhiaukuei we started to grasp, for the first time, the scale of church growth that was taking place amongst the Agar Dinka in the Diocese of Rumbek and Wau. We had known for some time about the growth of the church amongst the Bor Dinka and the role that Bishop Nathaniel had played in this. Rumours had been heard of similar growth amongst the Agar Dinka, but I do not think that any of us were prepared for the sheer scale of what we found in Akot and Dhiaukuei. In the Diocese of Rumbek and Wau in the early eighties there were six discouraged urban congregations and three preaching centres. In the Akot area when we visited there were 270 flourishing village congregations with an average size of around 500 adults. This represented an increase of over 130,000 church members in only a few years, amongst a people who, like the Bor Dinka, had been strongly resistant to the gospel. How did it happen? Amongst the Bor Dinka Bishop Nathaniel stood out as a prophetic, charismatic leader who clearly played a crucial role in the growth of the church there. In Akot there seemed to be no one of similar prophetic stature, and it was only after patient questioning that we started to uncover something of how it all happened.

Archdeacon Reuben Machir told us that in 1987 he was called to Khartoum to be consecrated bishop by Bishop Elenana. However, he told us in a quite matter-of-fact way: 'I did not see what was the use of being a bishop in Khartoum. The work that needed to be done was here.' So he stayed put, the only priest in the entire diocese. Reuben quietly continued his work, travelling on foot to visit the scattered cattle camps, preaching the gospel at every opportunity. Animal sacrifices to make peace with God had always been a central part of traditional religious observance, and Reuben said that Dinka readily made connections with New Testament teaching on sacrifice and the concept of atonement through the crucified Christ. Jesus was seen as the fulfilment of their own culture. Healing had clearly played an important part as well, and Reuben spoke of laying hands on people who were healed from disease, barren women who subsequently bore children, and even (and very importantly for Dinka) cows that had been healed by prayer. In an area where there were virtually no medical or veterinary services this was a lifesaving ministry.

Soon there were a hundred churches and Reuben realised that many of the church leaders were illiterate and needed training. He called them to Dhiaukuei (a Dinka word meaning 'the cry of the fish-eagle') and started a remarkable Bible School. Training began with none of the recognised necessities. A taut cowhide and dried cassava provided the first blackboard and chalk. There were no books or library and only a small quantity of Dinka New Testaments and Prayer Books to help the teachers. At first all the food was provided by the churches, then later the college relied on relief food. At the time that we visited there were 160 students in training, including many women. Of the 270 church leaders that had emerged half were women, a remarkable emergence of women's ministry in a culture where men traditionally held the leadership roles. With no formal church structures in place, and no salaries, people simply recognised the gifts of the Spirit wherever they were given. The Agar Dinka used the same songs as the Bor Dinka, two thousand of which had already been composed. Reuben told us that the normal form of service started with singing. Then there was a time of prayer, after which the leader explained the biblical significance of the songs that had been sung. All services ended with the laying on of hands and prayer for healing. As with the Bor Dinka, this rapid church growth had happened at a time when they were isolated from the wider Christian community, so the liturgical patterns that emerged were freely shaped by local Dinka themselves.

From Dhiaukuei we travelled south again, first visiting Biling where there was a tiny hospital run by Dr Ezekiel. Dr Ezekiel was responsible for the hospital and for a number of health centres scattered across Bahr el Ghazal, an area roughly the size of Wales. He was the only doctor in that area and had no transport and few medical resources. He received no pay; the local community simply offered support in whatever way they could. Dr Ezekiel continued with his impossible work because of his deep faith and commitment to his people. He was just one of the many Sudanese we met who were serving their own community in costly ways, and we longed for them all to have the resources to make their work effective.

We stopped in Mundri where we rested for a short time, while food and drink were miraculously produced by the women, who were expecting us. Then off we set again to Maridi where we arrived well after dark. The Bishop of Maridi, Joseh Marona, was still in Dungu in Zaire (where I had visited him the year before) and many of his people had fled with him to Zaire. The church members who were still in Maridi seemed somewhat at a loss without any clear focus of leadership. The good news that we heard in Maridi was that Bishop Daniel Zindo had returned from the Central African Republic and was waiting for us in Yambio.

The next day we drove on towards Yambio and stopped en route at the small village of Bangaza where we had a wonderful reunion with both Bishop Seme and Bishop Daniel. Bishop Seme had set off for Yambio as soon as he heard that Bishop Daniel was back. He said that he felt twenty years younger when he heard the news. Bishop Daniel had been in exile in the CAR for some months and it was our arrival in Yambio that finally triggered his return. After a confirmation service and a feast at Bangaza we went on to Yambio where hundreds of people were waiting to welcome us even though it was long after dark. We were led straight in to the cathedral for prayers of welcome.

One of the places we visited the next day was the training centre, founded in 1979, where the Revd Yapeta Tabia was principal. Fifty-two pastors had been trained and many courses for women's workers and youth workers had been held. During all those years no outside help had been received and during the most recent period Pastor Yapeta had no salary and no oversight or support, but simply continued faithfully with his ministry on his own. We heard many such stories of service amongst the people of Yambio, none of whom had received a salary for years.

The Mothers' Union called me to meet with them in the cathedral in the afternoon and when I arrived it was packed out. The leader spoke passionately in Zande for some time and as I sat waiting for the translation I watched the faces of the women. They were the faces of those who had led hard lives and known much suffering, yet there was an astonishing serenity and strength there that revealed the depth of their faith.

I wondered what the woman who was speaking was saying and assumed that there would be requests for food, medicines and clothing. The translation, when it finally came, revealed that they were asking for none of these basic essentials, but wanted reading glasses. They explained that, as some of them were getting old, they needed glasses to read their Bibles. They knew it was their responsibility to take the Word of God to others, and when they went out into the villages to teach they were ashamed that they could only teach what they could remember, and not share the full riches of God's Word. When I commented to one of the women later that I had been expecting them to ask for food and clothing she looked at me in surprise and said, 'But God's Word is more important to us than food and clothing.'

The next day we went to Nzara, an hour's drive from Yambio, and as we approached the grass airstrip Heather's little plane appeared in the sky and dropped down to pick us up. The timing was immaculate. We filled the plane with the gifts that we had been given in so many places, including large quantities of the most delicious wild honey. We had been given so much honey on the way round that we poured it all into an empty four-gallon water container to take on the plane. As we took off from Nzara on a steep climb the container heeled over and the top fell off. Andy and I were sitting at the back of the plane and we suddenly saw a tidal wave of honey flowing towards us. When I was on retreat a few months later, still struggling to absorb all that we had experienced, I suddenly saw this amazing flow of honey as a symbol of the love that had been lavished on us by our Sudanese friends as we travelled round that desperately suffering area, a sacrament of the overflowing of God's love that had been poured out to us throughout that extraordinary journey.

CHAPTER 16

Sudan: politics and refugees

AFTER RETURNING TO LONDON following our February visits to the New Sudan my work became dominated by Sudan-related activities. I was involved in at least six different groups that met regularly to monitor developments in Sudan, and was in constant demand at meetings around the country. Ian Smith had come back with some excellent photographs and taped interviews that he put together in a short videotape for circulation around the CMS constituency. We then mounted an intensive campaign of advocacy for peace in Sudan, and encouraged those who saw the tape to write to their MPs about the plight of the Sudanese people. Bishop Peter and I visited the Foreign Office and the ODA, where we spent a full hour with Lynda Chalker.

In June Archbishop Benjamina and his wife Mariamu visited London and I was asked to escort them to tea at the House of Lords, where we were the guests of an Irish peer. As we sat eating cucumber sandwiches and strawberries and cream in the palatial grandeur of the dining room, surrounded by portraits of imperial figures that adorned the walls, I wondered what on earth Archbishop Benjamina and Mariamu were making of it all. They had just come from Juba where they had been living in a bomb shelter for the last few months, dependent on inadequate supplies of relief food.

Baroness Caroline Cox, deputy speaker of the House of Lords, had initiated a debate on Sudan the previous year and the government of Sudan, stung by the many critical things that were said, invited her to visit Sudan so that they could show her what was really going on. At Lynda Chalker's suggestion Caroline kindly invited me to join her, and in July we flew to Khartoum together with John Eibner of Christian Solidarity International and a journalist, Adam Kelliher. We spent a week in Sudan as guests of the government and were looked after by the Minister of State for Social Planning and put up in luxury at the Hilton Hotel overlooking the Nile. One of our many meetings the first day was with the Minister of State for Foreign Affairs, Bishop Gabriel Roric Jur, who seemed somewhat discomfited by the encounter. Later I met up with Rosaleen Bryson and Eric Jager, who were then working in Khartoum.

We found to our surprise and delight that plans had been made for us to fly to Juba the next day. We flew down in an ancient Boeing 707 that regularly took several tons of sorghum into Juba and then flew on to Nairobi to pick up more relief supplies. Six hours later it reappeared in Juba to offload the food and pick up some two hundred passengers for the final leg of the journey back to Khartoum. The passengers sat on the floor of the empty hold, though we were given space just behind the cockpit. As we approached the runway at Juba airport I kept thinking it must all be a dream. Only our first full day in Sudan and already we were landing in the place that had been inaccessible for so long. My last visit to Juba had been six years ago. There was less evidence of shell damage from SPLA bombardment than we had expected and the Nile Bridge had been repaired and was in use. Our host for the day was the Governor of Equatoria, who provided us with transport and left us free to meet the people we wanted to see in the six hours we had before the Boeing returned.

Our official escorts took us first to visit the home of Paulino Lukudu, the Roman Catholic Archbishop of Juba, who had been under house arrest since speaking out against the atrocities that were carried out by government forces against the civilian population the previous year. We were allowed to talk with him in private so he was able to speak freely and we learnt much about the situation from him. Many of the Roman Catholic leaders in both Juba and Khartoum were speaking out with great courage at that time, but sadly the leadership crisis in the ECS had greatly weakened the ability of the ECS to speak with a united and clear voice. The appointment of Bishop Gabriel as a government minister had further weakened the position of the ECS, as he regularly spoke in support of government polices in international fora.

We had a tantalizingly brief meeting with a rapidly assembled group from the ECS and were then taken to the office of the Peace and Development Commissioner. He gave us a rather rosier picture of the situation in Juba than we had heard from our RC and ECS friends. Our final meeting was with Adam Van der Knap of the World Food Programme who was the only westerner in Juba at that time. He was helping to coordinate the massive food distribution that was still needed to keep the population of Juba alive. The land around Juba was suitable for cultivation, but only a very small area was safe to work because of the anti-personnel mines that had been laid around the town to stop people leaving. The bulk of food was coming in by air as barges on the river were vulnerable to attack by the SPLA.

Camp for displaced families from the Nuba Mountains, Kadugli

On the return flight to Khartoum we flew directly over Malek and Bor and I could see the church compound at Malek quite clearly from the cockpit. The next day we flew off again, this time in a small private plane that took us to Kadugli in the Nuba Mountains. This was another unexpected visit; the whole area had been closed since the outbreak of war as the government launched genocidal attacks on the Nuba people. From the air we could see the hills and outcrops of rock that give the area its name.

We were welcomed by the Commissioner and then taken to see a camp for displaced people that had clearly been set up as a show camp for visitors. Almost all the people in the camp were women and children and when we asked where the men were we were told that they were working in the fields. This was a laughably implausible response and we later met local people who confirmed that when villages were destroyed, the men were either killed or recruited into the army, while the women and children were sent to camps or taken into slavery. Butrus Trille, an RC priest and the only priest left in Kadugli, told us he was free to worship in the one remaining church in Kadugli but not allowed to visit camps.

We had heard that Ishmael Gabriel, the only ECS priest left in the area, was under house arrest at Dilling, so we persuaded our escorts to let us land there on the way back to El Obeid. In the short time we had there we managed to find Ishmael and had a conversation with him in the church, but he was very nervous about being interviewed, and as soon as we had started talking local security men tried to force their way into the church and break up the meeting. Afterwards we were very concerned for his safety; he seemed to be the most vulnerable of those who spoke to us in private as his situation was so isolated.

After a night in El Obeid we had hoped to fly to Wau, but after a long wait we were told that the weather was too bad and we would have to return to Khartoum. We found out later that there was a big meeting of regional governors in Wau that day which was probably the real reason why they did not want us around. So after a rather frustrating day we returned to Khartoum. The British Ambassador, Peter Streams, kindly organised a gathering of international NGOs at the embassy that evening so we had time to meet with them and hear their problems.

The next morning there was a gap in the programme so I jumped into a taxi and went across to Omdurman to visit the ECS office. Amongst others I met with Bishop Khamis Mubarak who had pastoral oversight of the Nuba Mountains, so I brought him news of Ishmael Gabriel. There were still four ECS pastors in the SPLA-controlled areas of the Nuba Mountains, but all other pastors in that huge area had been killed or fled the fighting. When I got back to the Hilton I met our host, who asked with some asperity where I had been. He was normally a very attentive and charming host, but he became very jumpy whenever we moved outside the arranged programme. We spent the rest of the day having formal meetings with government officials and heard much about the preservation of political, civil, and religious rights. By that time we were getting used to such talk, but what disturbed us most was the complicity of some Christian leaders who were there meekly agreeing with all that was said. I worked off my frustration at having to be polite by spending an hour in the swimming pool at the Hilton with Rosaleen and Eric.

The next day we went out to Asalaam, a large camp for displaced Southerners that had sprung up in the desert outside Omdurman. The camp had been established the previous year when some of the settlement camps in the city were bulldozed and thousands of families were taken in trucks to an area well beyond the city boundaries and simply dropped in the desert. There was an international outcry at the time, as many people died during the operation, and we heard stories about women who dug shallow holes in the sand to find protection for their children from the desert winds. This was a city planning exercise that had earlier been described to us by the Minister for Planning as the government's 'Salvation Housing Plan'. Aid agencies came to the rescue with emergency supplies of food and water and gradually mud buildings were put up and wells were drilled for water. But it was an utterly bleak setting, especially for Southern Sudanese who were not used to a desert environment, and the camps were too far from the city for people to find employment.

On the Sunday morning I made my way up to the cathedral and met five of the bishops including Peter Birish, the area bishop of Kadugli, so I talked with him too about Ishmael Gabriel. Bishop Peter had just spent twenty-four hours in prison on what he assured me was a trumped up charge of adultery. He had been given the sharia punishment of ninety lashes in public, and although the physical damage had not been great it had been a public humiliation. Benjamin Ruate, an area bishop in the Diocese of Yambio, was very interested in all that I could tell him about Yambio. He had not been there since being consecrated. I stressed to them all the need of the churches in the south for Episcopal leadership and Bishop Benjamin did in fact move back the following year.

Peter Streams turned up at the end of the service and took us to the very gracious home of Sadiq el Mahdi for lunch. We sat in an arbour in the garden and Sadiq (a direct descendant of the Mahdi and former president of Sudan) talked freely about his own situation. He told us that all his friends were in exile or in jail and others were being harassed every day and called in for questioning. His wife Sarah, who joined us later, had been imprisoned for periods varying from two weeks to two months at completely arbitrary intervals, with no charges being brought. She woke up every morning not knowing whether or not she might be arrested that day. Sadiq himself was under house arrest and he assured us that most Muslims in Sudan did not accept 'this invention of Islam' of the National Islamic Front.

In the evening Peter took us to the house of Martin Malwal, until the previous year one of the few remaining Christians in the government. He had gathered to meet us a number of ex-Southern politicians who described Khartoum as an open prison for Southerners. Martin came from Akot and he had seen a copy of the video, taken during our visit in February, which someone had smuggled into Khartoum. Everyone was delighted about that visit so I was given a very warm welcome.

Our final meeting was with Dr Hassan al Turabi, leader of the National Islamic Front, architect of the policies of the current regime and undoubtedly the most powerful man in Sudan. This was the most chilling experience of the week. Dr Turabi is an Oxford graduate and he spoke eloquently for two hours in a flow of beautiful English. He was charming, plausible, and persuasive and every now and then flashed a beaming smile round the group to reinforce his words. He assured us that regional relationships within the country were excellent and that pictures of starving people shown on television in Europe had been taken in Ethiopia, not Sudan. When I questioned this in the light of my recent visits to the south, he swept my comments away with an elegant wave of his hands and said I had been brainwashed by the BBC.

It was all an extraordinary experience and afterwards we discussed the nature of what happens in society when truth is silenced. Some of our escorts were charming and thoughtful people, but they all parroted the government line when it came to explaining what was happening in the country. As the government controls the media we realised that many of the people we met simply did not know what was really happening in the south, or even in the prisons of Khartoum. But the more senior figures must have known the reality and simply ignored the truth, for reasons of political expediency. It felt rather like being in a Communist State.

Sudanese refugees in Uganda
In October 1993 I flew up to Northern Uganda via Entebbe with Carolyn Schrock of the NSCC and Alison Ayres of Christian Aid to visit the Sudanese refugee camps at Adjumani and Koboko. At Adjumani we were welcomed by Joseph and Karin Ayok, CMS mission partners, who had been working in the camp for some months and had set up home in a locally-built house on a plot owned by the Church of Uganda. They had already started growing fruit and vegetables and kept chickens and a pet monkey.

There were some 90,000 Sudanese refugees in settlement areas and reception camps in the Adjumani area, mainly from the Kajo-Keji area of Western Equatoria. The majority of the refugees had been there for two years, but new arrivals were still turning up because of the continuing fighting in Sudan. Joseph (a Dinka originally from Aweil) worked with the ECS in exile, giving support to the pastors, helping with lay training and overseeing a TEE programme. The Dinka are traditionally much feared by Equatorians, so Joseph's ministry was a real witness to the power of God's love to break down tribal differences. Karin worked four days a week at the Government of Uganda Hospital at Adjumani, where the majority of the patients were refugees, and one day a week she visited the camps to do health education.

Joseph then drove us across northern Uganda to Koboko, where we visited Bishop Seme Solomona and some 30,000 refugees from the Kaya area. Since our visit to Kaya in February Bishop Seme and his people had all had to leave Sudan and flee across the border to Uganda. As government forces had started to push out of Yei and threaten the border town, the SPLA had wanted to keep the people in Kaya, but Bishop Seme and Father Peter Dada realised that for the sake of their people they needed to move. So at 8 a.m. on 3 August the border barrier was lifted and some 30,000 people streamed across to the nearby village of Koboko in Uganda. Bishop Seme, watching the sight from his hilltop church in Kaya, compared it to the Exodus of the Children of Israel from Egypt. It was taken as a sign of God's protection that no life was lost that day and more than one baby was born on the road.

On page 569 of *Day of Devastation Day of Contentment*,[1] Andrew Wheeler describes the arrival of the people of Koboko.

> The re-establishment of the community in the camps around Koboko at the height of the rainy season brought many hardships and death from exposure, hunger and sickness. The churches were built first, followed by the homes of the people. A new community, centred around the new church buildings, was created. A saga in Biblical style was created – a story of Exodus and the provision of a home, a story of God's leading, protection and provision. It was a story that upheld the people, made meaning out of their sufferings and gave energy to live positively and hopefully.

We arrived in Koboko on 12 October, so the refugees had only had two months to establish their new homes. Most people had some kind of shelter over their heads, but there were not enough tarpaulins to go round, so many were still living in flimsy grass huts. It rained very hard the night we were there and the next morning everyone looked thoroughly soaked. Bishop Seme was constantly active, tirelessly going round the camp to encourage his people, and the camp was a hive of constructive activity as people tried to recreate their homes. The houses were very crowded, though, and there was little that anyone could do

---

[1] Roland Werner, William Anderson and Andrew Wheeler, *Day of Devastation Day of Contentment: The History of the Sudanese Church across 2,000 years* (Paulines Publications Africa – no. 10 of the Faith in Sudan series).

to start growing food until additional land had been made available. Aid agencies were working together well and the basic supplies needed for survival were reaching the people.

Northern Uganda was an insecure part of the world as the Khartoum Government encouraged violence along the border by giving support to Ugandan dissidents, notably the Lord's Resistance Army. Within the next two years Koboko was attacked, the Bible school that Bishop Seme had set up was burnt, and he and many of his people had to move yet again, this time to Arua in the West Nile region of Uganda. Despite having seen the training centres that he had built up in Yei, in Kaya, and in Koboko destroyed, Seme was undaunted and established the Bishop Alison Bible School in Arua. This centre became an important place for the training of clergy in the south, and has since grown and flourished.

As a young man Seme had to flee from Yei at the start of the first phase of the civil war, in 1965. After several weeks of walking through the bush without food he reached Kampala, and from there was sent to Umuahia in Eastern Nigeria for ordination training. The Biafran War then broke out and he had to run yet again, this time with his wife Esther and a young child. He completed his theological studies in Ibadan before returning to Sudan once peace had returned. He thus had to run from violence twice as a young man and three times as a bishop. Such a catalogue of catastrophes might well have broken the spirit of lesser people, but Seme and Esther's faith was deepened and strengthened in a remarkable way. Their steadfast hope and courage gave fresh life to all around them.

From Arua we returned to Nairobi by air and I was then able to attend an historic gathering of the Bishops of the Episcopal Church of Sudan at St Julian's, Limuru. Because of the divisions of the civil war, and also because of the internal split in the ECS, it was the first time that the ECS bishops had been able to get together for eight years. Watching the bishops embrace one another as they arrived at St Julian's was a very moving experience and the whole occasion was a cause for great thanksgiving. Simon Barrington-Ward led a four-day retreat before the meetings which gave a much needed opportunity to pray together for repentance and reconciliation. At the end of the meetings all the bishops expressed a heartfelt desire to carry their newly-found unity into the days of separation that still lay ahead.

The only dissonant dynamic came from the presence of Bishop Gabriel Roric Jur, still Minister of State for Foreign Affairs in the

Khartoum government. He looked extremely discomfited as the bishops from the south expressed their views freely about his government appointment and about his absence from his own diocese. He was not used to hearing such views expressed openly; in Khartoum everyone spoke very guardedly because of the power he carried.

The week before Christmas I was invited to lunch with the Archbishop of Canterbury, Dr George Carey, to talk about his forthcoming visit to Sudan. Following our own visit to the liberated areas in February, I had been to Lambeth Palace to ask for his support for the CMS advocacy campaign for peace in Sudan, and to discuss the situation in the South. Since then he had been invited to visit the liberated areas and to go to Khartoum and Juba. Andy Wheeler helped to facilitate an itinerary for him in the south, and the Government of Sudan planned his itinerary in the north. In the end the Government wanted such close control over his movements that he refused to go to the north. This caused something of an international incident and resulted in the expulsion of Peter Streams, the British Ambassador in Khartoum. However, the Archbishop did go to Dhiaukuei and Yambio, where he was given a huge reception.

As soon as I got back to London in the New Year (January 1994) the Archbishop asked me to come and see him. He had been greatly moved by all that he had seen and wanted to launch an immediate appeal to raise funds for Sudan. The staff at Lambeth Palace had no means of actually launching and running an appeal themselves, so he wanted CMS to do it on his behalf. In the end an appeal was launched jointly by CMS, CAFOD and Christian Aid on behalf of the Anglican and Roman Catholic Churches in Sudan and over half a million pounds flowed in.

On my final visit to Sudan as Regional Secretary I visited Khartoum for a week in February 1995. It was very useful to catch up again with the ECS leaders in Khartoum and try to help them to understand what was actually happening for the Christians in the SPLA-controlled areas. Those living in Khartoum were subjected to a constant stream of government propaganda on the radio and in the press and had no access to objective news reporting. Sudanese themselves could not cross from the SPLA to the government-controlled areas within Sudan, so people built up seriously distorted pictures of the conditions in the south. Southerners in Khartoum were all hungry for news about their own home areas, many of which I had recently visited.

Seven ECS bishops were based in Khartoum at that time, four of whom were appointed to dioceses in the South (Mundri, Rumbek,

Wau and Yirol). None of them had visited their dioceses since their consecration in Khartoum, and I tried to get across to them how badly they were needed in their dioceses. CMS put in considerable efforts during the next few years trying to help the Southern bishops go to their dioceses, which meant helping with complex problems of transport, housing and educational facilities for their families. I was delighted to hear that Bishop Benjamin Ruate was already on his way back to Ezzo in Yambio Diocese. Gabriel Roric Jur, the Bishop of Rumbek, clearly had no intention of returning to Rumbek, which left the diocese for many years without a bishop. Henry Riak, the Bishop of Wau, was currently in prison for alleged financial irregularities. I was not allowed to visit him in prison, but he was freed one evening to visit his family and came to see me. He seemed well and adequately fed and was hoping that he would be released after his case came to court. In fact he spent several years in detention and had an extraordinary ministry during that time amongst his fellow prisoners.

I spent the last two nights with Rosaleen and Eric who showed me the lighter side of Khartoum and when I left they escorted me to the airport at 3 a.m. by bicycle. We pedalled through the sandy streets by moonlight, my travel documents and money in a bag swinging from the handle bars, and felt quite carefree as the streets were totally deserted. It would have been madness to have done such a thing in Nairobi and left me with strange memories of the two faces of Khartoum.

By 1995 a CMS presence in the south had been re-established through the remarkable ministries of Andy Wheeler and Marc Nikkel, and Paul Savage was soon to start work in Yambio. Gradually the numbers of mission partners involved in Sudan increased, and CMS continued to support large numbers of Sudanese who were studying in Kenya, Uganda and Egypt. Leadership training was a clear priority in a church that was growing so rapidly, and we tried to help in this area by building up training centres in Sudan and in neighbouring countries. In Britain CMS continued to be much involved in advocacy for peace.

CHAPTER 17

New responsibilities

IN DECEMBER 1994 MICHAEL NAZIR-ALI LEFT CMS to become Bishop of
Rochester. The process for finding a new General Secretary was put
in hand and meanwhile an Acting General-Secretary was needed to
cover the interregnum. As I was planning to retire in 1996 it was clear
that I would not be a candidate for the post, and I was asked to be Acting
General Secretary until a new appointment had been made. It promised
to be an interesting swansong for my time with CMS. However, no
appointment was made at the interviews held in January; instead I was
invited to apply for the job. This suggestion threw me into considerable
confusion as it was an idea that I had never entertained. One night I had
a long phone conversation with Dame Diana Reader-Harris, who knew
both me and CMS well, asking her for advice about how to respond. I
spelt out all the reasons why I was not the right person for the job, but
she encouraged me to be open to the idea.

The next morning I read the first scripture reading set for the day and
it was the passage from Jeremiah 1 in which Jeremiah protests his
inadequacy for the work that God is calling him to. I nearly dropped the
book like a hot potato. There was Jeremiah saying exactly what I had
been saying the night before. After that I knew I had to take the
invitation seriously and very tentatively put in an application. A few days
before the final interviews in March, Archbishop Desmond Tutu came
through London and just before leaving my office he asked how the
appointment process for Michael's successor was going and if I was
involved. I said yes, but that I was not expecting to be chosen. 'Oh,' he
said, 'that's what Jeremiah said.' At that stage I felt that the Spirit had
already taken things well beyond my own control. When I was
appointed the next week he sent me a huge bouquet of flowers from
Cape Town.

My appointment was confirmed by the CMS Trustees at the end of
March and I was asked to take up the responsibilities immediately. This
was not easy as I was still carrying the work of the regional desk, and I
had some mad weeks handing these responsibilities on to Kevin
Huggett, who had been in his own job in the regional office for only a

few months. It all resulted in a very rushed handover and gave me little space in which to prepare for the new work. I was not quite the first lay person to hold the post, as a layman had been General Secretary for four years in the 1920s, but I was the first woman to be appointed in the two-hundred-year history of CMS. My four immediate predecessors had been bishops, so it was all very daunting, but hundreds of letters flowed in offering support and encouragement. At the end of May the Archbishop of Canterbury welcomed me into the role at a service in the CMS chapel.

During the course of 1995 there were a number of consultations and conferences that helped to clarify our thinking about the way forward for CMS, and in June we held a week-long consultation with our partners from around the world entitled WorldReach. The need for such a consultation arose from our awareness that two-thirds of the world's population had yet to hear the gospel, and we wanted to explore ways of responding to this challenge from within a clear commitment to working in partnership with the local church. The aim was to hear stories from our partners about their work amongst unevangelised groups, to encourage cross-fertilization of ideas about how to communicate the gospel within such groups, and to seek advice from our partners about CMS strategy for the future and identify specific initiatives that might be taken.

The rich diversity of those at the consultation generated an immense amount of creative interaction. We heard stories of evangelism amongst prisoners, police forces, political leaders, flat-dwellers, street children and drug addicts in the urban centres of Pakistan. From many parts of South and East Asia came stories of sending teams of people into villages, for example groups going to work in the paddy-fields alongside the local community in rural areas of Malaysia, and from Nepal we heard of a new freedom to reach remote mountain villages under a changed political regime. From Britain and Germany we were reminded of the spiritual void in the cities of Western Europe, and from Eastern Europe came the voices of those who were still so recently experiencing the freedom to express their faith openly. We heard much from those who were living in situations of civil war and from those who were trying to rebuild their countries after long periods of violence. We heard about refugees whose displacement had brought them in touch with Christians for the first time, and refugees who had themselves been bearers of the gospel. Repeatedly we were made aware that it is from the heart of suffering that new life in Christ most freely flows.

When we discussed all that was presented, many new and creative ideas flowed as possibilities for fresh approaches and shared initiatives were recognised. Delegates from Pakistan spoke of a call to work in some of the newly freed countries of ex-Soviet Central Asia and serious thought was given to how CMS could be supportive of such initiatives.

In September the Anglican Communion held a meeting to mark the mid point of the Decade of Evangelism at Kanuga in the USA. This was a huge gathering with representatives from around the world reporting on their experiences of the first five years of the decade, and much of what emerged affirmed and developed the insights of WorldReach. From South America, the Caribbean, from all over Africa, and across Asia we heard many exciting stories of dynamic evangelism and rapidly growing churches. From North America, Western Europe, and Australasia came reports of a very different kind, giving an overall picture of churches struggling to stem a decline in numbers. Yet around the conference room the only delegates representing agencies involved in international mission were people from North America, Western Europe, and Australasia – those very places where the churches were growing least. The anomaly of this situation was striking and it was clear that the rich spiritual gifts of those from the dynamic and growing churches of the world were not being made available for the World Church. The pattern of movement of people in mission had been shaped by the availability of financial rather than spiritual resources. At Kanuga it became clear that many more churches within the Anglican Communion needed the opportunity to share their gifts in mission. In CMS we had already been inviting people from our partner churches around the world to come and help with the task of mission in Britain for some years, and after Kanuga we became even more involved in encouraging our partner churches as they explored new ways of training and supporting their own members in international mission.

My first few months as General Secretary thus held important and stimulating events, and as I gradually adjusted to the new role I felt relief at no longer having to be involved in the detailed programmatic work that had swamped the regional desk. Also I had the luxury of excellent administrative support.

CHAPTER 18

Widening horizons (India, Romania, Afghanistan, Middle East)

India

REPRESENTATIVES FROM THE CHURCH OF SOUTH INDIA (CSI), the Mar Thoma Church, and the Indian Evangelical Mission were all at WorldReach, and together they extended a warm invitation for me to visit South India. The Mar Thoma Metropolitan then asked me to speak at the Maramon Convention in February 1996, so I arranged a visit to all three organisations at that time. One of my priorities at that stage was to gain some first-hand experience of our partner churches in Asia and in Eastern Europe, so these invitations provided a very helpful start to this process.

I flew to Madras where Bishop Azariah gave me a great welcome in the diocesan office and expanded with eloquence on the Dalit (formerly known as 'Untouchable') community in South India. Bishop Azariah is himself a Dalit and has done much to help his own people. He spoke movingly about the power of long-inherited, negative self-perception, and the difficulty that all Dalits have in overcoming this. He had clearly succeeded in making this radical shift in self-understanding for himself so I asked him how he had been able to do this. Without a moment's hesitation he smiled and said the root of this changed inner dynamic flowed from his new life in Christ.

From Madras I flew to Trivandrum and was then taken by road to Palayankottai. For four hours we wound our way through densely populated villages along congested, narrow roads. At Palayankottai I was given a very warm welcome by Jason Dhamaraj, the Bishop of Tirunelveli, and his wife Lydia, and met Mary Paterson, one of the few remaining CMS mission partners in India. Bishop Jason rushed me round the diocese at high speed to see some of the eight hundred schools and hospitals run by the CSI and to lay foundation stones for even more. The bishop expressed gratitude to CMS for founding so many of them, which surprised me as I knew that the legacy of institutions had become a millstone round the neck of churches in many other places. But in

Tirunelveli Diocese all the institutions seemed to be much appreciated and to be meeting a real social need. As well as laying foundation stones for a counselling centre, an extension to the cathedral, and a youth centre, I was asked to open two newly completed buildings (another counselling centre and a magnificent new hall for the deaf school). Bishop Dhamaraj told me that every time he opens a newly completed building he aims to lay the foundation stone for another building.

I was invited to preach in the cathedral on Sunday morning and was surprised to find that the form of service was basically Anglican. Although the CSI had been united for over fifty years many of the churches still seemed to have a loyalty to their founding traditions. As we travelled round the diocese we visited many smaller churches, and at each one the Bishop asked me to speak in the church and then to go into the churchyard to lay wreaths on the graves of early CMS missionaries.

When in Tirunelveli I visited the offices of the Indian Missionary Society (IMS), the first indigenous missionary society in India, founded in 1903. It was shaped along the same lines as CMS and the society was still flourishing, supporting 315 Indian missionaries for work amongst tribal groups all over India. I was then driven to Madhya Kerala for the Maramon Convention that was held on the sandbed of the River Pamba. This convention was then the largest Christian gathering in the world, attracting over 100,000 people every day for a week. Crowds of people covered a huge area, sitting on the hot sand of the river-bed. Some 50,000 were protected by palm-frond shading, but the rest sat in the full glare of the sun, patiently sitting and listening to hours of speakers with apparent rapt attention. I spoke on the subject of unity and shared a platform with Dr Feliciano, General Secretary of the Christian Conference of Asia. The Mar Thoma Syrian Church, that organises this gathering, is part of the oldest Christian community in India, tracing its origin back to St Thomas.

The centre of the CSI diocese of Madhya Kerala is at Kottayam, so after speaking at the convention I went on to Kottayam where I was very warmly welcomed by Bishop Sam Matthew. Bishop Sam took me to visit the CMS College, which is now one of the leading tertiary institutions in the area, and the CMS Press. There I was shown the original wooden press built in 1821 by Benjamin Bailey, a CMS missionary who arrived in Kottayam in 1816. The press is lovingly preserved and still works. Bailey started to translate the Bible into the Malayalam language and by 1839 he had printed a first copy of the whole Bible in Malayalam, an event that helped the growth of the Christian community and gave an enhanced sense of identity to the Malayalam-speaking people as a whole. His memory is still held in such respect by the Malayalam community (the majority of whom are Hindus) that a twice life-sized statue of him has recently been erected in the centre of Kottayam.

In Bangalore I was welcomed by Dr Gnana Robinson, principal of the United Theological College (UTC). The UTC is the leading ecumenical theological training centre in South India and serves all the churches, from Orthodox to Pentecostal, so it was an important centre to visit. Drought in recent months and low water levels in various dams meant that there were regular power cuts every day that seemed to come at rather odd times, and I was amused to discover that the timing of the cuts had been arranged so that they would not interfere with television coverage of the World Cup.

Romania

In October Metropolitan Daniel from the Orthodox Church of Romania came to Britain to preach the CMS Annual Sermon, and I travelled with him when he went by train to preach the sermon in Salisbury Cathedral. On arrival at Salisbury station Bishop Peter Vaughan was waiting to welcome us, together with the short and rather stout Mayoress of the city. It made a wonderful picture as Metropolitan Daniel swept down the platform in his flowing black robes and Peter, in flowing purple robes, and the Mayoress, with a huge mayorial chain bouncing on her chest, swept down the platform in the opposite direction to welcome us. Later in York I was with him again and we dined with the Archbishop of York before Metropolitan Daniel spoke in the church at Bishopscourt. We were staying with Ian Smith, the CMS representative in the area, and when we returned to Ian and Carol's house in York Metropolitan Daniel kicked off his shoes and relaxed on the sofa as Ian plied him with whisky. The rather formal Orthodox churchman then disappeared and we had a wonderfully relaxed time together into the small hours. This was happy timing for me as Mark Oxbrow had made plans for us to visit Romania the following month.

Following the collapse of Communism in the Soviet Union CMS had received a variety of invitations to open relationships with the Orthodox Churches of Eastern Europe. Mark, then the CMS regional secretary for Britain, was asked to follow up these invitations and initiated a survey of the possibilities. CMS first entered into active relationships with the

Orthodox Churches in Russia and Romania and later became involved with Orthodox Churches in other countries in Eastern Europe including the Czech Republic, Ukraine and Georgia. The churches in all these countries were emerging from years of being cut off from the international Christian community, and of having no freedom to exercise any outreach ministry within their own communities. The churches were looking for links with the wider World Church and for help in rediscovering how to minister to their own societies.

On arrival in Bucharest we were welcomed by Father Christian Poppa who had arranged our hospitality. Mark had helped Christian to broaden his experience a few years earlier by bringing him to Britain for six months and arranging for him to work alongside a number of hospital chaplains. This was a ministry to which Christian felt strongly called, but there was no one in Romania who had ever had experience of such work. After his time in Britain Christian returned to Bucharest and had since trained over two hundred Romanian priests to become hospital chaplains. From Bucharest we made a circuit of the country by train, visiting Brasov, Sibiu, Timisoara, Cluj-Napoca, Iasi, and Ploieşti. Travel by train was extremely cheap yet perfectly comfortable and the trains all ran on time. Most of the stations were poorly signed and sometimes at night we could see no place name at all as we came into a station. So we made sure that we knew the time we were supposed to arrive and simply got out of the train when it stopped somewhere at that time. We always found ourselves in the right place – I would not dare to use such a method in Britain!

AIDS is a huge problem in Romania and in Sibiu we were taken to visit a hospital that had a wing reserved for the care of children with AIDS. Most of them were orphans who had been infected before birth. We heard horrendous stories about the conditions that forced women to abandon their children and the desperately inadequate resources available to the orphanages. Slowly the situation did seem to be improving, and the Churches were certainly at the forefront of efforts to rebuild a caring society.

In Iasi Metropolitan Daniel took us to visit Durau, the new centre that he is developing in a beautiful mountain retreat as an ecumenical pastoral centre with a focus on lay training. He showed us the large conference hall and the smaller rooms that can be used by small discussion groups. 'This is for the changing of ideas,' he said as he delightedly showed us the first room. It was lovely to meet with him again there and he gave us a great welcome. We travelled overnight by

With Metropolitan Daniel and Mark Oxbrow at Tirgu Neamt

train from Cluj to Iasi so were feeling rather crumpled by the time we reached his residence at Tirgu Neamt, but from then on we were treated like royalty. He apologised for the food, explaining that they were keeping their Advent fast, but fasting only meant that meat was not allowed and seven fish courses appeared before us in the magnificent dining hall of the residence, introduced by a glass of very strong spirit. We each slept that night on a four-poster bed in a huge sleeping chamber with portraits of previous metropolitans gazing down on us from the walls.

We were shown the monasteries at Neamt and Durau and heard that over two hundred new monasteries had been opened in Romania since 1989. The word 'monastery' was used for communities of both monks and nuns. The churches that we visited were all full to bursting so the church in Romania was certainly growing. During the services that we went to there was some wonderful singing and in the larger churches and cathedrals the visual impact was quite stunning. But I did find it difficult having to stand for hours on end and at Ploieşti simply sank to the ground after three hours, admiring the stoicism of all the eighty-year-olds around me who stayed on their feet.

During our visit we met many church leaders who had been imprisoned during the Ceauşescu days and who had used their time in prison to share their faith with fellow prisoners. We were shown diaries that prisoners had written during those days, some of which have since been published, and sang hymns that had been written in captivity. Gheorghe Precupesco told us how he had been arrested in the classroom for teaching 'anti-state propaganda' in school. Before he left he told the children to remember all that he had taught them and as he was driven away the children came out of class and ran behind the car shouting out their support. He served five years in prison before being released in an amnesty.

When Metropolitan Daniel delivered the CMS Sermon he spoke of how the question in the Ceauşescu days was always 'How can we get our freedom?' Now, he said, the question is 'How can we use our freedom?' That question is of course an equally important challenge to western Christians. I left Romania with a greatly deepened appreciation of the riches of Orthodox Christianity.

Afghanistan

In May 1996 Bob Wilkes, CMS Regional Secretary for the Middle East and Pakistan, invited me to join him on a visit to Pakistan and Afghanistan for meetings in Kabul of the board of a partner organisation. It was an overnight flight to Islamabad and we woke to spectacular views of the soaring peaks of the Karakoram Mountains. Summits of rock and ice were silhouetted against the clear dawn sky and the sun shone on the glaciers beneath us. The high mountains then gave way to barren hills and finally dusty plains.

We extracted ourselves from the chaos of Islamabad airport and took a taxi that raced to Peshawar, weaving in and out of the colourful traffic. I stayed for three nights at Edwardes College with David and Julie Fletcher which gave me the opportunity to see something of Peshawar and the ministry of the Church of Pakistan. Then I went on to Kabul, flying by courtesy of the International Committee of the Red Cross (ICRC). The tiny plane gave us dramatic glimpses of the heights of the Hindu Kush before dropping down to the military airstrip north of Kabul. On the hour's drive to the city we crossed open plains and saw scattered tented encampments of nomads with their herds: long-haired sheep and goats and camels.

It was four years since the Soviet-backed government had fallen in 1992, and since then different factions of local forces had shelled each other as they fought for control of the capital city. As a result much of Kabul had been reduced to a ruin. Shattered buildings were visible everywhere and some areas had been almost totally flattened by rocket fire. At that particular time there was a lull in the fighting as the different groups in Kabul had come together temporarily to join forces against the Taliban. The Taliban were camped only a few miles outside Kabul, and rockets were still falling onto the city every night.

Kabul was full of the most extraordinary contrasts. The surrounding countryside was at its most beautiful as snow was still lying on the mountains, and valleys that had been cleared of mines were green with spring wheat. Snow-covered peaks formed the backdrop to shattered buildings, trees and shrubs lined the streets, and roses were in full bloom everywhere. The human cost of the fighting was visible in the number of amputees on every street. The casualties of anti-personnel mines struggled to get about on crutches, and fresh casualties were still coming in as people returned to their homes and tried to work the land. Many of the casualties were children who had simply been playing around their homes. Margaret Knill, with whom I was staying, took me to her local hospital where several wards were filled with children who had lost one or both legs. Margaret knew the family background of many of the patients and through her eyes I was able to grasp something of the devastation that mine and rocket injuries bring, not only to the victims themselves but also to the whole family network. Caring for disabled

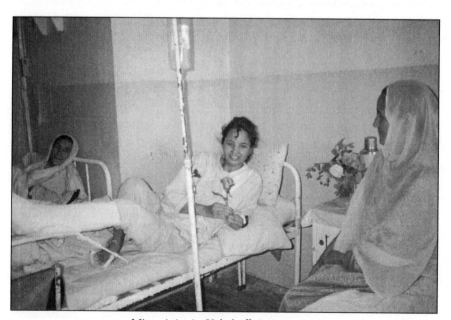

Mine victim in Kabul offering us a rose

children draws on the already overstretched resources of their families, and for adults the amputation of a limb probably means permanent unemployment and economic disaster for the whole family. One of the patients we talked to was a young girl who had a vase of roses beside her bed. Whe we left she took a rose from the vase and gave it to us as a farewell gift.

Margaret had been working in Kabul for some years amongst the visually impaired and was involved in training teachers of the blind. Many of those injured by anti-personnel mines had eye injuries, so this was a much needed ministry. She lived in an area of Kabul called Karte Seh that was on the opposite side of town from the hospital where she worked, and for a few months she had to cross the front line between two warring factions in order to reach the hospital. Every time she came to the frontier she would shut her eyes at the last military checkpoint, pray, and then put her foot on the accelerator and drive as fast as possible across no man's land. Her car was never hit by shells or bullets. One day when she came to the frontier one of the mujahidin greeted her by name and she asked how he knew who she was. He laughed and said that everyone there knew her, and that when she came through they radioed to the unit manning the guns on the hillside above and told them to hold their fire for the next two minutes to ensure that she arrived safely.

Most evenings I was given supper in Kabul and then driven back to Karte Seh before the curfew. It was an eerie feeling, driving through the deserted streets of the shattered city, stopping only for the occasional checkpoint. The first night this happened I was dropped at the end of the road where Margaret lived and had to walk down the dark, cratered, empty road on my own. Swathed figures clutching guns immediately appeared from the shadows and surrounded me and I wondered for a moment what was happening. Then the voices called out in greeting, 'Salaam aleikum!' and I realised that these mujahidin were friends of Margaret's who had come to escort me to her door to make sure that I arrived safely. For reasons of security the radio network around the city used initials, rather than names, for sorting out travel plans. I was amused to discover that I had become 'Delta Whiskey' and Bob did even better; his call sign was 'Bravo Whiskey'.

The board meetings took place in the Physiotherapy School of Kabul in the grounds of the Wazir Akbar Khan Hospital. Notices at the entrance forbade the carrying of guns into the hospital, the walls were all heavily protected with sandbags, and long queues of amputees waited for treatment outside the building. The board reviewed the work of the organisation that included educational work, such as vocational training for the disabled, education for the visually impaired, the training of mental health workers and the rehabilitation of drug addicts. Development initiatives included the installation and rehabilitation of wells, solar-heater workshops, micro-hydro power projects, and literacy classes. Medical work included responsibility for eye hospitals in Kabul, Herat and Mazar-i-Sharif, and the support of a mobile team, that frequently had to cross factional boundaries, for the running of eye camps. The logistics of keeping in touch across the organisation were formidable: availability of seats on internal flights was always uncertain and for access by road Kabul was reached from Pakistan, Mazar-i-Sharif from Uzbekistan, and Herat from Iran or Turkmenistan.

This remarkable organisation had been working in Afghanistan for thirty years so we celebrated its birthday at the end of the meetings and paid tribute to the courage of those who had kept humanitarian work going through so much violence over the years and through intense periods of shelling in Kabul. My 60th birthday happened to fall at the same time and Tim Aldred, a new CMS mission-partner, arrived from Jalalabad and gave me a jar of the highest quality local honey that was normally reserved for racing camels. I carried it back to London and it was delicious.

After the meetings five of us went on a fascinating drive up to and over the Salang Pass, the same one that I had crossed twenty-six years earlier riding on top of a cement lorry. This pass offers the only route for vehicles across the Hindu Kush that gives access to Kabul from the north. It was thus a strategic supply route for the Soviet forces during their years of occupation and the whole route was littered with the debris of shattered military hardware. In many places tanks had rolled over into the gorges below the road where they were immediately cannibalised by enterprising locals who used tank parts to make useful things like footbridges across the swirling rivers. The houses of the small villages clung to steep hillsides and the valley floors were available for grazing or cultivation only in areas that had been cleared of mines. As we were approaching the pass we came across a mine-clearing team under the leadership of one Colonel Aziz who offered to show us what they were doing. We put on flak jackets and visors and were led through a minefield to see a couple of recently detected mines that they were about to blow up. The intrepid Colonel Aziz said 'Follow me!' and set off across the mined area. I followed immediately behind him, taking the greatest care to put my feet exactly where he had just trodden.

Colonel Aziz on the north side of the Salang Pass

The road over the Salang Pass rises in a series of dramatic zigzags up to the snow-line and then disappears into a tunnel through the mountain for three miles before emerging on the northern side of the pass. Deep snow had been swept by the wind into both ends of the tunnel and the road surface was covered with rutted ice. There is no light in the tunnel, which is in total darkness, and at one point we narrowly missed decimating a herd of sheep and goats that was being driven blindly towards us by an adventurous herdsman. Uzbek forces controlled the northern approaches to the pass so we had not expected to go beyond the tunnel, but Colonel Aziz passed us at the top and invited us to follow him on down the north side of the pass to the front line to see another team at work. We followed him somewhat cautiously, watching the direction in which the rocket launchers were pointing to make sure we had not crossed the front line, and finally stopped, considerably lower down the valley, on the edge of no man's land. Here we met up with a second mine-clearing team and a group of Uzbek militia. The team were trying to clear the remaining stretch of four miles that separated the point we had reached from the nearest point that vehicles were able to reach from the north, thereby opening the road for a Red Cross convoy that was trying to reach Kabul from Mazar-i-Sharif.

The original plan was to fly back to Peshawar but there was something wrong with the landing gear of the ICRC plane so we all had to go by road. I was delighted by this as I had much wanted to see the spectacular Kabul Gorge as well as the Khyber Pass. The road through the Kabul Gorge is a superb piece of engineering, though we only had tantalising glimpses of the towering cliffs above us and the white water of the Kabul River below, cascading its way down to join the Indus. After emerging from the narrowest and most dramatic part of the gorge the road continued to follow the river, still high above the water, then wound its way across a high plateau. Dramatic rock formations appeared above the blue-green waters of a large reservoir, the striking colours of the water created by copper deposits in the rocks above. After the spectacular country we had already been through, the Khyber Pass seemed relatively tame, but it is rugged country still and hill forts overlook the road at every turn. Regimental plaques appear on the rocks at the side of the road, ensuring that the military history of the area is not forgotten.

Middle East

In February 1998 I visited the Anglican Diocese of Jerusalem which covers Lebanon, Syria, Jordan and Israel/Palestine. My visit happened at a moment of political tension as the US and British governments were considering taking military action against Iraq for impeding the work of UN arms inspectors. US warships were already gathering in the Gulf, and Tony Blair's announcement that Britain would support the threatened offensive came out the morning that I arrived in Beirut. During the two weeks' trip I was thus exposed to the full force of Arab opinion (Christian and Muslim) on the subject, which was a highly educative experience. I came back to London with an entirely new understanding of Arab perceptions of Western policies in the Middle East. Much anger was expressed about trade sanctions against Iraq and the suffering they were causing to thousands of ordinary people. The other comment was about double standards in the very different ways that the US government was responding to Iraq and to Israel. Israel was also failing to comply with UN directives by continuing to build settlements on the West Bank and I was repeatedly asked why the US was not sending warships to the Eastern Mediterranean. Although I did not agree with everything that was said, I sympathised with much of what I heard.

Much of Beirut had been rebuilt since the war, though some shelled buildings had yet to be demolished and looked dangerously unstable. Rubble from shelled buildings had been used to extend the seafront beyond the Anglican Church, so gone were the days when people could dive off the steps into the sea to cool off after the service. The international congregation seemed to be thriving and shared the building with the Arabic-speaking congregation that led the way in restoring the church after the war. Bishop Riah Abu El-Assal arrived in Beirut for a confirmation service, and together we met with the CMS folk in Beirut and Elizabeth Hume who flew in from Amman. I visited the Near East School of Theology and enjoyed talking with the Sudanese refugees who were studying there.

Bishop Riah and I travelled on together from Beirut and the diocesan driver took us up the mountainous road that crosses the Bekaa valley and then stopped short of the Syrian border. The road was open but snow was still lying on the verges and on the high peaks beyond. We met up with Stephen Griffith in a teashop, and he drove us on to Damascus. At the Syrian border there was some delay as Bishop Riah had no visa for Syria, but we were treated with the greatest courtesy and given somewhere comfortable to sit and tea to drink as the immigration formalities were completed.

Stephen took us round the wonderful old city of Damascus, with its narrow, bustling streets and ancient centres of worship. He also took us to meet with the Greek Orthodox Patriarch, who gave Stephen and myself a thorough dressing down on the way our government was behaving, and the Syrian Orthodox Patriarch, who expressed much appreciation of the work that Stephen had done in visiting the beleaguered Orthodox community at Tur Abdin in southern Turkey on his behalf. Bishop Riah took me to visit the Grand Mufti, the spiritual head of the Muslim community in Syria, and we sat with him for nearly two hours in his garden as this frail, elderly man spoke with passion of the need for Christians and Muslims, as people of faith, to come together to minister to the materialistic world around us.

The next day Stephen took Bishop Riah and myself to Krak des Chevaliers, the great crusader castle that stands guard over the main pass through the coastal mountains linking the eastern Mediterranean with northern Syria. For many years this was a strategically important access route for the crusading armies and the castle is a huge fortification, commanding sweeping views across the plains below. We explored the massive stone buildings, from the battlements to the underground cisterns, and saw the vast dimensions of the armoury, the stables, the banqueting halls, and sleeping quarters that housed the fighting men and their many camp followers. As we climbed around this massive fortification my thoughts went somewhat uneasily to the warships lying in the Gulf, and wondered where the parallels might lie. In the light of history the actions of the crusaders, who were confident in their God-given calling and believed that moral right was on their side, are now seen very differently. How, I wondered, would history judge the current military aggression against Iraq.

Bishop Riah and I were driven from Damascus to the Jordanian border in a vehicle supplied by the Syrian government, and on the way we stopped at the village of Izra where we visited two ancient, fourth-century churches. These had once been beautiful buildings but had fallen into disuse and the furniture was piled up and draped in cobwebs. The carrier of the huge key that effected our entrance told us that the centres had once been well-used places of worship, but that the last priest to live in the village had emigrated a few years back. We saw much sad evidence across the region of a diminishing Christian community.

At the Jordanian border a diocesan vehicle from Amman met us and took us across Jordan to the Shir Hussein crossing over the Jordan River into Israel. Having become accustomed to the warmth and courtesy of human interaction as we travelled through Lebanon, Syria, and Jordan, it was an extraordinary culture shock to arrive at the Israeli border. The young Israeli officials were sloppily dressed, gum-chewing, arrogant, and rude. All Bishop Riah's cases were opened at customs and the contents spilled out over the counter for all the world to see. High import tax was then demanded on personal items. After the respect with which he had been treated by the Muslim officials in Jordan and Syria I found it extraordinary that these young Israelis could behave with such complete lack of respect towards a senior church leader. The incident reminded me of the painful experience of travelling many years earlier with a respected Kenyan colleague in apartheid South Africa. The sad thing about this approach, which is common to all Israeli points of entry, is that it deepens fear and antagonism between Israel and her neighbours and thus runs directly counter to the long term search for peace.

The atmosphere in Israel/Palestine was very tense, as Israeli forces were mobilising for action. Jet fighters screamed overhead and military convoys were on the move on the roads. A curfew was in place and people were buying gas masks and stock-piling food. Bishop Riah's home is in Nazareth so I was based there for several days. One day he took me with him to Jericho to have lunch with Bishop Samir Kafity and Archbishop Edmund Browning from the US. Bishop Riah was very upset by the meeting and afterwards drove back to Nazareth at breakneck speed along the winding roads of the West Bank that were deserted except for some tanks on the move. I was thankful when we finally reached Nazareth in one piece.

After worshipping with the small Anglican congregation at Christ Church in Nazareth on Sunday morning, we had to drive back via a convoluted route to avoid bulldozers that were digging foundations for a huge mosque on a site close to the Basilica of the Annunciation. The authorities did nothing to stop this provocative initiative, well knowing that it would stir up yet more problems between the Christian and Muslim communities. Palestinian Christians are doubly marginalized in their own country; as Palestinians in Israel/Palestine, and as Christians in the Palestinian community. The time in Nazareth helped me to understand very much more clearly the difficulties that face Palestinian Christians and why so many Christians are emigrating elsewhere. Opportunities for education, employment, and trading are so limited that Christian families leave, hoping to build a better future for their children elsewhere.

Everywhere we went newly-built blocks of flats dominated the skyline, and as we drove out of Jericho towards Jerusalem our first sight of the serried ranks of high-rise blocks that flank the northern side of the city reminded me of our first sight of Krak des Chevaliers. These flats commanded a similarly impressive hilltop position overlooking the plains, but the blocks are houses for civilians, so I assumed that the parallel ended there. Later I learnt that the houses are made of large stone blocks protected by earth revetments and thick, steel-reinforced concrete. They have underground shelters, magazines and independent water supplies. The residents are armed and organised to defend the complexes. The blocks are effectively massive fortifications that encircle Jerusalem and cut the remaining land corridor between Jerusalem and Palestinian-administered territory.

The final leg of my journey was spent in Jordan where I stayed in Amman with Elizabeth Hume who taught at the Ahliyyah School for Girls. She was also involved in a small interfaith group and had been using her musical gifts by singing Christian songs in one of the internet cafés in Amman. The atmosphere in Jordan was much more relaxed than in Israel – the change was palpable as we crossed the border. Christopher Battiscombe, the British Ambassador, was very sympathetic for the difficult position that the Jordanians were in. Jordan is heavily dependent on Iraq for supplies of oil and feared a massive flow of refugees from Iraq into Jordan should hostilities break out.

As I sat at Amman Airport on the way back to London, television coverage of Kofi Annan's talks with Saddam Hussein in Baghdad was being shown in the departure lounge. We heard there had been a breakthrough and the Security Council had accepted a UN/Iraqi agreement. That was very welcome news.

CHAPTER 19

East Asia (China and Hong Kong, Japan, Nepal)

China and Hong Kong

IN NOVEMBER 1996 I WAS PART of a CMS delegation that visited China (Beijing, Nanjing and Guanzhou) for ten days at the invitation of the China Christian Council, and then spent another ten days in Hong Kong, as guests of the Anglican Church, for a mission consultation with our partners from South and East Asia. It was a fascinating experience and the visit was of some historic significance for the Society. We (Peter and Shirley Leung, Gordon Cryer, Philip Gartside, Barry Glover, David Urquhart, and myself) flew over the dusty hills of the Gobi Desert and landed in Beijing in a thick haze of pollution. We were met at the airport by Ten Hwa who had earlier spent a term at Crowther Hall and who stayed with us as we travelled on to Nanjing and Guanzhou. His cheerful face was framed by hair that tufted up at the back of his head and he was an indefatigable companion and guide throughout our time together. As we drove through the streets to our luxurious hotel we caught a first sight of the building boom that was going on in all the major cities; the sky-line was dominated by multi-storied buildings and the giant cranes that were raising them ever higher into the air. Bamboo scaffolding supported this enterprise which seemed a rather alarming marriage of technologies, but we saw no accidents. Neon advertisements hung from every available space, a clear sign that China had embraced a free market economy. We could well believe that the rate of economic development in the country was unprecedented in human history and we puzzled over how China's rulers could reconcile this uncontrolled free enterprise with a communist political system.

We were shown the sights and started with a visit to the Great Wall. It was a misty day so the watch towers along the wall and the surrounding mountains disappeared into the clouds, enhancing the dramatic effect of the scene. Having walked along part of the longest fortification in the world we then explored the most extensive royal palace in the world (the Forbidden City) and in the evening strolled around the largest civic space in the world (Tiananmen Square). Later, outside Nanjing, we crossed the longest single span suspension bridge in the world (the bridge over the Yangtze River) and our arrival in Beijing coincided with the completion of the coffer dam for the Three Gorges Dam, the largest hydro-electric and flood control enterprise in the world. Everything in China seemed to be happening on a huge scale, including the growth of the Church. We were graciously and generously hosted everywhere by the China Christian Council (CCC) and spent the entire three weeks eating huge meals of delicious Chinese food. We visited the Beijing Theological Seminary and the Religious Affairs Bureau and were feasted by the Beijing Christian Council, all of which helped to increase our understanding of the shape of the growing Christian communities in the country.

In Nanjing we disembarked at the luxurious and spacious new airport and were received by Dr Han Wenzao, President of the CCC. Later we were greatly privileged to spend two hours with Bishop Kuang Hsun Ting, one of the founding fathers of both the Three Self Patriotic Movement and the CCC. He had been a bishop of the Anglican Church and he delighted in reminding us that it was a former General Secretary of CMS, Henry Venn, who first articulated the three-self principle for churches (to be self-governing, self-supporting and self-propagating) that was adopted a century later by Chinese Christians trying to find their Chinese identity. Bishop Ting spoke movingly about his years of hard labour and isolation during the Cultural Revolution when all churches and seminaries were closed. It was a time when Christians learnt to 'pass through the shadow of death' and when men and women 'knew the reality of God with them and were sustained by continual prayer'. A younger generation of believers who had not had the same experience had by then flooded into the Church, and we came to realise what a huge generation gap lay between the elderly survivors of the Cultural Revolution and the young people who formed the majority of the Christian community. Bishop Ting spoke very graciously about the need for his own generation to give freedom in leadership to the young generation, but he also spoke with openness about the challenges that lay ahead.

We were taken to visit a village church one day and it was a relief to get out of the huge city into a rural environment. We lost our guide, who had driven on ahead, so we did not know where to go when we arrived in the village and had to ask our way. Eventually we were pointed to a large building at the top of a muddy lane that was indeed a church, but not the one that was expecting us. We were warmly welcomed by a small group of women who had come to practise their hymns for Christmas. We discovered that the church had been started just two years before and that some thousand people worshipped there on Sunday mornings. This encounter gave us a vivid picture of the way in which young people were flowing into the churches, as the situation was typical of what was happening in many villages across the country.

Prior to the communist takeover in 1949 there were some 700,000 Protestant Christians in China. Missionaries were expelled during the Korean War, the denominations were abolished, and during the Cultural Revolution Christian worship was prohibited. Yet by 1997 the official number of Protestant Christians had grown to ten million, and most observers put the actual number very much higher. The rapid growth in the size and number of congregations meant that leadership training was a very high priority for all the churches and while in Nanjing we visited the Nanjing Seminary which is the main theological training centre for the CCC. The acting-principal, a young woman, showed us round and introduced us to the 118 students. We were most impressed by all that was happening at the seminary and the commitment of staff and students. But they were still trying to build up a library and there was a real shortage of books that had been written by Chinese theologians. Most of the Biblical commentaries that they had were written by western theologians and translated into Mandarin.

The other important centre that we visited in Nanjing was the office of the Amity Foundation. The Amity Foundation was the first non-governmental organisation (NGO) in China when it started in 1985 and mission agencies in Britain, including CMS, had been supporting English teachers through this programme for several years. The Foundation was involved in medical work (mainly through the training of village doctors), in social welfare (such as the running of orphanages) and rural development (including helping farmers with terracing, irrigation, cattle rearing and the cleaning of water from wells.) The Foundation also had a printing press and had printed and distributed four million Bibles in a variety of Chinese languages the previous year.

From Nanjing we flew on to Guanzhou and found yet another huge city where multi-storey buildings were going up at every corner. Giant billboards on the banks of the Pearl River advertised consumer products of every conceivable kind, from Japanese cars to Coca-Cola. On the Sunday morning in Guanzhou we worshipped at the Shamian Church which was packed with young people, and once more we sensed the vitality of this growing church. From Guanzhou we travelled to Hong Kong by train, and although Hong Kong had just reverted to Chinese governance we had to go through full immigration and customs formalities before being allowed to board the train. We had not realised this would happen and nearly missed the train as a result. During the two-hour train journey we travelled through another vast building site, with huge high-rise blocks flanking the line on both sides for the whole journey.

Hong Kong is still a place where East meets West and is a vital link between mainland China and the rest of the world. We talked with those who lived in Hong Kong about the difference that the British handover to China had made, and many people spoke of a new freedom to discover their Chinese identity. We also had some interesting talks with the Anglican Church leaders about how the change would affect the Christian community in Hong Kong, and what their relationship would be with the China Christian Council. The answer always started with an explanation of the concept of 'one country, two systems'. But at the end of the day the Churches in Hong Kong, which are organised on a denominational basis, will have to work out how to relate to the post-denominational Church in China.

In Hong Kong we were the guests of the Anglican Church who generously offered hospitality to ourselves and to all the delegates who flew in from across Asia for the consultation. We were housed in St John's College and before the consultation started we were shown something of the ministry of the churches in the area. One day we were taken to Macao, speeding across the water on a fast 'TurboCat' and saw something of this Portugese-governed town that was about to revert to China in 1999 under provisions similar to those made for Hong Kong. In contrast to ultra-modern Hong Kong it had some of the stuccoed façades of Southern Europe. We visited the first Protestant church to be built in Macao and saw a photograph of Florence Tim Oi Li, the first woman to be ordained in the Anglican Communion in 1943.

The consultation, entitled 'Mission and Partnership in a Time of Change', was attended by delegates from Bangladesh, India, Japan, Korea, Malaysia, Myanmar, Nepal, Pakistan, the Philippines, Sabah, Singapore, Sri Lanka and Taiwan, together with our hosts from Hong Kong and a member of the China Christian Council. It was a very stimulating time, with keynote presentations from ecumenical visitors, and we grappled with an enormously wide range of issues. There was a real sense of common purpose (a deep commitment to mission) and a shared awareness of the growing sense of identity of Asian Christians and the new energy and vigour of the Asian churches. We became very much aware that the economic geography of the world was changing as financial centres moved from the Atlantic to the Pacific rim, and realised that technical achievement had become more visible in East Asia than in Western Europe. Yet the newly experienced confidence of the churches in the region did not spring only from being part of a growing economy: many of the most moving presentations that we heard came from contexts of great poverty.

The multi-faith nature of Asian communities constantly emerged. In Sri Lanka, where membership of all the religious groups transcends the ethnic differences that were still tearing the country apart, the setting up of an interfaith group to work for peace had brought Christians and Buddhists in particular into a close relationship as people of faith. From the Philippines we were reminded of the needs of migrant workers, the new economic refugees of East Asia, and churches in all the countries where the Filipino diaspora work were challenged to minister to their needs. From a rapidly growing church in Sabah came an enormous zest for evangelism, and from Korea came the longing of Christians in South Korea to make contact with Christians in North Korea. Many families had been separated for half a century by the political division of their country. From Japan came accounts of the ways in which the resolve to work for peace and reconciliation in the region was being expressed in practical ways. From an impoverished Bangladesh we heard of the commitment of the church to preach the good news to the poor. As we listened to one another we became more fully aware of the extraordinary richness of experience of Christians in South and East Asia, and at the same time of our deep oneness in Christ.

At the end of the consultation we asked all the delegates to draw out what for them had been the most important things to have emerged from our discussions. Etsuko Maruyama, the delegate from Japan, said she was tired of too many words by then and instead of writing anything down she drew a picture of a Chinese wok. In the wok were many varieties of good food: vegetables, fish and meat, representing the gifts that could be contributed by different churches. Then seasoning was added such as soy sauce, salt and pepper, representing the ideas arising from the discussions. Chopsticks (the Holy Spirit) were shown stirring up the contents of the wok together so that a good meal (the Gospel) could be served to the world.

The picture captured the whole dynamic of the consultation beautifully, and expressed our desire to be serious about the sharing of resources in the future. A financial 'wok' of resources was later agreed for the purpose of building up a centre for mission training in Singapore, and the whole principle of multi-lateral partnerships in mission was firmly endorsed. So ended a memorable experience for us all, and the consultation gave CMS guidelines for strategic thinking in relation to South and East Asia for many years to come.

Japan

In May 1998 I went to Japan, visiting five of the Dioceses of the Anglican Church in Japan, the Nippon Sei Ko Kei (NSKK). I found an unexpected similarity between Britain and Japan in that we are both a maritime people who are still trying to live down a recent history of colonialism. I was greatly impressed by the modern technology that was evident in the huge urban centres and by the Japanese genius for attention to detail revealed in the running of the railways. The average lateness of arrival for Japanese trains was under ten seconds and the sleek-nosed bullet train hit 300 mph without disturbing the coffee in my cup.

Etsuko Maruyama, who had represented the NSKK at our Asia conference in Hong Kong the previous year, met me and took me to the provincial offices where I was given a warm welcome. During conversations at the office much was said about people in the big cities feeling cut off from the roots of traditional society and uncertain of their identity. Materialism was said to be overtaking the traditional faiths of Japan. In new patterns of religious syncretism I was intrigued to discover that many people used Shinto rites at birth, Buddhist rites at death, and Christian rites on marriage. Wedding chapels were in evidence everywhere, including in the smartest hotels, and I was told that some priests augmented their income by officiating at secular weddings.

From Tokyo I flew on to Sapporo, the capital of Hokkaido, where Bishop Nathaniel Uematsu and his wife Michiyo gave me a very warm welcome. Nathaniel was the youngest bishop in the NSKK by about thirty years. Hokkaido Diocese covers the whole island of Hokkaido and Bishop Nathaniel has to drive six hours to reach some of the furthest corners of his diocese. During the winter months many of the roads disappear under metres of snow, and outlying places can only be reached by air. Many Japanese people holiday in Hokkaido during the summer months to escape the heat in the cities of Honshu and to enjoy the sparsely populated countryside that is scattered with beautiful forests, lakes, and volcanoes.

CMS was closely associated with the early history of the Anglican Church in Hokkaido and John Batchelor, an early missionary, is still remembered with great respect. The Ainu people living in the area around Biratori are the oldest inhabitants of Hokkaido, ethnically distinct from the majority of Japanese and with a language of their own. One of the reasons that John Batchelor is so well remembered is that he worked amongst the Ainu people, learnt their language, helped them to put it into writing, and then translated sections of the Bible into Ainu. The Ainu Museum at Biratori has many pictures of John Batchelor who clearly helped Ainu people to a new sense of their own identity by producing literature for the first time in the Ainu language. He is honoured amongst this minority community in Japan for the same reason that Benjamin Bailey is honoured by the people of Kottayam in South India. So often the assumption is made that the early missionaries were destructive of local culture, so I was delighted to find another clear example of the opposite being true.

On one of our car journeys together Bishop Nathaniel told me a moving personal story of reconciliation. As a young man he had been sent to Oklahoma to do post-graduate study at the university, and in the town where he lived there was only one small Anglican church. A senior warden in the church was a man called Bob who had been a bomber pilot with the US Air Force during the Second World War. His plane had been shot down over Japan and he and his crew were taken prisoner. All of them were tortured and half of them died. Bob survived to return home and become a pillar of the church, but he continued to nurse a deep hatred of all things Japanese. When Nathaniel arrived, Bob's response to him was hurtfully cold, and although Nathaniel tried to be friendly nothing in Bob's attitude seemed to change. After two years Nathaniel's fiancée Michiyo arrived to marry Nathaniel, but her parents were too elderly to make the journey so she had no one to give her away. When Bob heard about this he asked Nathaniel if he could stand in for her father. Nathaniel was taken aback by the request but rather hesitantly agreed. At the start of the wedding, as Bob came down the aisle with Michiyo, Nathaniel saw that Bob was weeping. Later he said to Nathaniel, 'For me, today, the war has ended.'

From Sapporo I flew nearly a thousand miles south to the port of Fufuoka where Bishop Iida welcomed me to Kyushu Diocese. He gave me dinner in a restaurant on the top floor of the tallest building in the city where we had a spectacular view across the brilliantly lit docks and out to sea. Then I travelled on by train to Nagasaki where I was hosted by David Busk, a USPG missionary doing a much appreciated job as a parish priest. David kindly showed me round Nagasaki, starting with a visit to the Atom Bomb Museum which was an exceedingly thought-provoking experience. Among the many appalling photographs was a transcript of the words used by the US military chaplain who prayed with the bomber crew before they set off, asking God to bless their mission. One of the many tragedies of that terrible day was that cloud covered the docks (the planned target), so the bomb was dropped on a munitions factory in the area where most of the small Christian community lived. They were virtually wiped out.

Close to the Atom Bomb Museum is the Martyrs Memorial which marks the place where twenty-six Christians were crucified in 1597 after a long forced march across Japan. From 1600 onwards Christianity in Japan was suppressed and believers were forced underground to become 'hidden Christians'. The faith was passed on secretly from generation to generation until 1868 when the laws of suppression were repealed and these hidden Christians, who had kept the faith over two centuries, were able to reveal themselves once more. David showed me the church where they had first made contact with a newly-arrived priest who was astonished when they came to him and said, 'Our hearts are one with yours.'

From Nagasaki I travelled by ordinary train along the coast to Fufuoka and then caught the 'Shin-Kan-Sen' (bullet train) to Osaka. There I was welcomed by Evelyn Wroe and Pam Cooper who were both teaching in the Poole Gakuin High School, the leading Anglican girls' school in Japan, originally founded by CMS. I visited the school and Poole Gakuin University that had grown out of the school and housed some 1,500 students in a new campus on the outskirts of Osaka. Christopher Kikawada, the retired Bishop of Osaka, showed me the parallel institutions for boys: St Andrew's Boys' School and the St Andrew's University (also known as the Momoyama University). The university moved three years earlier to a new campus outside the city and the buildings and the facilities represented state of the art technology. The library alone occupied five floors and had seating for 750 students. The sports centre had every kind of equipment imaginable. It was one of the best-equipped and liveliest universities in Western Japan. At the heart of this huge modern university is a chapel where regular services are held, even though only a very small proportion of the students are Christians. As we marvelled at the scale and sophistication of the whole enterprise Bishop Christopher delighted in reminding me that it was all fruit of the founding of St Andrew's School by CMS.

My final visit was to Kyoto where I was welcomed by Bishop Mutoh and Claire Debenham who was working with the Centre for the Study of Japanese Religions. Bishop Mutoh asked me to address the students of the Bishop Williams Theological College and we had a stimulating time together. Later Bishop Mutoh took us both to visit the Ryogen-In Zen Temple, a beautiful and peaceful Zen Buddhist place of meditation in the old part of the city. We lingered in the stone gardens and sat cross-legged for the traditional Japanese tea ceremony. The temple afforded a real haven from the fast-moving life of the city outside that is such a feature of modern Japan. After visiting the temple we drank tea again in an old wooden tea house nearby that we were told had been run by the same family for the last 900 years.

Nepal

In November 1998 I spent a week in Kathmandu visiting the United Mission to Nepal (UMN) and leaders of the Nepali Churches, particularly those involved in the National Churches Fellowship of Nepal (NCFN). When I visited Nepal as a tourist in 1969 Kathmandu was an exotic place of temples, palaces, and ancient wooden houses. Doors, windows, and balconies everywhere were covered with intricate carving, and moss flourished on the overhanging rooftops. Cows and tricycle rickshaws (non-motorised) filled the streets. People could still remember the arrival of the first motorcar in Kathmandu when it was carried over the mountains from India on poles by relays of porters. The scene in 1998 was very different. Old buildings were lost in a plethora of new houses and apartments that had mushroomed round the city – Nepal at that time was experiencing one of the highest rates of urbanisation in the world. Cars and trucks filled the streets with noxious diesel fumes that lay heavily over the city, trapped in the valley by the surrounding mountains. Satellite dishes flourished on the rooftops in place of the moss. Not an easy environment, but the capital still proved a lure for Nepalis struggling with the harsh demands of remote rural areas.

A major turning point for Nepal was the revolution of 1951 that ended the dictatorship of the Rana family and opened Nepal to the outside world. Nepali and Indian Christians were then able to enter the country and the tiny Christian community (twenty or thirty Christians actually in Nepal at that time) started to grow despite opposition from the Hindu government. Laws against conversion and proselytism were introduced and many Christians were imprisoned or killed. Following the revolution of 1990 a new constitution was introduced that allowed freedom of religion, but conversion from one faith to another was not allowed. The penalty for talking to someone of another religion about the Christian faith was three years in prison. New Christians also suffered ostracism from their families in a tightly knit Hindu community, and some were murdered. Despite these difficulties Nepali Christians continued to witness boldly to their faith and by 1998 the Christian community in Nepal had grown to around 200,000 believers.

The Nepal Ebenezer Bible College was the main training centre for the Nepali Churches and ran three-year courses in Theology. I was taken round this centre and met the students, many of whom were the first Christians in their families. Some were also the first Christians in their village communities and were preparing to go back to their villages as evangelists. They were well aware of the risks involved, as the murderer of a Christian was rarely brought to justice by the local authorities. I asked some of the students if the risks they were facing deterred them from taking up their Christian ministry, and they simply said, 'We know the power of God in our lives. How can we not want to share that with others?' Only two weeks after I left Nepal news came through that two recent graduates of the college, Sikh Ham and Gopal Buddha, had been killed by police.

★ ★ ★

July that year was an almost uninterrupted party as waves of bishops from around the world flowed through London on their way to the Lambeth Conference. I went to one gathering after another, as the bishops circulated around the country during the weeks immediately before Lambeth, and during the Conference itself all the bishops were invited to a garden party at Buckingham Palace where I spent a non-stop two hours embracing bishops from all over the world. Salisbury Diocese invited all the Sudanese bishops to a huge service in the Cathedral where I had been installed as a Canon earlier in the year.

At the end of that summer bad news came in from many quarters. First we heard that tall, strong Marc Nikkel, who had been doing such important work amongst the Dinka of southern Sudan, was seriously ill with bowel cancer and had been given only two weeks to live. Then news came through of the bombing of the American Embassies in Nairobi and Dar-es-Salaam. When the US government launched retaliatory attacks in Sudan and Afghanistan, that made more difficulties for everyone in Khartoum and forced the temporary withdrawal of CMS personnel from Afghanistan and northern Pakistan. Then we heard of yet more violence in Zaire that affected many CMS mission partners, and of violence in Sierra Leone in which Clare and Ronnie Williams were caught up and Ronnie's brother was killed. Finally in October we heard of the death of the newly elected Archbishop of Sudan, Daniel Zindo. He was killed in a car accident just outside Nairobi on his way to meetings in Kampala. At very short notice David Stancliffe and myself flew to Yambio for the funeral.

CHAPTER 20

Bicentenary celebrations (Britain, New Zealand, Australia)

NINETEEN NINETY-NINE MARKED THE TWO HUNDREDTH anniversary of the founding of CMS so there were many celebrations across the country during the year. Services of thanksgiving for the past and renewed commitment to God's mission for the future were held all over Britain and I spent most of the year from 12 April (the actual birthday) onwards attending such celebrations. By the time I came to Lincoln and Norwich Cathedrals at the end of November I had just about exhausted my capacity for talking about the bicentenary ever again. But it was a good year, with many people rediscovering their CMS past, and much thinking and praying went on about the ways in which God was calling the Society to move forward into the third millennium.

The Bicentenary year began on 12 April when we had a gathering of staff past and present at Partnership House. Together we thanked God for the day two hundred years earlier when a group of men who were deeply concerned to share the Gospel across the world met at the Castle and Falcon Inn and decided that they must stop asking the question 'What ought the Church to do?' and address the question 'What can *we* do?' Amongst them was William Wilberforce, who was already deeply involved in fighting for the abolition of the slave trade, an activity that contradicted every Gospel principle.

The central event of the year was a service held in a marquee on Clapham Common. The venue was chosen because John Venn, chairman of the founding fathers of CMS, was rector of Holy Trinity Clapham for many years. The church adjoins the Common so many exhibits were displayed in the church, and lunch for the VIPs was served in the Wilberforce Hall. The marquee itself held 2,000 people, and friends of CMS from all over the world gathered that day to worship God together. Archbishops George Carey and David Gitari (from Kenya) preached, and the worship was led in many languages. Fifty Japanese Christians from Hokkaido and Osaka had come to Britain especially for the event and they sang wonderful Japanese songs before the main service started. In fact they enjoyed themselves so much that we had difficulty in getting them to leave the stage so that the service could begin. Musicians from all over the world provided a rich variety of music, and there was a great roll of Kaago drums from Africa as we all processed into the marquee. The weather held till the crowds had dispersed and then a massive thunderstorm broke and flooded the marquee. The floods subsided just in time for an evening performance of Handel's *Creation*, a work that was first published in 1799. The next day I preached at the morning service in Canterbury Cathedral and all the Japanese visitors came on down to the service which was wonderful.

CMS members in the north of England mounted an excellent exhibition at the Maritime Museum in Liverpool which stayed open for several months and was visited by thousands of school children and other visitors. The exhibition focussed on the hundreds of missionaries who had sailed from Liverpool over the years as they set off for places all over the world, many of them never to return. An example of the dangers faced by early travellers is vividly captured by Eugene Stock in his history of CMS,[1] as he describes the journey of three German Lutheran missionaries (Nylander, Butscher and Prasse) as they set out in 1806 to sail to Sierra Leone.

> After five weeks of waiting at Liverpool, their ship sailed on 12 February 1806, but was stranded on the Irish coast. After seven more weeks' delay in Ireland they sailed again on 22 April from Bristol, but the ship had to put into Falmouth to join others sailing under convoy. While the brethren were on shore, the captain suddenly weighted anchor without giving them notice and resumed his voyage. They hastily engaged an open boat, hoping to catch up the vessel, which, before steam made ships independent of wind, was generally possible; but the attempt failed and after being tossed about by a violent gale, and in imminent peril, they had the mortification of being obliged to return to Falmouth. Providentially the wind changed, and the whole fleet had to put back. Thus they were enabled to embark again, and after losing the convoy, and narrowly escaping a French privateer, they reached Madeira on 2 June. There the captain, who had been drinking, suddenly died, and the ship was detained for more than three months until fresh orders could come from England. At last, on 22 September, they safely reached Sierra Leone, more than seven months after their first sailing.

After spending time at the museum I joined some three hundred CMS supporters to sail out across the Mersey on a ferry, following in the path of so many who had gone before. We held a service of thanksgiving on

[1] Eugene Stock, *History of the Church Missionary Society* published by The Church Missionary Society in 1899, Volume 1, page 86.

the boat, thanking God for all the men and women of faith who had sailed over those same waters to so many unknown destinations over the years. We also remembered the links that Liverpool had with the slave trade and gave thanks for the life and work of William Wilberforce.

The main service for the Province of York was held in Kingston-upon-Hull, the birthplace of William Wilberforce. The Mayor welcomed us to a civic reception then we (ecclesiastical and civic dignitaries) processed through the streets of Hull from the Guildhall to Holy Trinity Church for a splendid service. One of the guest speakers was Julius Lynch, Bishop of Freetown in Sierra Leone, and amongst the congregation was a direct descendant of William Wilberforce. In an unforgettable moment after the service Bishop Julius and Mrs Wilberforce met and embraced each other.

Graham Kings organised a walk from Oxford to Cambridge with two camels to raise money for mission in northern Kenya and I went along to cheer them on their way as they left Oxford. The local press wanted the Vice-Chancellor and myself to stand as close to the camels as possible for a good photo opportunity and we both got dribbled on in the process. The camels came from a zoo so they were unused to walking such distances and the police did not allow them to cross the MI, so they made part of the journey by camelbox. However, a group of enthusiastic human walkers made it all the way. In Kenya Bishop Alfred Chipman organised a rather longer walk in the footsteps of Johannes Krapf from the Kenya coast at Mombasa to the summit of Mount Kenya. The journey took six weeks and culminated in a celebration of the eucharist in the snow on Point Lenana. Krapf was another of the many German Lutherans who played such an important part in the early history of the Society.

These and many other events filled my diary that year and Rosemary Keen kindly mined the archives on my behalf so that I could speak at each place about the people associated with that locality. I learnt some fascinating bits of CMS history in that way. For instance I read with great interest a letter written by the Rev Horace Price who arrived in Osaka in 1890 and managed to establish a small school for boys. In 1892 he wrote, 'Of the prospects of the school it is difficult to write with confidence. Our numbers have not risen as some hoped they would. I see no likelihood of the school becoming anything like self-supporting.' I realised that the school he spoke about was the St Andrew's School that I had visited in Osaka the year before, from which the huge Momoyama University had grown. It was amazing to realise how much fruit had come from this initially uncertain beginning.

During the course of 1998 and 1999 we drew as many people as possible into a process of consultation about the future of CMS in order to hear as clearly as possible what it was that God was calling CMS to do and to be, as we launched into our third century in mission. Group discussions were held in Britain and many people from around the world were invited to make individual contributions. The material amassed as a result of this was brought to a meeting in Swanwick in May where a microcosm of the Society gathered and we spent three days together listening to one another and to the voice of the Spirit.

During this time a strong call came to recover the **centrality of evangelism**, to do so joyfully and to 'stop apologising'. The meeting also called for a renewed commitment to standing beside our partner churches in war-torn and other suffering places and to work with them in programmes of conflict resolution, and we agreed to give issues of **justice, peace, and reconciliation** a high priority. Thirdly we affirmed the importance, in our religiously plural world, of developing in-depth, long-term **relationships with those of other faiths**. There was also much discussion about the ways in which CMS is organised and a commitment was made to **decentralising** and **internationalising** the structures of the Society. These findings were tested with CMS members and international partners at a large Bicentenary Conference at Leicester University in September, and at a consultation with our African partners at a venue outside Kampala in November.

The Africa consultation was the final major event in the CMS envisioning process, and for me it was a wonderful opportunity to meet with friends from across Africa just a few months before retiring. We spent a week together in the relaxed surroundings of a hotel overlooking Lake Victoria and as we walked, talked and prayed together we enjoyed a rich time of fellowship. We also took time out to see something of the surrounding countryside and many of us visited the Church of Uganda centre at Namugongo. Delegates from all over Africa were visibly moved as we gathered round the shrine of the Ugandan Martyrs and listened intently as a young Ugandan related the story of the faith of the boy martyrs and the courage with which they met their death.

The bicentenary year was very demanding for all the staff and we did rather collapse in a heap when it was over. But it was all immensely worthwhile, and for myself it was very fulfilling to have such a year as my last one before retiring.

During July and August our sister societies in the Antipodes, New Zealand CMS (NZCMS) and CMS Australia (CMSA), invited me to share in their own bicentenary celebrations. It was a memorable trip and provided an important opportunity to strengthen links with both societies.

On arrival in New Zealand I was welcomed in Auckland by the General Secretary of NZCMS, Michael Lawrence and his wife Susan, then together we flew to Kerikeri in the Bay of Islands where the Maori Bishop, Ben Te Haara, hosted us for the first few days. Bishop Ben led us on a wonderful pilgrimage to visit places linked with the coming of the Christian faith to New Zealand and the early history of CMS. We started by visiting Matauri Bay where Samuel Marsden landed on 19 December 1814, together with the young Maori chief Ruatara and the CMS artisans William Hall, Thomas Kendall, and John King. Only five years before this historic landing a ship called *The Boyd* had been attacked while at anchor in the nearby harbour of Whangaroa and set on fire, and the whole crew had been killed and eaten. This had understandably deterred other ships from visiting the coast of New Zealand and Marsden was only able to land in the area with some assurance of safety because of his friendship with Ruatara, whose people lived at Rangihoua in nearby Oihi Bay. The party was held up by a storm in Matauri Bay for three days before they were able to sail on to Rangihoua, and the Marsden Memorial Church was later built in Matauri Bay to commemorate this first landing by the party on New Zealand soil. On our arrival we were welcomed into the church by traditional Maori singing and hand-quivering and prayed together. As we sat in the little church, enjoying a magnificent view of the sea through the window above the altar, I was moved to hear Archdeacon Wiritai saying, 'We welcome you amongst us with joy because your ancestors brought the Gospel of Jesus Christ to our ancestors.'

The next day we were taken by boat to Oihi Bay itself. A smart launch carried us smoothly across the sparkling blue sea to a remote peninsula and as we neared the bay we saw the conical hill that was the site of Rangihoua, Ruatara's fortified village, and then the great stone cross that stands near the beach in memory of Marsden and Ruatara. We splashed through the shallows to reach the foreshore and gathered round the cross as Bishop Ben led us in an act of thanksgiving and prayer. He read an account of the original landing as Marsden and his party arrived from Matauri Bay on 22 December, and of the service that was held on Christmas Day 1814 on the very beach where we were gathered. It was the first act of Christian worship on New Zealand soil. I thought back to that day earlier in the year when I had sailed across the waters of the

With Elizabeth Ludbrook (left), healing the hurt of 150 years

Mersey and remembered the start of so many voyages of faith. At Oihi Bay I was privileged to see the place at the end of one of those journeys, and to appreciate its far-reaching historical significance. The place name *Rangihoua*, which had been used for many years before Marsden and his companions sailed into Oihi Bay, translates into English as 'gateway to heaven'.

After the expedition to Oihi Bay we had lunch at a beautiful farm overlooking the sea and there were a few informal speeches after the meal. I took the chance to thank our hosts and to say something about Henry Williams. Henry Williams was the first ordained missionary to be sent to New Zealand and he had a remarkable ministry amongst the Maori people. Under his leadership the church really started to grow. He also played a crucial role in persuading Maori chiefs to sign the Treaty of Waitangi that brought New Zealand under British sovereignty in 1840. A few years later accusations were brought against him of land-grabbing and stirring up war amongst the people. Henry had in fact bought land quite legally for his large family and he had acted in many courageous ways as a peacemaker amongst warring Maori groups. However, the accusations were backed by the Governor, Lord Grey, and by Bishop Selwyn. CMS in London accepted these accusations at their face value and Henry was disconnected from the Society. This was bewilderingly painful for him and deeply damaging to the work of CMS and the growing young church. The mistake was recognised five years later, but by that time the damage had been done. A great-grand-daughter of Henry Williams, Elizabeth Ludbrook, was at the lunch and I felt moved to say how deeply I regretted the great injustice of what CMS had done to Henry. Later that day Elizabeth spoke to us about her great-grandfather and said that my words had made her realise how much pain she was still carrying on his behalf. We prayed together in the church and it was a truly Spirit-filled moment of healing.

The final part of Bishop Ben's pilgrimage was to the Treaty House at Waitangi. Before we were allowed to approach the *marai* (meeting house) we had to demonstrate that we were coming in peace. We walked across a beautiful expanse of lawn overlooking the sea, the grass still chilly with early morning dew, and were then challenged by three Maori warriors who leapt out from the trees in turn to perform a *haka*. The *haka* was originally designed to terrify strangers to such an extent that they would run away instead of fighting, and as they rushed towards us with amazing grunts and grimaces I might well have taken to my heels, had the reassuring figure of Bishop Ben not been beside me. After his *haka* each warrior threw a small branch on the ground and then retreated and watched warily to see how it would be picked up. Each time the branch was thrown down a little further from where the party was standing, so the one who picked it up had to expose himself in greater vulnerability. Having established our peaceful intentions we were then welcomed to the *marai* and shown round the Treaty House.

On our return to Auckland I was invited to address a combined meeting of NZCMS and the Anglican Historical Society about how the three-self principles of Henry Venn were applied in the CMS with-drawal from New Zealand. It was a somewhat daunting assignment as there were professional historians in the audience who knew far more about local church history than myself, but what I said was kindly received and the preparation for the event led me into some interesting background reading. In Auckland and elsewhere I marvelled at the clarity of the light as clean air swept in unpolluted from across thousands of miles of Pacific Ocean. Michael Lawrence escorted me to a series of meetings at centres round North Island, then we flew to Christchurch where Michael and Susan lived and where they kindly offered me hospitality for the rest of my stay. Once the formal speaking engage-ments were over they took me to see something of the beauty of South

Island. We made a day visit to Hanmer Springs then travelled towards the Southern Alps and enjoyed views of snow-covered peaks from across the still waters of Lake Tekapu and Lake Pukaki. A few miles west of Oamaru we discovered Teaneraki House where my maternal grand-mother was born in 1873. That was a very exciting moment and the owner of the house kindly gave me a recently-published local history which had a photograph of my great-grandfather on the first page.

In Australia I was whirled round the six state centres where CMSA has regional offices (Melbourne, Launceston, Adelaide, Sydney, Brisbane, and Perth) and swept into a non-stop round of speaking engagements. It was very interesting, but as I jetted from one State capital to the next I had little opportunity to explore the beauties of the Australian countryside. My kind hosts and hostesses did their best to show me something of the local beaches and tolerated my eccentricity in wanting to swim in mid-winter. As I travelled round New Zealand and Australia I was encouraged by the open discussions that I had and the desire on the part of many people to move into new patterns of mission.

By a happy coincidence of centenary celebrations the Episcopal Church of Sudan celebrated its centenary the same year that CMS celebrated its bicentenary.

1898 was the year when Kitchener regained control of Khartoum following the debacle of the siege of Khartoum and the death of General Gordon, and this opened the door for CMS and others to work in Sudan. Llewellyn Gwynne arrived in Omdurman in 1899 to open this major new area of involvement for CMS and the ECS dates its birth from that year. Major celebrations were held in December 1999 in Khartoum and Juba (for those living in government-controlled areas of Sudan, in Yambio (for those living in areas of southern Sudan controlled by the SPLA) and in Nairobi (for Sudanese refugees in Kenya). I was invited to the celebrations in Yambio, together with Bishop Peter Hullah, the Bishop of Ramsbury.

Ten of the southern bishops were at the service and we all robed in the cathedral before processing across the grass to the area where the service was to be held. As guest preacher I was invited to process with the bishops, and as we walked through two long lines of welcoming pastors and other church workers, the faces of the Mothers' Union workers lit up as they saw a woman walking amongst the men. It was rather like watching the sunrise, seeing the faces of the women break into expressions of delight and joy, and those closest stretched out their hands to touch me. It was so moving I was almost in tears before we

Gathering of CMS General Secretaries at my farewell service. L to R: Simon Barrington-Ward, Michael Nazir-Ali, George Carey, Diana Witts, John Taylor, Tim Dakin, Harry Moore (photo CMS)

reached the end of the line. The women in the ECS have borne much of the pain of their people in recent years as their sons and husbands have been killed in the fighting and they have borne the brunt of responsibility for caring for their battered communities. They form the backbone of the ECS, as all the bishops testify, and their worn faces show a strength and calmness that springs from their faith and years of patient endurance.

The following February the ECS held a synod in Kenya to elect a new Archbishop and Joseph Marona, Bishop of Maridi, became the new Archbishop of the Province. The other major topic that was discussed was the ordination of women to the priesthood. Each diocese had been asked to discuss the issue and delegates reported the views of their diocese to the synod. No real theological objections were raised and finally a delegate from Yei Diocese commented that some people thought women who were pregnant should not be allowed to lead worship, but that he himself did not see that as a problem as they could wear cassocks. 'Anyway,' he said, 'many men priests have very large bellies.' This comment brought the house down and everyone laughed so much that the motion that women should be allowed to become priests was passed by a clear majority.

I was very glad to be at the synod as it gave me an opportunity to say goodbye to the many members of the ECS whom I had come to know well over the years. When I sent an official letter to all the bishops letting them know of my retirement date, one of them replied, 'You may retire from your job, but you won't retire from friendship.'

During the spring I concentrated on getting ready to hand over to Tim Dakin who had been appointed to succeed me. There were many leaving parties and Archbishop George Carey came to my farewell service at Partnership House, as did all my living predecessors as CMS General Secretary: Bishops John Taylor, Simon Barrington-Ward, Harry Moore and Michael Nazir-Ali. Tim was also there so it was a unique gathering. John Taylor died early the next year, so I was especially happy that he had been able to be with us that day. He and Peggy had been a constant support to me during my time in office. I retired formally on my birthday, 14 May, thus ending an extraordinarily rich twenty-five years with CMS.

Afterword

SINCE RETIRING FIVE YEARS AGO life has been very much quieter and I can now reflect a little more clearly about the challenges that retirement presents. At first I was delighted to have time to relax, to enjoy friends and to do a little more travelling. I was offered a couple of one-term fellowships (one in the States and one the following year in the UK) that helped me to keep in touch with the international mission scene, and I continued to be involved with Salisbury Cathedral and the local church in Kew. I became a trustee of the Lee Abbey Fellowship and the St Augustine's Foundation, and started to become involved in Ignatian Spirituality. But this was a huge gear change after over forty years of full-time, demanding, and absorbing work. Jobs had provided a regular sense of purpose and, to a certain extent, of identity. I resisted the assumption of our society that to retain one's self-worth it is necessary to be 'busy', yet found it difficult not to equate my decreasing capacity to be active in the World Church with a diminished sense of self-worth, even though I knew this to be a delusion.

Earlier this year I came across that wonderful little book by Rowan Williams entitled *Silence and Honey Cakes*[1] in which he talks about self-justification. On page 33 he writes:

> The church is a community that exists because something has happened which makes the entire process of self-justification irrelevant. God's truth and God's mercy have appeared in concrete form in Jesus Christ and, in his death and resurrection, have worked the transformation that only God can perform and told us what only God can tell us: that he has already dealt with the dreaded consequences of our failure, so that we need not labour anxiously to save ourselves and put ourselves right with God.

Later, on page 60, he writes:

> We don't know what we shall be, what face God will show to us in the mirror he holds up for us on the last day, but we can continue to question our own (and other people's) strange preference for the heavy burden of self-justification or self-creation, and weep for our reluctance to become persons and to be transfigured by the personal communion opened for us by Jesus.

These words became particularly meaningful for me after having major surgery for cancer in October 2003. I was in hospital for a month before starting on four months of chemotherapy, and throughout this time was too weak to reach my third-floor flat in Kew. Ailsie looked after me wonderfully in her own flat in Kensington, where her husband Dennis had died earlier in the year after many years of illness. At Easter I returned to Kew and it was a real resurrection experience to have legs that started to work again and to be able to enjoy the spring beauty of Kew Gardens. During those five months I was totally dislocated from my normal surroundings and could not even try to 'do' things by way of self-justification. In a strange way I think that experience has freed me to embrace more deeply the reality that Rowan Williams so helpfully talks about. The central purpose of my life seems much clearer, and at the heart of the journey that I am now on is a desire for the transfiguration of which he speaks. I feel like a stumbling beginner in this enterprise, but am fortified by gratitude to God for the rich memories of past experience that I have endeavoured to share in this memoir.

---

[1] Rowan Williams, *Silence and Honey Cakes. The Wisdom of the Desert*. A Lion Book, an imprint of Lion Hudson plc. First published 2003.

Index

Abuja 118, 124
Accra 111
Acheson, Judy 129
ACROSS 140–148, 156
Adetiloye, Archbishop Joseph 120, 123
Adjumani 174–5
Adrale, Bishop Ephraim 126
Akinola, Peter (later Archbishop) 118, 124
Akot 162, 163, 164, 173
Aldred, Tim 190
Andrew, HRH Prince 46, 47
Amman 28, 193–6
Angi-Koti 142, 144
Aru 105, 125–129
Arua 105, 159, 176
Auckland 212, 214
Ayieko, Mrs 64, 66, 67, 75, 87
Ayok, Revd Joseph, and Karin 174–5
Ayres, Alison 174
Aziz, Colonel 190, 191

Bailey, Benjamin 183
Bamiyan 42
Bangalore 184
Banjul 116
Barrington-Ward, Bishop Simon 51, 176, 216, 217
Barrington-Ward, Dr Jean 51
Bataaga, Revd Ben 81, 91, 92
Batchelor, John 203
Beaumont, Hubert 47, 107
Beaumont, Lord Tim 47, 107
Beaver, Margaret 51
Beijing 197, 198
Beirut 28, 192–3
Ben Te Haara, Bishop 212, 214
Beeby, Dan 51
Bingham, Philip 129
Birish, Bishop Peter 173
Birley, Hilary 25
Blacker, John 21, 43

Bo 113
Boga 76, 81–88, 94–96, 103–107, 125, 129, 130, 146
Bor 138, 150, 153, 156, 163, 165, 171
Bray, Marie 122
Browne, Archbishop George 111, 115, 116
Bruce, Mary 30, 31
Bryson, Rosaleen, and Jager, Eric 74, 109, 169, 172, 178
Bucharest 185
Bukavu 76, 81, 86, 87, 90, 91, 96, 103, 129
Bunia 77, 86, 104, 129
Burgess, Fred 32, 74
Burgess, Jenny (née Bryson) 25, 32, 74
Busk, David 204
Bwakadi 84, 85, 104

Cairo 28, 48, 124, 148, 150, 151
Cape Town 95, 136, 179
Carey, Archbishop George 109, 110, 177, 208, 216, 217
Carey, Revd Christopher 52, 74, 100, 132, 151
Carey, Rosemary 52, 74
Carlisle, Penny 99
Chambers, Robert 21
Chipman, Bishop Alf 210
Charles, Eirene 23
Ciobetea, Metropolitan Daniel 184–187
Conakry 114, 115
Cooper, Pam 204
Corble, Dennis 44, 48
Corble, Ailsie (née Witts) 1, 2, 4, 5, 8, 9, 11, 13, 16, 18, 32, 44, 48
Cowx, Judy 48
Cox, Baroness Caroline 169
Cox, Dr Peter, and Liza 33
Crowther Hall 49, 51, 76, 88, 197

Dada, Father Peter 159, 175
Dakin, Revd Tim 216, 217

Damascus 28, 193, 194
Daniell, Patrick 38
Daniell, Susan 14, 16, 18, 38
Darfur 142, 144
De Wind, Christina 101
Dhamaraj, Bishop Jason, and Lydia 182, 183
Dhiaukuei 164–166, 177
Diggs, Bishop Ronald 116
Diropka Balufuga (later Archbishop) 90, 95
Dungu 130, 131, 166

Eglin, Lorna 57
Eldoret, Highlands School 20, 21
Essam, Sue 124
Ethiopia 23, 151, 161, 174

Fallowes, Carol 147
Farafenni 116
Fletcher, David and Julie 187
Freetown 112–114

Gabriel, Revd Ishmael 172, 173
Gaines 1–6, 8, 9, 11, 12, 22
Garang, Bishop Nathaniel 141, 150–158, 160, 162, 164, 165
Gathua, Shelometh 33
Gitari, Archbishop David 208
Gordonstoun 43, 45, 46, 48, 49, 51, 59, 72
Goma 81, 126
Griffith, Stephen 193
Guanzou 197, 199, 200

Harare 26, 151
Hassan Al Turabi, Dr 174
Hayward, John and Kathleen 90, 103
Hillman, Revd Jesse 76, 77
Hinds, Jeremy and Wendy 118, 119
Hokkaido 202, 203, 208
Holder, Lucy 74
Hong Kong 197, 200, 202
Horsfall, Anne 22, 32, 33, 35–7, 40, 48, 59
Housman, Georgina 48
Hume, Elizabeth 193, 195

Iasi 185, 186
Ibadan 120, 124, 176
Idjwi 95, 96

Janda, Revd Clement 142
JCMWA 122, 124
Jeavons, Revd Richard 121
Jennings family 129
Jerusalem 28, 192, 195
Johannesburg 134
John, Revd Arun 134
Jones, Beverley 102, 153, 155
Jos 116–118, 124
Juba 128, 139, 140–142, 145–147, 149, 152, 153, 161, 163, 170, 177, 215
Julius (Maasai cook) 64, 66, 70

Kabul 42, 187–189, 190, 191
Kabarole, Nyangoma 125
Kabarole, Nyakato 125, 130
Kadugli 148, 171, 173
Kaduna 117, 119, 121, 123
Kamau, George 64, 66, 68, 70, 87
Kampala 98–102, 176, 207
Kaniama 93
Kano 117, 119, 122
Kanuga 181
Karamoja 100, 101
Katara, Revd Buleta 103, 104, 106
Kathmandu 40–42, 205
Kauma, Bishop Miseari, and Geraldine 100
Kaya 153, 159, 160–162, 175, 176
Keili, Bishop Michael, and Agnes 113
Kelly, Dan 142, 144, 146, 147, 148
Kempe, John 43
Kew 47, 107
Khartoum 138, 142–151, 153, 156, 159, 160, 163, 165, 169, 171–174, 176–178, 207, 215
Kikawada, Bishop Christopher 204
Kikuyu, Alliance Girls High School 28–33, 39, 43
Kilifi 33
Kinshasa 78, 82, 90–93, 128, 129
Kirk, Maggie 35
Kisangani 80–83, 90, 91, 128, 129
Kivebulaya, Apolo 80
Knill, Margaret 188, 189
Koboko 160, 174–176
Kottayam 183, 184, 203
Krak des Chevaliers 28, 193, 195
Krapf, Johannes 210
Kuang Hsun Ting, Bishop 198

Kyoto 205

Lagos 120, 122, 124
Lake Baringo 26, 32
Lake Kivu 81, 86, 95
Lake Turkana 74
Lamb, Revd Dr Christopher, and Tina 51
Lane, Bridget 84
Lapsley, Revd Michael 133, 136
Lawrence, Revd Michael, and Susan 212, 214
Lee Abbey 25, 29
Lee, Bishop Peter 134
Lesotho 132, 136
Leung, Revd Dr Peter, and Shirley 197
Loewen family 2, 4
Lokichoggio 155
Lonmon, Aylie 46
Lubumbashi 92–94, 109, 125–127, 129
Ludbrook, Elizabeth 213, 214
Lugor, Bishop Michael 146, 150
Lukudu, Archbishop Paulino170

Mabula, Bishop Joseph 94
Machir, Reuben (later Bishop) 165, 166
Mackay, Cynthia 99
Macao 200
Madras 182
Main, Clive 128, 129
Main, Judith (née Wilson) 128, 129, 147
Makuku, Bishop Philip 136
Malau, Bishop John 144
Malek 156–158, 171
Malwal, Martin 173
Maramon Convention 182, 183
Maridadi, Gideon 52, 54, 57–60, 65, 70, 75
Maridi 127, 130, 141, 166, 216
Marona, Joseph (later Archbishop) 130, 141, 166, 216
Marsden, Revd Samuel 212
Maruyama, Etsuko 201, 202
Mbona, Kolini (later Archbishop) 86, 90–94
McCoy, Revd Mike, and Lorna 136
Metcalfe-Gibson, Ann 10, 13–18
Meto 51–77, 87, 108
Mexico City 16
Miller, Colonel 91
Modderpoort 132, 134

Montgomery, Caroline 46
Montreal 13–16
Moore, Bishop Harry 216, 217
Mount Everest 40
Mount Kenya 28, 33, 210
Mount Kilimajaro 22, 33
Mount Mulanje 109
Mountain Club of Kenya 21, 26, 32
Mukono 101
Mundri 140, 162–164, 166, 177
Mukulungani, Revd Robeni 84, 85, 104

Nagasaki 203, 204
Nairobi 20, 21, 26, 51, 87, 98, 103, 108, 126, 140, 145–151, 160, 170, 176, 178, 206, 207, 215
Nambulong 54, 55, 59, 66, 75, 87
Nanjing 197–199
Natana, Bishop Ephraim 146
Nazareth 194, 195
Nazir-Ali, Bishop Michael 116, 132, 179, 216, 217
Ndahura, Archbishop Bezaleri 81, 86, 87, 90
Negus, Arthur 12
Newbigin, Bishop Lesslie 51
Ngalamu, Archbishop Elenana 140, 145, 146, 148, 152, 165
Nickson, Dr Pat (later Revd) 88–90, 94–97, 125, 129
Nikkel, Revd Dr Marc 140, 141, 163, 178, 206
Njojo, Archbishop Patrice 88, 89, 92, 103, 105, 106, 129, 130
Njonjo, the Hon Charles 58
Njonjo, Margaret 52
Nwankiti, Bishop Ben 120
Nyala 142, 144

Oamaru 215
Oetztal 17
Okinda, Jackson 64, 66, 68, 87
Olang, Archbishop Festo 52, 61
Ol Doinyo Lengai 27
Olofusoye, Archbishop Timothy 120
Omdurman 142, 148–150, 172, 215
Onitsha 120, 124
Onyemelukwe, Bishop Jonathan 120
Osaka 204, 208, 210

Owerri 120
Oxbrow, Revd Mark 183–186

Palmer, Elizabeth 16
Pasha, Dr Emin 82
Paterson, Mary 182
Pearce, Pat 22
Pearson, Dr Nigel 129
Peppiatt, David 129
Peshawar 187, 191
Petra 28
Pitt family 129
Poggo, Revd Benaiah 140
Poppa, Fr Christian 185

Rangihoua 212
Reader-Harris, Dame Diana 51, 179
Riah Abu El-Assal, Bishop 193, 194
Riak, Bishop Henry 178
Richards, Elizabeth 21
Richards, Dr Charles 21, 25, 27, 43, 44, 49,
    50, 59
Richards, Idwal 119
Ridsdale, Bishop Philip, and Lucy 81–83
Risi, Yolanda 87
Ritchie, Agnes (Nanny) 1, 5, 13
Roric Jur, Gabriel (formerly Bishop) 151,
    152, 164, 169, 170, 176, 178
Rous, Judy (née Somerville) 106, 130,
    131
Rous, Tim 88, 89, 90, 95, 96, 104, 106,
    125, 130, 131
Royal Hospital, Chelsea 6, 39
Rowney, Doris 98
Ruate, Bishop Benjamin 173, 178
Ruwenzori Mountains 33, 37, 78, 82, 96

Sadiq el Mahdi 173
Salang Pass 42, 190, 191
Sato, Grace 29
Savage, Paul 178
Schrock, Carolyn 155, 174
Schrock, Roger 153, 155, 159
Sengulane, Bishop Dinis 133
Sharland, David 127–129
Shaw, Archdeacon Archibald 158
Shepherd, Mildred 4
Slade, Joan and Robin 52, 61, 63
Smith, Ian and Carol 161, 169, 184

Smith, Norma 46
Solomona, Bishop Seme 128, 141, 149,
    153, 159, 160, 162, 163, 167, 175, 176
South, Tony 28, 32
Stancliffe, Bishop David 207
Stanley, Henry Morton 82
Streams, Peter 172, 173, 177
St Beuno's 108, 109, 129

Taban, Bishop Paride 150, 153, 155
Tambaki, Madame 91
Tarrant, Revd Ian, and Barton, Sally
    126–129
Taylor, Bishop John 216, 217
Tibafa, Bishop Mugera, and Edreda 82, 90,
    91
Tipape Ole Seitah 55, 56, 87, 108
Tirunelveli 182, 183
Tokyo 202
Torit 141, 150, 153, 155, 156, 159, 161
Tutu, Archbishop Desmond 132–134, 179

Uematsu, Bishop Nathaniel, and Michiyo
    202, 203
Urquhart, David (later Bishop) 197
Upper Slaughter 11, 12, 42, 44, 48, 76, 108

Victoria Falls 26
Vaughan, Elizabeth 51
Vaughan, Bishop Peter 51, 161–163, 169,
    184
Vause, Eve 84, 94
Venn, Revd Henry 198, 214
Venn, Revd John 208

Waite, Terry 87, 109
Walker, Pauline 140
Wheeler, Revd Andrew, and Sue 51, 140,
    150, 161, 163, 168, 175, 177, 178
Wiersum, Dr Joanna and Revd Tim 115
Wilberforce, William 208, 210
Wilkes, Revd Bob 187, 189
Wilks, Derek and Pat 52, 61, 74, 77, 87
Williams, Revd Henry 213, 214
Witts, Major-General Frederick 1, 6, 7,
    9–12, 38, 109
Witts, Alice (mother of Diana) 1–3, 6, 9,
    12, 39, 42, 44, 48, 59, 108, 109
Witts, Elizabeth 1–9, 11, 13, 38, 48, 49, 59

Witts, Francis 2, 3, 5, 8, 16, 26, 38, 48, 62,
    63, 104, 105, 109, 110
Witts family at Upper Slaughter 11, 12
Wright, Louise 128, 147
Wrigley family at Gaines 2, 5, 6, 11
Wroe, Evelyn 204
Wusasa 119, 121, 122

Yambio 146, 162, 166, 167, 173, 207, 215
Yamufaya 83, 128

Yei 127, 141, 147, 149, 153, 159, 162, 175,
    176
Yugusuk, Archbishop Benjamina 145, 146,
    148, 152, 153, 169

Zaria 117, 121, 122
Zindo, Archbishop Daniel 166, 167, 207
Zomba 26, 109
Zunguluka 84, 104